TALKING DIRTY

A collection of sexual innuendo, toe-curling
confessions and sexy bons mots

CAROLE McKENZIE

MAINSTREAM
PUBLISHING

EDINBURGH AND LONDON

This edition, 2013

Copyright © Carole McKenzie, 2013
All rights reserved
The moral right of the author has been asserted

First published in Great Britain in 2013 by
MAINSTREAM PUBLISHING COMPANY
(EDINBURGH) LTD
7 Albany Street
Edinburgh EH1 3UG

ISBN 9781780575964

No part of this book may be reproduced or transmitted in any form or by any other
means without permission in writing from the publisher, except by a reviewer who
wishes to quote brief passages in connection with a review written for insertion in a
magazine, newspaper or broadcast

The author has made every effort to clear copyright permissions but where this has
not been possible and amendments are required the publisher will be pleased to
make any necessary arrangements at the earliest opportunity

A catalogue record for this book is available
from the British Library

Printed in Great Britain by
Clays Ltd, St Ives plc

1 3 5 7 9 10 8 6 4 2

INTRODUCTION

'It's only kinky the first time.'

The interpretation of sex and sexual pursuits seen as harmless to some is sure to be condemned as an outrage to others. Sex is promoted everywhere. No longer hidden and forbidden, it is now direct and often leaves nothing to the imagination.

Women in particular have sexual freedom as never before and waste no time in advertising themselves. *X Factor* judge and former Pussycat Dolls singer Nicole Scherzinger, reflecting on her showbiz career, said: 'I sometimes wish I were more slutty. I would probably be a lot more successful.' Actress Joanna Lumley, however, issued some no-nonsense advice to young women: 'Don't look like trash, don't get drunk, don't break your heels and stagger about in the wrong clothes at midnight.'

In the medium of popular music, artist Beyoncé aims to look sexy: 'At the Billboard awards my skirt was so tight they had to lift me on stage.' Others like singer Adele take a different approach: 'The focus on my appearance has really surprised me. I've always been a size 14–16. I don't care about clothes. I'd rather spend my money on cigarettes and booze.'

Even politicians are not immune to the lure of sexual activity. Some find it fascinating, like politician Jacqui Smith admitting 'pornography fascinates us – media and public alike'. This proved true, as her husband admitted inadvertently charging pornographic videos on expenses. Others like Chief Secretary to the Treasury Danny Alexander, commenting on the love life of a former Lib Dem MP, are baffled: 'I just don't know where people find the time.'

Pleasure comes in many forms, and even royalty are happy to indulge: 'There is nothing like a good bong ' – The Prince of Wales on being the first to test the Royal Jubilee Bells, 2012.

It is clear that, whatever our age or status, sexuality in all its forms is a popular activity, hard work, entertaining and often bizarre. Actress Felicity Kendal acknowledges its popularity in response to a report that revealed women over 50 are having more sex than in their youth: 'They couldn't have had more than I had, but it was only ever one at a time.'

According to author Kathy Lette, sexuality is often entertaining and challenges old stereotypes: 'I doubt that any man would have trouble multi-tasking at, say, an orgy.'

Finally, Lady Gaga, no stranger to the bizarre, explains her unique style: 'So basically I did this whole show carrying 100 lbs, looking out of one eye, dancing. Then my tits explode at the end. 'It's not as easy as it looks.'

✳

In any collection of quotations there is a need for accuracy – quotations are frequently attributed to people who never said them, or who said them in quite a different form or context to the one in which they are represented.

The quotations in this book are derived from a variety of sources: books, magazines and interviews. The quotes are assumed to be accurate and all were obtained from previously published or broadcast sources. The quotes are, of course, the opinion of those who first spoke or wrote them. As much information about the speaker is included as has been possible to find.

ACRONYMS

SIECUS
Sex Information and Education Council of the United States.
SIECUS was founded in 1964, when one in two marriages was
warped by sexual problems.

SINBADS
Women who are: Single In Need of Blokes, in Absolutely Desperate
State

USWISOMWAGMOHOTM
United Single Women In Search Of Men Who Aren't Gay, Married,
Or Hung-up On Their Mothers

SCUM
Society for Cutting Up Men manifesto

The PC is the LSD of the '90s
Timothy Leary, American psychologist

WIFE
Washing, Ironing, Fucking, Etc.

SHICPMP
So Happy I Could Piss My Pants

THTH
Too Hot To Handle

IMFAO
In My Fucking Arrogant Opinion

ACTING

Strip Club Shock – Magistrates May Act on Indecent Shows
Daily Mirror **headline**

I'm glad you like my Catherine. I like her too. She ruled 30 million

people and had 3,000 lovers. I do the best I can in two hours.
Mae West (1893–1980), American actress, speaking from the stage after her performance in *Catherine the Great*

Dramatic art in her opinion is knowing how to fill a sweater.
Bette Davis (1908–1989), American actress, on Jayne Mansfield

I just pretended I was a cartoon. I exaggerated every move. Every time I made a movement, I would think like a cartoon.
Kim Basinger, American actress, on her role as a cartoon seductress

All those actresses who turned the film away are stupid. I believe that if you have the right equipment and a point of view, that's a deadly combination.
Sharon Stone, American actress, on her role in the film *Basic Instinct*

Some American producers discuss actresses as if they were a load of cows.
Jackie Collins, British novelist

A good actress lasts, and sex attraction does not.
Brigitte Bardot, French actress turned animal-rights campaigner

I have made enough faces.
Greta Garbo (1905–1990), Swedish actress, refusing ever again to perform, c.1946

Acting is not very hard. The most important things are being able to laugh and cry. If I have to cry, I think about my sex life. And if I have to laugh – well, I think of my sex life.
Glenda Jackson, British Labour Party politician and former actress, describing her acting technique

Everybody's attracted to sex. So I'm learning to use it a lot better than I used to, because if we ain't using it, we're wasting it.
Kim Basinger, American actress

A man can be a great lover, but no matter how well he performs, sex won't compensate for personality, intelligence, consideration, and whatever else you may be looking for. You may think you're in love when the passions of sex get hold of you, but if you didn't love the man before, you won't love him after. Like him, maybe – but not love him!
Mae West (1893–1980), American actress

Ladies, here's a hint; if you're playing against a friend who has big boobs, bring her to the net and make her hit backhand volleys. That's the hardest shot for the well-endowed.
Billie Jean King, American tennis player, winner of 12 Grand Slams

The strongest possible piece of advice I would give to any young woman is: don't screw around and don't smoke.
Edwina Currie, British novelist and former Conservative MP

Never be possessive. If a female friend lets on that she is going out with another man, be kind and understanding. If she says she would like to go out with all the Dallas Cowboys, including the coaching staff, the same applies. Tell her 'Kath, you must go right ahead and do what you feel is right.' Unless you actually care for her, in which case you must see to it that she has no male contact whatsoever.
Bruce Jay Friedman, American novelist and screenwriter, in *The Lonely Guy's Book of Life*, **extracted in** *Esquire* **magazine, 1977**

So this gentleman said a girl with brains ought to do something else with them besides think.
Anita Loos (1893–1981), American screenwriter of *Gentlemen Prefer Blondes*, **1953**

The only time to believe any kind of rating is when it shows you at the top.
Bob Hope (1903–2003), American comedian, in *Playboy* **magazine, 1973**

You must try harder at your French letters.
Phillip Schofield, British TV presenter and actor, advising children on writing in French

Don't try! You have too luscious a bosom to keep the conversation general.
Madame Aubernon de Nerville (1825–1899), French hostess known for her salon

In lovemaking, feigning lovers succeed much better than the really devoted.
Ninon de Lenclos (1620–1705), French author and courtesan

Men should keep their eyes wide open before marriage, and half-shut afterwards.
Madeleine de Scudéry (1607–1701), French writer

When you're bored with yourself, marry and be bored with someone else.
David Pryce-Jones, British writer, in *Owls and Satyrs*, **1961**

You don't want to work here. After all, how many ways are there to say 'big tits'?
Shel Silverstein (1930–1999), American singer and children's writer

Never hurt a man whom you respect nor a woman whom you do not deeply love.
George C. Scott (1927–1999), American actor and director, in *Esquire* **magazine, 1965**

A woman seldom asks for advice until she has bought her wedding clothes.
Joseph Addison (1672–1719), British writer and politician, in the *Spectator*, **1712**

There are two guidelines in good sex: don't do anything you really don't enjoy, and find out your partner's needs and don't balk if you can help it.
Dr Alex Comfort (1920–2000), British sexologist and author of *The Joy of Sex*, **1972**

Trust your husband, adore your husband, and get as much as you can in your own name.
Joan Rivers, American comedienne, repeating advice from her mother

Why should we take advice on sex from the Pope? If he knows anything about it, he shouldn't.
George Bernard Shaw (1856–1950), Irish playwright

Some women choose to follow men, and some women choose to follow their dreams. If you're wondering which way to go, remember that your career will never wake up and tell you that it doesn't love you any more.
Lady Gaga, American singer

If he invited you out, he's got to pay.
Beyoncé, American singer

AFFAIRS

What I have seen of the love affairs of other people has not led me to regret that deficiency in my experience.
Mrs Clandon, in *You Never Can Tell* **by George Bernard Shaw (1856–1950), Irish playwright**

Just how difficult it is to write a biography can be reckoned by anybody who sits down and considers just how many people know the real truth about his or her love affairs.
Rebecca West (1892–1983), British writer

I don't remember any love affairs. One must keep love affairs quiet.
Wallis Simpson, Duchess of Windsor (1896–1986)

I knew about the affair . . . [I] told Paddy . . . 'Look, kiddo, you've got to come clean or people will think that it's something much worse.'
Jane Ashdown, wife of former Liberal Democrat leader Paddy Ashdown, on his much-publicised affair

Baloney!
Barbara Bush, wife of President George Bush, on the allegations that he had an affair

I don't sleep with married men, but what I mean is that I don't sleep with happily married men.
Britt Ekland, Swedish actress

Some of the greatest affairs I've known involved one actor unassisted.
Wilson Mizner (1876–1933), American playwright

[Americans are] better at having a love affair that lasts ten minutes than any other people in the world.
Stephen Spender (1909–1995), American poet laureate

Alex, I can't see why having an affair with someone on and off is any worse than being married for a course or two at mealtimes.
Bob, in Sunday Bloody Sunday **by Penelope Gilliatt (1932–1993), British screenwriter**

Sara could commit adultery at one end and weep for her sins at the other, and enjoy both operations at once.
Joyce Cary (1888–1957), Irish novelist, in The Horse's Mouth, **1944**

Mick screws many but has few affairs.
Bianca Jagger, model, activist and ex-wife of Mick Jagger

In Europe, extramarital affairs are considered a sign of good health.
Jean-Pierre Detremmerie, Belgian politician, commenting on Bill Clinton's alleged affairs

If I had as many love affairs as you have given me credit for, I would now be speaking to you from a jar in the Harvard Medical School.
Frank Sinatra (1915–1988), American singer

I used to date the lead singer of the Cranberries, but she cheated on me. Turns out she had some turkey on the side.
Jarod Kintz, American writer, in It Occurred to Me

I haven't trusted polls since I read that 62 per cent of women had affairs during their lunch hours. I've never met a woman in my life who would give up lunch for sex.
Erma Bombeck (1927–1996), American writer

AGEING

Now that I'm over 60 I'm veering toward respectability.
Shelley Winters (1920–2006), American actress

I refuse to admit that I'm more than 52, even if that does make my sons illegitimate.
Lady Nancy Astor (1879–1964), first woman to sit as an MP in the House of Commons

The lovely thing about being 40 is that you can appreciate 25-year-old men more.
Colleen McCullough, Australian writer

A man's as old as he's feeling, a woman as old as she looks.
Mortimer Collins (1827–1876), British writer

When a woman tells you her age, it's all right to look surprised, but don't scowl.
Wilson Mizner (1876–1933), American playwright

The age of a woman doesn't mean a thing. The best tunes are played on the oldest fiddles.
Ralph Waldo Emerson (1803–1882), American writer

Middle age is the time when a man is always thinking that in a week or two he will feel as good as ever.
Don Marquis (1878–1937), American humorist and writer

You know, when I first went into the movies Lionel Barrymore played my grandfather. Later he played my father and finally he played my husband. If he had lived, I'm sure I would have played his mother. That's the way it is in Hollywood. The men get younger and the women get older.
Lillian Gish (1893–1993), American actress

The older one grows the more one likes indecency.
Virginia Woolf (1882–1941), British writer

I've always been a bit more maturer than what I am.
Samantha Fox, former British glamour model

When a woman in love reaches a certain age, though her heart may cease to sing, her eyes remain veiled with gratitude.
Colette (Sidonie-Gabrielle, 1873–1954), French writer

I'm 40 and no woman knows what falling in love can mean until she's 40.
Marie Lloyd (1870–1922), British music-hall singer

The great thing about being 30 is that there are a great deal more available women. The young ones look younger and the old ones don't look nearly so old.
Glenn Frey, American singer and founding member of The Eagles

A lot of people start to fall to bits at 30 . . . quite honestly once you are able to reproduce you're over the hill. You start to go downhill at 18 physically.
Mick Jagger, lead singer of the Rolling Stones

Time and trouble will tame an advanced woman, but an advanced old woman is uncontrollable by any earthly force.
Dorothy L. Sayers (1893–1957), British writer

Every man over 40 is a scoundrel.
George Bernard Shaw (1856–1950), Irish playwright, in Maxims for Revolutionists

She may very well pass for 43 in the dusk, with a light behind her!
Mortimer Collins (1827–1876), British writer, in The Unknown Quantity, **1876**

A man is only as old as the woman he feels.
Groucho Marx (1880–1977), American comedian

One searches the magazines in vain for women past their first youth. The middle-aged face apparently sells neither perfume nor floor wax. The role of the mature woman in the media is almost entirely negative.
Janet Harris, American writer, in The Prime of Ms America, **1975**

AIDS

Take the wife.
Edwina Currie, British writer and former Conservative MP, advising businessmen travelling abroad on how to avoid catching AIDS

It could be said that the AIDS pandemic is a classic own-goal scored by the human race against itself.
Anne, Princess Royal

Every time you sleep with a boy, you sleep with all his old girlfriends.
AIDS poster, 1987

Several times a day they show a television cartoon in which a lustful-looking bee flies from flower to flower while a voice-over says, 'There is a disease that spreads through sex.' At the end of the cartoon the bee drops down dead. We would like to make it quite clear that bees are not promiscuous. They do not carry AIDS. And they do not visit flowers for sex, but for nectar. We feel bees and flowers are too gentle a topic to be associated with AIDS.
Ton Kemps, secretary of the Dutch Beekeepers' League, protesting against the Dutch Government's anti-AIDS campaign

The most frightening fact about AIDS is that it can be spread by normal sex between men and women. This is still rare in Scotland.
Scottish Sunday Mail

For the first time in history, sex is more dangerous than the cigarette afterwards.
Jay Leno, American chat-show host

ALIMONY

You never realise how short a month is until you pay alimony.
John Barrymore (1882–1942), American actor

If the income tax is the price you have to pay to keep the government on its feet, alimony is the price we have to pay for sweeping a woman off hers.
Groucho Marx (1880–1977), American comedian

Alimony is the curse of the writing classes.
Norman Mailer (1923–2007), American writer and political activist

The high cost of leaving.
Anon

Bounty after the mutiny.
Johnny Carson (1925–2005), American television host and comedian, on NBC's *Tonight Show*, **1984**

The claim for alimony . . . implies the assumption that a woman is economically helpless.
Suzanne La Follette (1893–1983), American feminist writer

ART

Why should I paint dead fish, onions and beer glasses? Girls are so much prettier.
Marie Laurencin (1883–1956), French painter, quoted in *Time* **magazine, 1956**

A painting of a nude Mick Jagger, taken from the rear by Cecil Beaton, was sold by London auctioneers Bonham's yesterday for £1,050.
Report in the *Evening Standard*, **16 July 1986**

I called the drawing 'HRH Royal Britannia': I wanted the image to have a romantic title and also be strong and sexy and strident.
Tracey Emin, British artist, on her latest drawing of HM Queen Elizabeth, 2012

BAD

I believe that it's better to be looked over than it is to be overlooked. And that a girl who keeps her eyes open is always the kind to look out for. I know the difference between a good man and a bad one, but I haven't decided which I like better.
Mae West (1893–1980), American actress

I don't think that the wrath of God descends on bad girls. No, I think bad girls have a ball and die having a ball. The life my characters lead – having affairs, living from one party to the next . . . and going shopping – this is their idea of a ball. It's not up to me to say, 'Girls, this isn't the sort of ball you should be having.'
Shobhaa De, Indian writer

There is no worse evil than a bad woman; and nothing has ever been produced better than a good one.
Euripides (c.480–406 BC), Greek playwright, in *Melanippe,* **fifth century BC**

It's the good girls who keep the diaries; the bad girls never have the time.
Tallulah Bankhead (1902–1968), American actress

I'm not a bad girl, I'm just a good girl who does bad things.
Anon

I just sort of wish people would dance differently. It reminds me of teenage sex.
Laurie Anderson, American musician

There's nothing better than good sex. But bad sex? A peanut butter and jelly sandwich is better than bad sex.
Billy Joel, American singer

The worst sex I've ever had has always been great.
Vince McMahon, American sports commentator, in *Esquire,* **2005**

BACHELORS

We are lads. We have burgled houses and nicked car stereos, and we like girls and swear and go to the football and take the piss.
Noel Gallagher, British singer, in interview, *Melody Maker,* **1996**

A bachelor's virtue depends upon his alertness; a married man's depends upon his wife's.
H.L. Mencken (1880–1956), American writer and humorist

Never trust a husband too far, nor a bachelor too near.
Helen Rowland (1875–1950), American writer and humorist

Bachelors are not fashionable any more. They are a damaged lot. Too much is known about them.
Lord Caversham, in *An Ideal Husband* **by Oscar Wilde (1854–1900), Irish playwright**

Being a bachelor is the first requisite of the man who wishes to form an ideal home.
Beverley Nichols (1898–1983), British writer

A bachelor never quite gets over the idea that he is a thing of beauty and a boy forever.
Helen Rowland

A bachelor has to have inspiration for making love to a woman, a married man needs only an excuse.
Helen Rowland

I'm o'er young, I'm o'er young,
I'm o'er young to marry yet!
I'm o'er young, 'twod be a sin
To tak me frae my mammy yet.
Robert Burns (1759–1796), Scottish poet, in *Aye Waukin O*

People always assume that bachelors are single by choice and spinsters because nobody asked them. It never enters their heads that poor bachelors might have worn the knees of their trousers out proposing to girls who rejected them or that a girl might deliberately stay unmarried because she didn't want to spend the rest of her life filling a man's stomach with food and washing his dirty shirts.
Jilly Cooper, British novelist, in *Angels in a Rush*

No unmarried woman can be polite to a bachelor without beginning to speculate how he would look in a wedding coat. This fact, which is too obvious to need proof, makes friendly dealings with them somewhat strained.
H.L. Mencken (1880–1956), American writer and humorist

Most men are [married]. I say countries go to war. The question is – is it a good idea? I live alone (a bachelor flat in Teddington) and

any woman would love to get their hands on it and do it over. But I have freedom and the only person I have to please is me.
Benny Hill (1924–1992), British comedian

BEAUTY

For the butterfly, mating and propagation involve the sacrifice of life; for the human being, the sacrifice of beauty.
Johann Wolfgang von Goethe (1749–1832), German writer

Is it too much to ask that a woman be spared the daily struggle for superhuman beauty in order to offer it to the caresses of a subhumanly ugly mate?
Germaine Greer, Australian feminist writer

I love being a woman. You can cry. You get to wear pants now. If you're on a boat and it's going to sink, you get to go on the rescue boat first. You can wear cute clothes. It must be a great thing, or so many men wouldn't be wanting to do it.
Gilda Radner (1946–1989), American actress

We have to have faith in ourselves. I have never met a woman who, deep down in her core, really believes she has great legs. And if she suspects that she might have great legs, then she's convinced that she has a shrill voice and no neck.
Cynthia Heimel, American feminist writer

There's a difference between beauty and charm. A beautiful woman is one I notice. A charming woman is one who notices me.
John Erskine (1879–1951), American educator

It's a good thing that beauty is only skin deep or I'd be rotten to the core.
Phyllis Diller (1917–2012), American actress

When I go to the beauty parlour, I always use the emergency entrance. Sometimes I just go for an estimate.
Phyllis Diller

Beauty is altogether in the eye of the beholder.
Margaret Wolfe Hungerford (1855–1897), Irish novelist, in *Molly Bawn*, **1878**

I admit that I think that it is better to be beautiful than to be good. But on the other hand, no one is more ready than I am to acknowledge that it is better to be good than to be ugly.
Lord Henry, in *The Picture of Dorian Gray* **by Oscar Wilde (1854–1900), Irish playwright**

Beauty for some provides escape
Who gain happiness in eyeing
The gorgeous buttocks of the ape
Or Autumn sunsets exquisitely dying.
Aldous Huxley (1894–1963), British writer

The epithet beautiful is used by surgeons to describe operations which their patients describe as ghastly, by physicists to describe methods of measurement which leave sentimentalists cold, by lawyers to describe cases which ruin all the parties to them, and by lovers to describe the objects of their infatuation, however unattractive they may appear to the unaffected spectators.
George Bernard Shaw (1856–1950), Irish playwright

Beauty. The power by which a woman charms a lover and terrifies a husband.
Ambrose Bierce (1842–1914), American writer

If beauty isn't genius it usually signals at least a high level of animal cunning.
Peter York, British journalist

The feminine vanity-case is the grave of masculine illusions.
Helen Rowland (1875–1950), American writer and humorist

Life belongs to the pretty woman.
Lady Isobel Barnett (1918–1980), British television personality

One girl can be pretty – but a dozen are only a chorus.
F. Scott Fitzgerald (1896–1940), American novelist, in *The Last Tycoon,* **1941**

Manners are especially the need of the plain. The pretty can get away with anything.
Evelyn Waugh (1903–1966), British novelist

My love in her attire doth show her wit. It doth so well become her:
For every season she hath dressings fit, for winter, spring and summer.
No beauty she doth miss, when all her robes are on:
But beauty's self she is, when all her robes are gone.
Sixteenth-century madrigal

You're the most beautiful woman I've ever seen, which doesn't say much for you.
Groucho Marx (1880–1977), American comedian, in *Animal Crackers*, **1930**

In Britain, an attractive woman is somehow suspect. If there is talent as well, it is overshadowed. Beauty and brains just can't be entertained; someone has been too extravagant.
Vivien Leigh (1913–1967), British actress

That although artificial teeth are a great blessing, and although a suitable wig may be a charitable covering for a bald head, yet she is committing a sin against her personal appearance as well as against her self-respect if she dyes her hair.
Mary Scharlieb (1845–1930), British gynaecological surgeon and writer, in *The Seven Ages of Woman*, **1915**

It's not fair the emphasis put on beauty, or on sexuality.
Rosanna Arquette, American actress

Everyone wants to look like her. Chick with a dick.
Cheryl Cole, British singer, on Lily Allen

BED

The happiest part of a man's life is what he passes lying awake in bed in the morning.
Dr Samuel Johnson (1709–1784), British writer and lexicographer

The cool kindliness of sheets, that soon smooth away trouble; and the rough male kiss of blankets.
Rupert Brooke (1887–1915), British war poet

For I've been born and I've been wed – all of man's peril comes of bed.
Charles Henry Webb (1834–1905), American journalist

She isn't a bad bit of goods, the Queen! I wish all the fleas in my bed were as good.
Miguel de Cervantes (1547–1616), Spanish writer, in *Don Quixote,* **1605**

It is getting too squeaky. The technicians are worried one of the legs might fall off.
Anonymous BBC Radio 4 source, on the bed used in the radio programme *The Archers*

Always buy a good pair of shoes and a good bed – if you're not in one you're in the other.
Gloria Hunniford, British television presenter, repeating advice from her mother

This morning my girlfriend was so loud in bed that we woke up the neighbours. So I told them to roll over and go back to sleep.
Jarod Kintz, American writer, in *It Occurred to Me*

BEHAVIOUR

If women are supposed to be less rational and more emotional at the beginning of our menstrual cycle when the female hormone is at its lowest level, then why isn't it logical to say that, in those few days, women behave the most like the way men behave all month long?
Gloria Steinem, American feminist writer

The mother-in-law thinks I'm effeminate; not that I mind because, beside her, I am!
Les Dawson (1934–1993), British comedian

There is a tide in the affairs of women,
Which, taken at the flood, heads – God knows where.
Lord Byron (1788–1824), British Romantic poet, in *Don Juan,* **1819**

He was the rudest, meanest man I've ever seen. He was terrifically hostile – maybe because he was blind – and everybody hated him but that one secretary he was going to bed with. She was the ugliest thing you've ever seen, but he didn't care because he couldn't see her.
Truman Capote (1924–1984), American writer, on James Thurber

Funny really. When you look at the things that go on these days, my story reads like Noddy.
Diana Dors (1931–1984), British actress

My candle burns at both ends;
It will not last the night;
But Ah, my foes, and Oh my friends –
It gives a lovely light!
Edna St Vincent Millay (1892–1950), American poet, in *A Few Figs From Thistles*, **1922**

I'm proud that I was never vulgar. There's no way I'd need a tattoo or [to] dress up in some surgical appliance to give folks a good night out.
Tina Turner, American singer, referring to Cher

I repent of my diets, the delicious dishes rejected out of vanity, as much as I lament the opportunities for making love that I let go because of pressing tasks or puritanical virtue.
Isabel Allende, Chilean writer

The behaviour of a human being in sexual matters is often a prototype for the whole of his other modes of reaction in life.
Sigmund Freud (1856–1939), Austrian psychoanalyst, in *Sexuality and the Psychology of Love*

BELIEF

Contrary to popular belief, English women do not wear tweed nightgowns.
Hermione Gingold (1897–1987), British actress

I've always been famous, it's just no one knew it yet.
Lady Gaga, American singer

Understand that sexuality is as wide as the sea. Understand that your morality is not law. Understand that we are you. Understand that if we decide to have sex whether safe, safer, or unsafe, it is our decision and you have no rights in our lovemaking.
Derek Jarman (1942–1994) British film-maker and gay activist

People take sex far too seriously.
Christina Aguilera, American singer, in *Newsweek,* **2006**

I don't want to be horny when I'm seventy, because it will be so hard to fulfil.
Neil Simon, American playwright and screenwriter

I'm not going to lose weight because someone tells me to. I make music to be a musician, not to be on the cover of *Playboy* or *Vogue*.
Adele, British singer

I would never know how to sell myself as a sex symbol. That's not how I'm programmed.
Jude Law, British actor

BIRTH CONTROL

. . . wherefore, since if the parts be smooth, conception is prevented, some anoint that part of the womb on which the seed falls with oil of cedar, or with ointment of lead or with frankincense, commingled with olive oil.
Aristotle (384–322 BC), Greek philosopher

The remedy for preventing conception shocks the mind of woman, at the first thought; but prejudice soon flies.
Richard Carlile (1790–1843), British campaigner for universal suffrage and the emancipation of women, in *Every Woman's Book; or, What is Love?*

If instead of birth control everyone would preach drink control, you would have little poverty, less crime and fewer illegitimate children . . . I speak feelingly; for as my brother Harold John Tennant and I were the last of twelve children, it is more than probable we should never have existed had the fashion of birth control been prevalent in the eighties.

Margot Asquith (1865–1945), wife of Prime Minister Herbert Henry Asquith, in *Places and Persons*, 1925

We want far better reasons for having children than not knowing how to prevent them.
Dora Russell (1894–1986), British socialist campaigner and writer

The contraceptive pill may reduce the importance of sex not only as a basis for the division of labour, but as a guideline in developing talents and interests.
Caroline Bird, American writer, in *Born Female*, 1968

He no play-da-game. He no make-a-da rules!
Earl Butz (1909–2008), US Secretary of Agriculture under Presidents Nixon and Ford, referring to the Pope's stricture against contraception

Vasectomies and condoms are as safe for women as anything based on men's behaviour can be.
Spare Rib **magazine**

Skullion had little use for contraceptives at the best of times. Unnatural, he called them, and placed them in the lower social order of things along with elastic-sided boots and made-up bow ties. Not the sort of attire for a gentleman.
Tom Sharpe, British novelist, in *Porterhouse Blue*, 1974

My girlfriend just found out she's been taking aspirins instead of the pill. Well, at least she doesn't have a headache – but I do.
From *Laugh-In*, NBC TV, 1969

The pill came to market and changed the sexual and real estate habits of millions: motel chains were created to serve them.
Herbert Gold, American novelist, in the *New York Times*, 1972

Young girl: Have I had any side effects from the pill?
Doctor: Only promiscuity.
Don Orehek, American cartoonist, caption in *Playboy* magazine, 1969

I wonder how he feels, his first game in a Dutch cap.
Barry Davies, British sports commentator, discussing a member of the Holland football team during the 1990 World Cup

Even if a condom in your purse was approaching the sell-by date, it would still be worth having it.
Ben Elton, British writer and comedian

Some women behave like harlots when they feel the life of a child in their wombs. They induce herbs or other means to cause miscarriage, only to perpetuate their amusement and unchastity. Therefore I shall deprive them from everlasting life and send them to everlasting death.
Bridget of Sweden (1303–1373), Swedish nun and visionary, in *Revelations*

The command 'be fruitful and multiply' was promulgated according to our authorities, when the population of the world consisted of two people.
William Ralph Inge (Dean Inge, 1860–1954), British professor of Divinity at Cambridge and Dean of St Paul's, in *More Lay Thoughts of a Dean,* **1931**

Protestant women may take the pill, Roman Catholic women must keep taking *The Tablet.*
Irene Thomas (1919–2001), British radio personality (*The Tablet* **is a Roman Catholic newspaper)**

Family Planning – please use rear entrance.
Sign outside the Barnstable Health Centre

Let us have a vast condom within us to protect the health of our soul amid the filth into which it is plunged.
Gustave Flaubert (1821–1880), French writer

The unbelieving repulsion on her face was fixed forever for me like Kean's Macbeth.
John Osborne (1929–1994), British playwright, recalling his meeting with Lynn Reid Banks, author of *The L-Shaped Room,* **after he had offered her a sandwich into which he had inserted a used condom**

The best contraceptive is a glass of cold water: not before or after, but instead.
Pakistani delegate at the International Planned Parenthood Conference

It is now quite lawful for a Catholic woman to avoid pregnancy

by a resort to mathematics, though she is still forbidden to resort to physics and chemistry.
H.L. Mencken (1880–1956), American writer and humorist

Contraceptives should be used on all conceivable occasions.
Spike Milligan (1918–2002), British comedian

I want to tell you a terrific story about oral contraception. I asked this girl to sleep with me and she said 'No'.
Woody Allen, American actor and film-maker

If nature had arranged that husbands and wives should have children alternatively, there would never be more than three in a family.
Lawrence Housman (1865–1959), British writer and illustrator

Don't wreck a sublime chocolate experience by feeling guilty. Chocolate isn't like premarital sex. It will not make you pregnant. And it always feels good.
Lora Brody, American celebrity chef

BISEXUALITY

Bisexuality is not so much a cop-out as a fearful compromise.
Jill Johnston (1929–2010), American feminist writer, in *Lesbian Nation***, 1973**

I can't understand why more people aren't bisexual. It would double your chances for a date on Saturday night.
Woody Allen, American actor and film-maker

A Bay Area bisexual told me I didn't quite coincide with either of his desires.
Woody Allen

If you swing both ways, you really swing . . . double your pleasure.
Joan Baez, American folk singer

OK, OK, if you're asking me am I one, I'll go that route – good public relations. If it's good enough for Gore Vidal and Elton John, it's good enough for me. I am bisexual, happy and proud. A woman

in every bed . . . and a man too.
Rock Hudson (1925–1985), American actor

There's nothing wrong with going to bed with somebody of your own sex. People should be very free with sex – they should draw the line at goats.
Elton John, British singer

I was too polite to ask.
Gore Vidal **(1925–2012), American writer and wit, when asked whether his first sexual experience had been heterosexual or homosexual**

I am not bisexual. I am not gay. I have never had sex with men.
Matt LeBlanc, American actor

BLONDES

Blondes have the hottest kisses. Red-heads are fair-to-middling torrid, and brunettes are the frigidest of all. It's something to do with hormones, no doubt.
Ronald Reagan (1911–2004), American actor and 40th President of the United States

Is it possible that blondes also prefer gentlemen?
Mamie Van Doren, American actress who modelled herself on Marilyn Monroe

Who can resist a date with a blonde? She always wanted me to come back. By God I've been lucky, haven't I?
Professor Sir Alan Walters (1926–2009), on his appointment as Chief Economic Advisor to Margaret Thatcher

Sex makes you get real.
Pamela Anderson, Canadian actress and model, in *Playboy* **magazine**

We are born sexual creatures, thank God, but it's a pity so many people despise and crush this natural gift.
Marilyn Monroe (1926–1962), American actress

BODY

Really that little dealybob is too far away from the hole. It should be built right in.
Loretta Lynn, American country music singer, on the female body

Woman has ovaries, a uterus . . . It is often said that she thinks with her glands. Man superbly ignores the fact that his anatomy also includes glands, such as the testicles, and that they secrete hormones.
Simone de Beauvoir (1908–1986), French writer

Our [women's] bodies are shaped to bear children and our lives are a worship out of the processes of creation. All ambition and intelligence are beside that great elemental point.
Phyllis McGinley (1905–1978), Canadian-born poet

My bust was visible under the negligée in one scene. Suddenly, there were Barbra Streisand's breasts and I was worried that people might concentrate on my body instead of my acting.
Barbra Streisand, American actress and singer, on seeing rushes of the sex scenes with Nick Nolte in the film *The Prince of Tides*, **1991**

. . . Much like the stump-end of a whist-card pencil.
From *The Mastery of Sex Through Psychology and Religion* **by Leslie Weatherhead and Dr Marion Greaves, 1931**

He must have had a magnificent build before his stomach went in for a career of its own.
Margaret Halsey (1910–1997), American writer

When the life of the party wants to express the idea of a pretty woman in mime, he undulates his two hands in the air and leers expressively. The notion of a curve is so closely connected to sexual semantics that some people cannot resist sniggering at road signs. The most popular image of the female, despite the exigencies of the clothing trade, is all boobs and buttocks, a hallucinating sequence of parabolas and bulges.
Germaine Greer, Australian feminist writer, in *The Female Eunuch*, **1970**

Like a drawing by a student in a life class who was sitting at the back without his specs.
Victoria Wood, British comedienne, describing someone's appearance

I would have preferred to omit this chapter, that women might not become all the more arrogant by knowing that they also, like men, have testicles, and that they not only suffer the pain of having to nourish the child within their bodies . . . but also that they too put something of their own into it.
Juan Valverde de Amusco (c.1525–1588), Spanish anatomist, in *Historia de La Composicion del Cuerpo Humano,* **1556**

The two women gazed out of the slumped and sagging bodies that had accumulated around them.
Nadine Gordimer, South African writer and winner of the 1991 Nobel Prize for Literature, in *Vital Statistics,* **1965**

The womb of a woman is in the number of the insatiable things mentioned in the Scriptures. I cannot tell whether there is anything in the world its greediness may be compared unto; neither hell fire nor the earth being so devouring, as the privy parts of a lascivious woman.
Nicolas Venette (1633–1698), French physician, quoted in *The Mysteries of Conjugal Love Revealed*

Fat is not about lack of self-control or willpower. Fat is about protection, sex nurturance, mothering, strength and assertion. Fat is a social disease.
Susie Orbach, feminist psychotherapist, in *Fat is a Feminist Issue,* **1978**

I want to ask Tim if he's been manscaped.
Jenni Murray, host of BBC Radio 4 *Woman's Hour,* **on meeting presenter Tim Samuels**

I'm aware of my body.
Joanna Lumley, British actress

Abs are overrated anyway . . . What u know about this Bart Simpson body?
Bruno Mars, American singer, on Twitter

If you have a boyfriend and he loves my body then I'm not worried.
Adele, British singer

BOOKS

I didn't know, truly I didn't know. Mine is a life sheltered to the point of stuffiness. I attend no movies, for any motion picture theatre is an enlarged and magnificently decorated lethal chamber to me. I have read but little of Madame Glyn. I did not know that things like it were going on. I have misspent my days. When I think of all those hours flung away in reading Henry James and Santayana, when I might have been reading life, throbbing, beating, perfumed life, I practically break down. Where, I ask you, have I been, that no true word of Madame Glyn's literary feats has come to me?
Dorothy Parker (1893–1967), American wit, on Elinor Glyn, *New Yorker,* **1927**

Women who love men who hate women who love men too much but love men and on and on . . . you have to feel sorry for the women who buy this stuff and believe it. Even under the best of circumstances men are hard creatures to trap. Women who flatter themselves into thinking they've trapped one are like people who believe they can get rid of the cockroaches in their kitchen. They're in for a big surprise late one night when they turn on the light.
Harry Shearer, American actor and voice artist, giving his views on 'relationship' books

A lot of bad novels in which the clitoris is described as the red pearl and the penis is always described as engorged and throbbing. Mercy.
Rita Mae Brown, American feminist writer, on the sexual revolution

Is this a book that you would ever wish your wife or servants to read?
Mervyn Griffith-Jones QC (1909–1979), British prosecuting counsel at the trial for obscenity of D.H. Lawrence's novel *Lady Chatterley's Lover,* **1960**

Sister Susie built her hopes on the book of Marie Stopes but I fear from her condition she must have read the wrong edition.
Madge Kendall (1848–1945), British actress

Fair crack of the whip, who reads dictionaries anyway? You've guessed it, sport – old ladies doing the *Women's Weekly* crossword and audio-typists who can't spell 'receive'. Correct me if I'm wrong but case in point: A red-blooded digger puts the hard word on the homy little tart down the local rubbidy . . . she looks like she'll come across so he whips her up to his brick veneer unit and they're both starkers before the froth's gone flat on his Fosters. She's screaming for it, so what does this rat-bag do? He sticks his nose (wait for it) in a copy of the *Australian Pocket Oxford Dictionary*! Viewed dispassionately thus, I ask you, readers, what strange minority need does this flaming book meet?

Sir Les Patterson (aka Australian comedian Barry Humphries), in the *Sunday Times*

An interviewer asked me what book I thought best represented the modern American woman. All I could think of to answer was: *Madame Bovary*.

Mary McCarthy (1912–1989), American writer, in *On the Contrary*, **1962**

I'm going to introduce a resolution to have the Postmaster General stop reading dirty books and deliver the mail.

Gale W. McGee (1915–1992), US Senator of the Democratic Party

At last an unprintable book that is readable.

Ezra Pound (1885–1972), American poet, on Henry Miller's *Tropic of Cancer*, **1934**

Perversity is the muse of modern literature.

Susan Sontag (1933–2004), American writer and political activist

We romantic writers are there to make people feel and not think. A historical romance is the only kind of book where chastity really counts.

Barbara Cartland (1901–2000), British novelist

The modest and chaste woman may be assured that nothing in here is meant to offend her. Instruction, upon a matter, of which both men and women are by far too ignorant, for their welfare and happiness, is the sole object of this publication. It may shock

prejudices, but it will be approved by reason and due deliberation.
Richard Carlile (1790–1843), British campaigner for universal suffrage and the emancipation of women

Reading about sex in yesterday's novels is like watching people smoke in old films.
Fay Weldon, British writer, in an interview in *The Guardian*

A dirty book is rarely dusty.
Anon

Literature is mostly about having sex and not much about having children. Life is the other way round.
David Lodge, British writer and critic, in *The British Museum is Falling Down,* **1965**

BOREDOM

Who wants normal? I would get bored.
Nancy Dell'Olio, Italian lawyer and media personality, when asked about her relationships with men

BREASTS

It's impossible to be more flat-chested than I am.
Candice Bergen, American actress

Uncorsetted, her friendly bust gives promise of pneumatic bliss.
T.S. Eliot (1888–1965), American writer

There are two good reasons why men go to see her. Those are enough.
Howard Hughes (1905–1976), American business magnate, on Jane Russell

A fine woman shows her charms to most advantage when she seems most to conceal them. The finest bosom in nature is not so fine as imagination forms.
Dr John Gregory (1724–1773), British physician, in *A Father's Legacy to His Daughters,* **1774**

It was not a bosom to repose upon, but it was a capital bosom to hang jewels upon.
Charles Dickens (1812–1870), British writer, describing Mrs Merdle in *Little Dorrit,* **1857**

Of course I flaunt my assets. They are big, but I've always had 'em, pushed 'em up, whacked 'em around. Why not make fun when I've earned a fortune with 'em?
Dolly Parton, American country music singer

If I hadn't had them, I would have had some made.
Dolly Parton

Even today, every time I open a magazine I get depressed looking at cleavages which look as if they should be offering day trips. If it wasn't for men's infantile obsession with large breasts, women wouldn't experience these humiliating scenarios in the first place.
Jaci Stephen, British journalist, in *If Men Had More Up Top We'd Need Less Up Front*

Boys, I've got an idea. Let's fill the whole screen with tits.
Hunt Stromberg (1894–1968), American film producer, discussing a documentary about the South Seas

I came to London during the '70s with the Three Degrees and was staying at the Hilton Hotel. After a day's shopping, I breezed into reception to collect my key when I noticed a man in front of me staring with his eyes so wide open they were nearly falling out of his head. I thought maybe I knew him, so I said: 'Hello.' When I looked down, I realised the boob tube I was wearing had slipped and I was standing topless in front of a complete stranger.
Sheila Ferguson, American singer, describing her most embarrassing moment

MORDELL LECTURE, 1978. Professor J. Tits, of the Collège de France, will deliver the Mordell lecture at 5 p.m. on Monday 24th April in the Babbage lecture theatre, New Museums site. The title of the lecture will be 'Rigidity'.
Cambridge University Reporter

Miss World has always had its fair share of knockers.
Julia Morley, British chairwoman of the Miss World contests

A vacuum with nipples.
Otto Preminger (1905–1986), Austro-Hungarian film director, on Marilyn Monroe

To read the papers and magazines, you would think we were almost worshipping the female bosom.
Billy Graham, American Christian evangelist, 1966

If anything happens to me, please arrange for me to be buried topless.
Ann Stevens (1910–2004), mother of American actor George Hamilton, after she revealed that, at the age of 73, she had just had her breasts enlarged by silicone implant

Big breasts à la Pamela Anderson are one thing, but ones that look more like old socks with tangerines dropped in the bottom are an entirely different kettle of poison.
Arabella Weir, British actress and writer, in Does My Bum Look Big in This?**, 1997**

This country is into tits and ass.
Neil Simon, American playwright and screenwriter

I used to be so top-heavy that I leaned forward.
Loni Anderson, American actress

God bless Fergie for bringing back boobs and hips. Every fat farm girl should kiss Sarah Ferguson's chubby thighs.
Joan Rivers, American comedienne

My breasts aren't actresses.
Liv Ullman, Norwegian actress and director, on nudity in the theatre

It's not my fault they're pert.
Cheryl Cole, British singer, on her breasts

BULLSHIT

First, we see how women have been the cause of many troubles, have done great harm to those who govern cities, and have caused in them many divisions . . . among the primary causes of the

downfall of tyrants, Aristotle puts the injuries they do on account of women, whether rape, violation or the breaking up of marriages.
Niccolò Machiavelli (1469–1527), Italian philosopher, in *Discourses on the First Decade of Titus Livius*

The wife is entirely under the power and subjection of her husband.
James Balfour (c.1525–1573), British judge and politician, in *The Practiks of Sir James Balfour of Pittendreich***, 1550**

Woman in her greatest perfection was made to serve and obey man, not to rule and command him.
John Knox (c.1514–1572), British clergyman and leader of the Protestant Reformation, in *First Blast of the Trumpet Against the Monstrous Regiment of Women*

How is it that woman, who is soulless herself, can discern the soul in man? How can she judge about his morality who is herself non-moral? How can she grasp his character when she has no character herself?
Otto Weininger (1880–1903), Austrian religious writer, in *Our Church Review*

It is even possible, quite often, to spot women on the pill from a certain deadness about their flesh, lustiness about their eyes and lifelessness in their movements.
Malcolm Muggeridge (1903–1990), British writer and satirist, speaking on BBC television, 1965

Anyone who ever thought that Ellen and I broke it off because of sexuality couldn't be more mistaken. And for anyone who thought my mother's prayers had anything to do with me marrying a man, forget it.
Anne Heche, American actress

Just because I look sexy on the cover of *Rolling Stone* doesn't mean I'm naughty.
Britney Spears, American singer

I hate the whole reluctant sex-symbol thing. It's such bull. You see these dudes greased up, in their underwear, talking about how they don't want to be sex symbols.
Ben Affleck, American actor

I'm forcing more men into my company to get more sexual tension into the business – because I love the buzz and the sexuality of verbal foreplay.
Anita Roddick (1942–2007), founder of Body Shop International

My business is a love story with the world.
Luciano Benetton, Italian clothing magnate and founder of the Benetton Group

Like sex in Victorian England, the reality of Big Business today is our big dirty secret.
Ralph Nader, American attorney and activist

I have a tremendous charge out of business. I get the same sort of feeling that women must have when their babies pop out.
Sir Terence Conran, British designer and founder of Habitat

I often get invited to boardroom lunches as the token woman: I find it tempting to say something outrageous.
Jennifer d'Abo (1945–2003), British former chairwoman of Ryman Ltd

A lot of businesses are being started by women who have been working for idiots for years. They know they can do their boss's job, but they know they will never be given it.
Jean Denton, Baroness Denton of Wakefield (1935–2001), British businesswoman and politician

If you love your customer to death, you can't go wrong.
Sir Graham Day, Canadian-British businessman and former CEO of the Rover Group

If there was a good deal or a woman – I would probably go after the woman.
David Wickins (1921–2007), British founder of British Car Auctions and four times married

I'll tell you what: if you become our Playmate for July, I'll get you that new addressograph for your department.
Hugh Hefner, American founder of *Playboy* magazine, to his subscription manager, Charlaine Karalus; after some coaxing, she agreed

I sell projects but I try not to fall in love with them. If someone says to me, 'I love you', I have more suspicion of him than the guy who says, 'I just want to make money', God bless him. He's the guy I want to deal with.
Adnan Khashoggi, Saudi Arabian businessman

Where? When? How much?
Your place, tonight, free.
Business-like exchange between Francois d'Orleans, Prince de Joinville (1818–1900) and actress Rachel Felix

Advertising is the most fun you can have with your clothes on.
Jerry Della Femina, Italian-American advertising executive

Don't tell my mother I work in an advertising agency . . . she thinks I play piano in a whorehouse.
Jacques Séguéla, French publicist, 1979

Falling in love with the boss is the cardinal sin in the office. A girl must look after her boss – be a friend, public relations officer, colleague and nanny – but never love him. Nothing is more boring or irritating to his friends and colleagues than an adoring and possessive secretary.
Raine Spencer, Lady Dartmouth, British politician and socialite, addressing a group of secretarial students in 1966

Men will try to use secretaries as status symbols. They hire them for ornamental reasons. Every time a young one leaves to get married, they swear they'll go for someone older and steadier. Then they go right ahead and hire the next pretty face with 40-40 speeds.
Katharine Whitehorn, British journalist

Industrial relations are like sexual relations. It's better between two consenting parties.
Vic Feather (1908–1976), British former General Secretary of the TUC, in the *Guardian Weekly***, 1976**

Employees make the best dates. You don't have to pick them up and they're always tax deductible.
Andy Warhol (1928–1987), American artist, in *Exposures***, 1979**

In a society where people get more or less what they want sexually, it is much more difficult to motivate them in an industrialised context, to make them buy refrigerators and cars.
William S. Burroughs (1914–1997), American writer, in *The Guardian*, **1969**

Professionalism, if you like, is not having sex on Thursdays or Fridays.
Don Revie (1927–1989), British football manager, in *The Guardian*, **1976**

It's a historic moment for our company and for athletic supporters in general.
Randy Black, vice-president of Bike Athletic, on selling their 300-millionth jockstrap

Sex is not taxed, but it can be taxing.
John Barrymore (1882–1942), American actor

The sex element is the most important in the business. You must sell sex.
Bobby Darin (1936–1973), American singer

BUTTOCKS

A mystery man on a bicycle is being sought by police following two incidents in which Reading women have been jabbed in the buttocks. The police have been told that a man rode up behind young women in the town, stuck what is believed to be a school compass into them, and rode off.
From *Punch*'s 'Country Life' column

The buttocks are the most aesthetically pleasing part of the body because they are non-functional. Although they conceal an essential orifice, these pointless globes are as near as the human form can ever come to abstract art.
Kenneth Tynan (1927–1980), British theatre critic

The essence of life is the smile of round female bottoms, under the shadow of cosmic boredom.
Guy de Maupassant (1850–1893), French short-story writer

He kissed the plump mellow yellow smellow melons of her rump, on each plump melonous hemisphere, in their mellow yellow furrow, with obscure prolonged provocative melonsmellonous osculation.
James Joyce (1882–1941), Irish writer, in *Ulysses*, **1922**

How brave a prospect is a broad backside!
Henry Vaughan (1621–1695), British writer and physician

Mary: Which would you say is my best side, Mr Hitchcock?
Alfred: My dear, you're sitting on it.
Conversation between Mary Anderson, American actress, and Alfred Hitchcock (1899–1980), British film director, on a photoshoot for the 1944 film *Lifeboat*

It was a stupid compromise.
The explanation of a man with three previous convictions for indecent exposure, when arrested for baring his buttocks to a group of girls

Buttock fetishism is comparatively rare in our culture . . . Girls are often self-conscious about their behinds, draping themselves in long capes and tunics, but it is more often because they are too abundant in that region than otherwise.
Germaine Greer, Australian feminist writer, in *The Female Eunuch*, **1970**

George Moore unexpectedly pinched my behind. I felt rather honoured that my behind should have drawn the attention of the great master of English prose.
Ilka Chase (1900–1978), American actress and novelist

Do you scratch your bottom while taking a bath? Have it reglazed by the professionals.
Advert in the *Edinburgh Advertiser*

CANADA

Somebody who knows how to make love in a canoe.
Pierre Berton (1920–2004), Canadian writer, giving his definition of a Canadian

I can't give too many kisses. The Press is watching. Perhaps later.
Pierre Trudeau (1919–2000), fifteenth Prime Minister of Canada, to a female campaign worker

CAREER

A caress is better than a career.
Elisabeth Marbury (1856–1933), American playwright, in *Careers for Women*, **1933**

I trained to be a priest – started to. I went to seminary school when I was 11. I wanted to be a priest but when they told me I could never have sex, not even on my birthday, I changed my mind.
Johnny Vegas, British comedian

A career is a wonderful thing, but you can't hold on to it on a cold night.
Marilyn Monroe (1926–1962), American actress

They say an actor is only as good as his parts. Well, my parts have done me pretty well, darling.
Barbara Windsor, British actress

Sexual harassment at work. Is it a problem for the self-employed?
Victoria Wood, British comedienne

CAUTION

Beware of men on aeroplanes. The minute a man reaches 30,000 feet, he immediately becomes consumed by distasteful sexual fantasies which involve doing uncomfortable things in those tiny toilets. These men should not be encouraged; their fantasies are sadly low-rent and unimaginative. Affect an aloof, cool demeanour as soon as any man tries to draw you out. Unless, of course, he's the pilot.
Cynthia Heimel, American feminist writer

Woe to the man who tries to be frank in lovemaking.
George Sand **(Amantine Lucile Dupin, 1804–1876), French writer**

Anger repressed can poison a relationship as surely as the cruelest words.
Joyce Brothers (1927–2013), American psychologist and advice columnist

Among external causes are springtime, which is a particularly dangerous season, warm climates, improper clothes, rich food, indigestion, mental overwork, nervousness, habits of defective cleanliness, especially of the local kind, prolonged sitting or standing, too monotonous walking, sitting cross-legged, spanking, late rising, petting and indulgence corsets that produce stagnation or hyperaemia of blood and great straining of memory.
Professor G. Stanley Hall (1844–1924), pioneering American psychologist, talking about lust in *Adolescence*, **1904**

The itemized phone bill ranks up there with suspender belts, Sky Sports channels and *Loaded* magazine as inventions women could do without.
Maeve Haran, British writer, in interview, 1999

Beware of the man who denounces women writers; his penis is tiny and cannot spell.
Erica Jong, American writer

I used to be told if I talked about my sexuality in any way that we wouldn't have a tennis tour.
Billie Jean King, American tennis player, winner of 12 Grand Slams

Don't get married to an actress, because they're also actresses in bed.
Roberto Rossellini (1903–1977), Italian film director

When authorities warn you of the sinfulness of sex, there is an important lesson to be learned. Do not have sex with the authorities.
Matt Groening, American cartoonist and creator of *The Simpsons*

Katie Graham is going to get her teat caught in a big fat wringer.
John N. Mitchell (1913–1988), US Attorney General under President Nixon, on the *Washington Post***'s pursual of the Watergate story**

CENSORSHIP

The British Board of Censors will not pass any seduction scene unless the seducer has one foot on the floor. Apparently sex in England is something like snooker.
Fred Allen (1894–1956), American comedian and wireless star

If a man is pictured chopping off a woman's breast, it only gets an 'R' rating; but if, God forbid, a man is pictured kissing a woman's breast, it gets an 'X' rating. Why is violence more acceptable than tenderness?
Sally Struthers, American actress, in *Life* **magazine, 1984**

Censorship feeds the dirty mind more than the four-letter word itself.
Dick Cavett, American chat-show host, in *Playboy* **magazine, 1971**

It is appalling that naked women cannot be kept out of the nation's living room.
Billy Graham, American Christian evangelist, in support of censorship

I've got nothing against sex, it's a marvellous human activity; but it was watching others do it all the time that got me down.
John Trevelyan (1903–1986), former Secretary of the Board of British Film Censors, explaining why he resigned, 1974

That must be removed. It clearly portrays a male orgasm.
Margaret Thatcher (1925–2013), first female British Prime Minister, when chairwoman of the Finchley Arts Society, standing before a canvas with a single white splash on it

The steamy film *9½ Weeks* has been temporarily banned from Worthing's Dome cinema until it has been privately viewed by Worthing council's moral watchdogs. The film *Body Lust*, the best bit of crumpet in Denmark, will be shown instead.
Reported in the *Worthing Guardian*

Censorship, like charity, should begin at home; but unlike charity it should end there.
Clare Boothe Luce (1903–1987), American writer and politician

What's wrong with appealing to prurient interest? I really want the Supreme Court to tell me that fucking is dirty and no good.
Lenny Bruce (1925–1966), American comedian

I couldn't bend down to put a dish in the dishwasher without him seeing it as an invitation for a shag.
Denise Welch, British actress, *Loose Women*, **'Girls Night Out'**

You know that old saying: once you go dead, no one's better in bed.
Jeaniene Frost, American novelist, in *One Foot in the Grave*, **2008**

I'm as confident as Cleopatra's pussy.
Bette Midler, American actress

I think pop music has done more for oral intercourse than anything else that has ever happened, and vice versa.
Frank Zappa (1940–1993), American musician

CHANGE

A century and a half ago there were no knickers and girls read the Bible; now they wear impenetrable bodystockings and read *Portnoy's Complaint*.
Kenneth Tynan (1927–1980), British theatre critic

I don't think he has changed that much. He still eyes a pretty lady – and why not? This is part of his magnetism. This is Warren. What has changed, I hope, is that he doesn't seem to have that urge to bed these lovely ladies. Now that's a major change.
Annette Bening, American actress, on being asked what convinced her that marriage had changed Warren Beatty

We're living in an age where you have to call a chick and ask her if she'll wear a dress tonight. And they say: 'You're weird.'
Tim Rose (1940–2002), American singer

It's hard for me to get used to these changing times. I can remember when the air was clean and the sex was dirty.
George Burns (1896–1996), American actor and comedian

We were born in an era in which it was a disgrace for women to

be sexually responsible. We matured in an era in which it was an obligation.
Janet Harris, American writer, in *The Prime of Ms America,* **1975**

This Ken Starr report is now posted on the internet. I bet Clinton's glad he put a computer in every classroom.
Jay Leno, American chat-show host, referring to the report investigating Bill Clinton's misdemeanours in the *Sunday Times,* **1998**

Sex and older women used to be considered an oxymoron, rarely mentioned in the same breath.
Gail Sheehy, American writer and social critic

CHARM

'Charm' – which means the power to effect work without employing brute force – is indispensable to women. Charm is a woman's strength just as strength is a man's charm.
Havelock Ellis (1859–1939), British physician and writer

It's a sort of bloom on a woman. If you have it, you don't need to have anything else; and if you don't have it, it doesn't much matter what else you have.
J.M. Barrie (1860–1937), British writer

Charming women can true converts make
We love the precepts for the teacher's sake.
George **Farquhar (1677–1707), Irish playwright**

She lacks the indefinable charm of weakness.
Lord Henry, in *The Picture of Dorian Gray* **by Oscar Wilde (1854–1900), Irish playwright**

Men get to be a mixture of the charming mannerisms of the women they have known.
F. Scott Fitzgerald (1896–1940), American novelist

You know what charm is: a way of getting the answer yes without having asked any clear questions.
Albert Camus (1913–1960), French-Algerian Nobel Prize-winning writer

You know what, I'm very attracted to someone who makes me laugh and is that charming. Really, I could be charmed by anyone. I'm just a sucker for somebody that is charming.
Beyoncé, American singer

Simon is the most charismatic man I've met – it's like he's trancing you. It's actually quite scary.
Cheryl Cole, British singer, on Simon Cowell

CHASTITY

Lord, give me chastity – but not yet.
Saint Augustine (AD 354–430), early Christian theologian

As a child of eight, Mr Trout had once kissed a girl of six under the mistletoe at a Christmas party, but there his sex life had come to an abrupt halt.
P.G. Wodehouse (1881–1975), British writer, in *Bachelors Anonymous,* **1973**

Of all sexual aberrations, perhaps the most peculiar is chastity.
Remy de Gourmont (1858–1915), French writer and critic

A woman's chastity consists, like an onion, of a series of coats.
Nathaniel Hawthorne (1804–1864), American novelist

An unattempted woman cannot boast of her chastity.
Michel de Montaigne (1533–1592), French writer

In the old days poverty kept Latin women chaste: hard work, too little sleep, these were the things that saved their humble homes from corruption.
Juvenal (AD 60–130), Roman poet

Only one woman in thousands has been endowed with the God-given aptitude to live in chastity and virginity . . . God fashioned her body so that she could be with a man, to have and to rear children. No woman should be ashamed of that which God made and intended her.
Martin Luther (1483–1546), German Catholic priest and seminal figure in the Reformation

Nothing makes women more esteemed by the opposite sex than chastity; whether it be that we always prize most those who are hardest to come at, or that nothing beside chastity, with its collateral attendants truth, fidelity and constancy, gives the man a property in the person he loves, and consequently endears her to him above all things.
Anonymous contributor, in *Spectator*, **1711**

She is chaste who nobody has asked.
Ovid (43 BC–AD 17), Roman poet

The common man believes that in order to be chaste, a woman must not be too clever; in truth it is doing chastity too little honour to believe it can be found beautiful only by the blind.
Marie le Jars de Gournay (1565–1645), French feminist writer, in *Le Promenoir de M. de Montaigne*, **1594**

Those who choose matrimony do well; those who choose virginity or voluntary abstinence do better.
Pope Paul II (1417–1471)

Filth and old age; I'm sure you agree, are powerful wardens upon chastity.
Geoffrey Chaucer (1343–1400), British poet, known as the Father of English Literature

CHASTITY BELT

There is no doubt that the practice is a means of suppressing and controlling the sexual behaviour of women. Female circumcision is a physiological chastity belt.
Sue Armstrong, South African journalist, on assignment for the World Health Organisation, in *New Scientist*, **1991**

The advantages are manifold. Not only will the purity of the virgin be maintained but the fidelity of the wife exacted. The husband will leave the wife without fear that his honour will be outraged and his affections estranged.
A French advertisement for a chastity belt, from *The Girdle of Chastity* **by Eric Dingwall, 1931**

Made of iron, and consisting of a belt and a piece which came up under and was locked in position, so neatly made that once a woman was bridled it was out of the question for her to indulge in the gentle pleasure, as there were only a few little holes for her to piss through.
Pierre de Bourdeille, Seigneur de Brantôme (1540–1614), French writer, describing the chastity belt, in *The Lives of Gallant Ladies*

The Crusaders, we are told, put their wives into chastity belts before they sailed off for the Holy Land. They did not, for certain, put their own sexual equipment out of action for the duration.
Mary Stott (1907–2002), British journalist and feminist

Chastity – the most unnatural of sexual perversion.
Aldous Huxley (1894–1963), British writer

Someone told me the delightful story of the Crusader who put a chastity belt on his wife and gave the key to his best friend for safekeeping, in case of his death. He had ridden only a few miles away when his friend, riding hard, caught up with him saying, 'You gave me the wrong key!'
Anaïs Nin (1903–1977), American writer

CHILDBIRTH

None of the 15 legal men, comprising judge, senior and junior barristers and solicitors, had ever witnessed childbirth. Is it possible, the judge was to ask, for a woman to give birth standing up? Women have given birth underwater, in aeroplanes, in comas, lying unnaturally flat on their backs in hospital beds and even after death, but this man wondered if they could do it standing up . . .
Nell McCafferty, Irish playwright and feminist campaigner

Somewhere on this globe, every ten seconds, there is a woman giving birth to a child. She must be found and stopped.
Sam Levenson (1911–1980), American writer and television host

Simpson succeeded in proving that there was no harm in giving anaesthetics to men, because God put Adam into a deep sleep when he extracted his rib. But male ecclesiastics remained

unconvinced as regards the sufferings of women, at any rate in childbirth.
Bertrand Russell (1872–1970), British philosopher

My obstetrician was so dumb that when I gave birth he forgot to cut the cord. For a year that kid followed me everywhere. It was like having a dog on a leash.
Joan Rivers, American comedienne

To enter life by way of the vagina is as good a way as any.
Henry Miller (1891–1980), American writer

I have an intense desire to return to the womb. Anybody's.
Woody Allen, American actor and film-maker, in interview with *Esquire*

To my embarrassment, I was born in bed with a lady.
Wilson Mizner (1876–1933), American playwright

If men had to have babies they would only ever have one each.
Diana, Princess of Wales (1961–1997)

Often women have babies because they can't think of anything better to do.
Lord Beaumont of Whitley (1928–2008), Liberal Party politician and Anglican clergyman

I had a Jewish delivery: they knock you out with the first pain and they wake you up when the hairdresser shows.
Joan Rivers

Dr Snow gave that blessed chloroform and the effect was soothing, quieting and delightful beyond measure.
Queen Victoria (1819–1901), describing her labour in her journal of 1853

Publication is the male equivalent of childbirth.
Richard Ackland, British journalist, 1974

The artificial insemination of animals is taken for granted to improve the breed and product. Human insemination is a different ball-game.
The Catholic Register of Canada

Dear Mary,
We all knew you had it in you.
Dorothy Parker (1893–1967), American wit, congratulating a friend on the successful outcome of her pregnancy, 1915

I'm a woman of a certain age who doesn't have kids and never really settled down . . . I enjoy kids but not for long periods. I think they're adorable and funny and sweet, and then I have a headache.
Kim Cattrall, American actress

CHILDREN

Sometimes when I look at my children I say to myself, 'Lillian, you should have stayed a virgin.'
Lillian Carter (1898–1983), mother of President Jimmy Carter

An ugly baby is a very nasty object, and the prettiest is frightful when undressed.
Queen Victoria (1819–1901)

It takes a woman 20 years to make a man of her son, and another woman 20 minutes to make a fool of him.
Helen Rowland (1875–1950), American writer and humorist

A loud noise at one end and no sense of responsibility at the other.
Father Ronald Knox (1888–1957), British clergyman and BBC broadcaster

From the moment of birth, when the Stone-Age baby confronts the twentieth-century mother, the baby is subjected to these forces of violence called love, as its father and mother and their parents and their parents before them have been. These forces are mainly concerned with destroying most of its potential.
R.D. Laing (1927–1989), British psychiatrist

Babies are the enemies of the human race.
Isaac Asimov (1920–1992), American science-fiction writer

Don't take up a man's time talking about the smartness of your children; he wants to talk to you about the smartness of his.
E.W. Howe (1853–1937), American writer and editor

Before I got married I had six theories about bringing up children; now I have six children, and no theories.
John Wilmot, 2nd Earl of Rochester (1647–1680), British poet and courtier

Men are generally more careful of the breed of their horses and dogs than of their children.
William Penn (1644–1718), real-estate entrepreneur and founder of the state of Pennsylvania

I learned to walk as a baby, and I haven't had a lesson since.
Marilyn Monroe (1926–1962), American actress, when asked about her famous wiggle

Oh my son's my son till he gets him a wife, but my daughter's my daughter all her life.
Dinah Mulock Craik (1826–1887), British writer, in *Young and Old*, **c.1887**

I want to have children and I know my time is running out. I want to have them while my parents are still young enough to take care of them.
Rita Rudner, American actress and comedienne

No matter how much cats fight, there always seem to be plenty of kittens.
Abraham Lincoln (1809–1865), 16th President of the United States

After doing *One Fine Day*, and playing a paediatrician on *ER*, I'll never have kids. I'm going to have a vasectomy.
George Clooney, **American actor**

Familiarity breeds contempt – and children.
Mark Twain (1835–1910), American writer, in *Notebook*, **published posthumously in 1935**

I only have two rules for my newly born daughter: she will dress well and never have sex.
John Malkovich, American actor

CHIVALRY

Remember, men, we're fighting for this woman's honour, which is probably more than she ever did.
Groucho Marx (1880–1977), American comedian, in *Duck Soup*, **1933**

Every man I meet wants to protect me. I can't figure out what from.
Mae West (1893–1980), American actress

CLASS

There is no middle-class sexual style for men. What would it be based on? Golfing? Discussing stock options? Attending church? Downing highballs?
Edmund White, American writer

Diana Ross is a big inspiration to all of us. We all grew up watching everything about her – her mic placement, her grace, her style and her class.
Beyoncé, American singer

I think there's a fine line between being a slut and being classy. I walk in between that line.
Adele, British singer

COMFORT

I'm at the age where food has taken the place of sex in my life. In fact, I've just had a mirror put over my kitchen table.
Rodney Dangerfield (1921–2004), American comedian

COMMUNICATION

Whereas a lot of men used to ask for conversation when they really wanted sex, nowadays they often feel obliged to ask for sex even when they really want conversation.
Katharine Whitehorn, British journalist

I try to talk to one person. I've got this picture of a woman, a housewife, young or young at heart. She's probably on her own virtually all day. She's bored with the routine of housework and her own company, and just for her I'm the chatty, slightly cheeky romantic visitor.
David Hamilton, British radio broadcaster, quoted in *Is This Your Life?: Images of Women in the Media*, **edited by Josephine King and Mary Stott, 1977**

Love is just a system for getting someone to call you darling after sex.
Julian Barnes, British writer, in *Talking It Over*, **1991**

The trouble with talking about acting is that it's like sex. It's enormously fun to do but just dreadfully embarrassing when you have to talk about it.
Paul Bettany, British actor

I think sex is very interesting for most people, but I'm interested in sex as a way of communication. I'm not interested in the fantasy version of a sex scene.
Maggie Gyllenhaal, American actress

COMPLIMENTS

There are only two superlative compliments you can receive from a woman: 'I think you're a master chef, and I think you're a good lay.' The two basic drives in life.
Rod Steiger (1925–2002), American actor

Women are never disarmed by compliments. Men always are. That is the difference between the sexes.
Mrs Cheveley, in *An Ideal Husband* **by Oscar Wilde (1854–1900), Irish playwright**

The Queen did fish for men's souls, and had so sweet a bait that no one could escape her network.
Sir Christopher Hatton (1540–1591), British politician and Lord Chancellor of England, on Queen Elizabeth I

CONSCIENCE

The only time I worry is when I'm fishing. When I'm standing in the river for hours, I sometimes have a pee in the water. I'm always petrified some cameraman is going to catch me at it.
Prince Charles, Prince of Wales

CONVERSATION

I told him I've been too fucking busy – or vice versa.
Dorothy Parker (1893–1967), American wit

If you don't ring me, I'm going to kick you in the bollocks next time I see you.
Victoria Beckham, British fashion designer and former Spice Girl, to husband David after giving him her phone number, from *The Beckhams* **by Andrew Morton**

I think men talk to women so they can sleep with them and women sleep with men so they can talk to them.
Jay McInerney, American writer

Sex is better than talk. Ask anybody in this bar. Talk is what you suffer through so you can get to sex.
Val, played by Woody Allen, in *Hollywood Ending*, **2002**

COSMIC

The sex organ has a poetic power, like a comet.
Joan Miró (1893–1983), Spanish artist

I have been led to imagine that the few extraordinary women who have rushed in eccentrical directions out of the orbit prescribed to their sex were male spirits, confined by mistake in female frames.
Mary Wollstonecraft (1759–1797), British feminist writer, in *A Vindication of the Rights of Women*, **1792**

One may see a girl in her mother-nakedness dancing around a hippy guy, and another looking at the spectacle with passing amusement. Her boobs and the hirsute 'pelvic triangle' look

prominent in the soliciting gestures.
Som Deva, Indian sexologist, describing the sexual habits of the alternative society in *The Marching Eros*, **1983**

The underground was rather shy and inhibited. Later, though, when 'horizontal recruitment' became the more favoured form of recruitment on the libbo left, then it really did get going. The libertarian loony left scene of the early '70s was very strong on rogering and leg-over: it was a leg-over-based scene.
David Robins (1944–2007), British sociologist

A show is like having an orgasm. It's like having an incredible, natural climax. And then suddenly, it's all finished and you don't know what to do next.
Rod Stewart, British singer

So basically I did this whole show carrying 100 pounds, looking out of one eye, dancing. Then my tits explode at the end. It's not as easy as it looks.
Lady Gaga, American singer

I love tackling, love it. It's better than sex.
Paul Ince, former professional footballer

COURAGE

It gave me a taste for comedy again. I kissed him in *EastEnders* and I kissed his bum in *Hustle*, so you could say I've topped and tailed him. He looks quite alarmed when he sees me now.
Sheila Hancock, British actress, on her reunion with fellow actor Martin Kemp, in *Woman*, **2012**

I like nice clothes whether they're dodgy or not.
David Beckham, British footballer

CREATIVITY

We don't call it sin today – we call it self-expression.
Baroness Stocks (1891–1975), British writer and campaigner for women's suffrage

In a non-permissive age, she made remarkable inroads against the taboos of her day, and did so without even lowering her neckline.
Leslie Halliwell (1929–1989), British film critic, on Mae West

I've got a nurse's outfit and a policewoman's uniform, and a naughty housewife costume. I am a naughty housewife, anyway, because I don't clean the house enough.
Coleen Nolan, British singer and television presenter, on *Loose Women*

CRITICS

Western man, especially the Western critic, still finds it very hard to go into print and say: 'I recommend you go and see this because it gave me an erection.'
Kenneth Tynan (1927–1980), British theatre critic, in *Playboy* **magazine, 1977**

It is better to be thought of as a heart-throb than as a pig.
Tom Conti, British actor

Bill Clinton has a small penis and Hillary has broad ankles.
Gennifer Flowers, American model and actress, alleged to have had an affair with Bill Clinton

It's one thing to shoot a man, quite another to cast aspersions upon his lovemaking.
Teresa Medeiros, American romance novelist, in *The Vampire Who Loved Me,* **2006**

One magazine said that no one writes sex in the back of a Bentley better than Jackie Collins.
Jackie Collins, British novelist

DATING

I took a gentleman on a beautiful trail ride. He wasn't a good rider so I put him on the safest, slowest horse in the barn. As luck would have it, his horse stepped in a hornet's nest. After that episode, in which his horse ran faster than Secretariat, ardour hit the deep freeze. My second-worst date occurred when a quite pretty lady asked me out and I was thrilled that she had noticed me. I met her at the appointed time at a posh restaurant only to be greeted by her and her husband. I was shocked.

Rita Mae Brown, American feminist writer

Men generally pay for all expenses on a date . . . either sex, however, may bring a little gift, its value to be determined by the bizarreness of the sexual request to be made later that evening.

P.J. O'Rourke, American writer and political satirist, in *Modern Manners*, **1983**

Anything my mother had anything to do with goes in the 'worst' category. But the very worst was when my sister was at the University of Wisconsin and I was a teenager and my girlfriend and I came to visit her for the weekend and she fixed us up with two of her discards, in my case a very tall gentleman named 'Moose'.

Alice Kahn, professor in speech-language pathology at Miami University, Ohio

It's terrific if you're a computer.

Rita Mae Brown, American feminist writer, on computer dating

Dates used to be made days or even weeks in advance. Now dates tend to be made the day after. That is, you get a phone call from someone who says, 'If anyone asks, I was out to dinner with you last night, okay?'

P.J. O'Rourke, American writer and political satirist, in *Modern Manners*, **1983**

A date, at this juncture in history, is any pre-arranged meeting with a member of the opposite sex towards whom you have indecent intentions . . . One does not have to sleep with or even touch someone who has paid for your meal. All those obligations are hereby rendered null and void, and any man who doesn't think so needs a quick jab in the kidney.

Cynthia Heimel, American feminist writer, in *Sex Tips for Girls*, **1993**

While at Cambridge, a friend of mine – a friend, you understand – had been fixed up with a blind date. Being an optimist, he called at a chemist on the afternoon of the big day and bought himself a packet of contraceptives. That evening he met his date. He recognised her. She had sold him the contraceptives.
Tim Brooke-Taylor, British actor and member of The Goodies

If you want to get to know someone better, you shouldn't take them out for a candlelit dinner, you should watch them at work. When they're full of concentration, only not concentrating on you.
Julian Barnes, British writer, in *Love, etc*, **2000**

It's hard for me to meet someone, because guys are intimidated. They see the glamour, and the security guys, and don't know how to deal. Honestly, even if I give a guy my number, they don't call.
Beyoncé, American singer

It's hard to take showers with only one of five guys you're dating.
Cher, American singer

I'd go out with women my age, but there are no women my age.
George Burns (1896–1996), **American actor and comedian**

Accept every blind date you can get, even with a girl who wears jeans. Maybe you can talk her out of them.
Abigail Van Buren (Pauline Phillips, 1918–2003), American journalist and 'Dear Abby' advice columnist

DEPRAVITY

The mother complained that her son, an only child, was becoming truculent, had started smoking, had been seen entering a public house and was keeping company with a girl. Inspector McCann began to investigate. 'I found that the son was 36,' he stated.
The Birmingham Post

At both services in the morning, it is intended to preach a series of sermons on the 'deadly sins', omitting lust.
Our Church Review

Beware of veneryous acts before the first sleep, and specially beware of such things after dinner or after a full stomach, for it doth engender the cramp and the gout and other displeasures.
Andrew Boorde (1490–1549), British physician, in *Here Foloweth a Compenyous Regiment or Dyetary of Health, Made in Mountpyller,* **sixteenth century**

I believe in the total depravity of inanimate things . . . the elusiveness of soap, the knottiness of strings, the transitory nature of buttons, the inclination of suspenders to twist and of hooks to forsake their lawful eyes and cleave only unto the hairs of their hapless owner's head.
Catherine Walker (1840–1916), British poet

The worldwide web is fantasyland. There is no way that anyone can find anything in the web without having to adopt the thought patterns of a weirdo.
Germaine Greer, Australian feminist writer, in *Independent,* **2001**

There will be sex after death, we just won't be able to feel it.
Lily Tomlin, American actress and comedienne

My mother was like a sister to me, only we didn't have sex quite so often.
Emo Philips, American comedian

DESIRE

Where they love they do not desire and where they desire they do not love.
Sigmund Freud (1856–1939), Austrian psychoanalyst

The man's desire is for the woman; the woman's desire is for the desire of the man.
Samuel Taylor Coleridge (1772–1834), British poet

Those who restrain desire, do so because theirs is weak enough to be restrained.
William Blake (1757–1827), British poet and painter, in *The Marriage of Heaven and Hell,* **1793**

Some desire is necessary to keep life in motion.
Dr Samuel Johnson (1709–1784), British writer and lexicographer

I have to find a girl attractive or it's like trying to start a car without an ignition key.
Jonathan Aitken, former Conservative MP

Ever since my childhood I have been accustomed to see the face of every man who has passed me light up with desire. Many women will be disgusted to hear that I have always taken this as homage. Is it despicable to be the flower whose perfume people long to inhale, the fruit they long to taste?
Caroline 'La Belle' Otero (1868–1965), Spanish actress and courtesan

It is a barbarous custom that forbids the maid to make advances in love, or that confines these advances to the eye, the fingers, the gesture, the motion, the manner . . . And now let us examine the carnal desires of the body itself, whence has arisen unconscionable harm to human life. Justly may we say with Cato of Utica: if the world could be rid of women, we should not be without God in our intercourse. For truly without the wickedness of women, to say nothing of witchcraft, the world would remain proof against innumerable dangers.
Heinrich Kramer (c. 1430–1505) and Jakob Sprenger (c. 1436–1495), German Catholic clergymen, in *Malleus Maleficarum: The Classic Study of Witchcraft,* **1487**

Want is the mistress of invention.
Susanna Centlivre (1667–1723), British actress and poet

He wondered why sexual shyness, which excites the desire of dissolute women, arouses the contempt of decent ones.
Colette (Sidonie-Gabrielle, 1873–1954), French writer

I write to be sexually desirable.
Kenneth Tynan (1927–1980), British theatre critic, to his wife

I'd like a wealthy older man who adores me, a passionate middle-aged man, and a 30 year old who'd come by twice a week (I wouldn't have to know his name).
Liza Minnelli, American actress and singer, in interview with *You* **magazine**

The more successful I become, the more I need a man.
Beyoncé, American singer

Sex . . . or lack thereof . . . is at the centre of everyone's identity, and once you've cracked someone's desires, you understand them in full.
Arianne Cohen, American writer, in *Marie Claire* **magazine, 2008**

My favourite thing in the world is a box of fine European chocolates which is, for sure, better than sex.
Alicia Silverstone, American actress

DIFFERENCES

The main difference between men and women is that men are lunatics and women are idiots.
Rebecca West (1892–1983), British writer

God made men stronger but not necessarily more intelligent. He gave women intuition and femininity. And, used properly, that combination easily jumbles the brain of any man I've ever met.
Farrah Fawcett (1947–2009), American actress

Women represent the triumph of matter over mind: men represent the triumph of mind over morals.
Lord Henry, in *The Picture of Dorian Gray* **by Oscar Wilde (1854–1900), Irish playwright**

Men always want to be a woman's first love. That is their clumsy vanity. We women have a more subtle instinct about things. What we like is to be a man's last romance.
Mrs Allonby, in *A Woman of No Importance* **by Oscar Wilde**

Women are not men's equals in anything except responsibility. We are not their inferiors either, or even their superiors. We are quite simply different races.
Phyllis McGinley (1905–1978), Canadian-born poet

The reason husbands and wives do not understand each other is because they belong to different sexes.
Dorothy Dix (Elizabeth Meriwether Gilmer, 1861–1951), American journalist

I believe in the difference between men and women. In fact, I embrace the difference.
Elizabeth Taylor (1932–2011), British actress

Mr Darwin . . . has failed to hold definitely before his mind the principle that the difference of sex, whatever it may consist in, must itself be subject to natural selection and to evolution.
Antoinette Brown Blackwell (1825–1921), American feminist writer and first female minister to be ordained in the USA, in *The Sexes Throughout Nature*, **1875**

The little rift between the sexes is astonishingly widened by simply teaching one set of catchwords to the girls and another to the boys.
Robert Louis Stevenson (1850–1894), British writer

Man's love is of man's life a thing apart,
'Tis woman's whole existence.
Lord Byron, (1788–1824) British Romantic poet, in *Don Juan*

Semen maketh man . . . sex merely expresses the totality of differences between male and female.
Sir Solly Zuckerman (1904–1993), British zoologist

For him she is sex – absolute sex, no less. She is defined and differentiated with reference to man and not he with reference to her; she is the incidental, the unessential as opposed to the essential. He is the subject, he is the absolute – she is the other.
Simone de Beauvoir (1908–1986), French writer, in *The Second Sex*, **1949**

When a man goes on a date he wonders if he is going to get lucky. A woman already knows.
Frederick Bushnell 'Jack' Ryder (1871–1936), American football coach and sportswriter

Women are programmed to love completely, and men are programmed to spread it around.
Beryl Bainbridge (1932–2010), British writer, in an interview in the *Daily Telegraph*, **1996**

The difference between sex and love is that sex relieves tension and love causes it.
Woody Allen, American actor and film-maker

The difference between pornography and erotica is lighting.
Gloria Leonard, former pornographic actress and editor of *High Society* **magazine**

Women were excited after sex, wired because in their minds the relationship was only beginning. Men went to sleep, because for them the relationship was done.
Eric Jerome Dickey, American novelist, in *Pleasure,* **2008**

Sexuality and sensuality are completely different things. Sensuality is something that you're born with. But sexuality is something I leave for my own mirror.
Ricky Martin, Puerto Rican singer

DISEASE

President Amin of Uganda, in his capacity as his country's Health Minister, has nicknamed venereal disease 'Good Hope' so that sufferers will not be embarrassed when seeing a doctor.
Report in the *Daily Telegraph*

Viv Richards is giving Patrick Patterson the clap.
Richie Benaud, Australian sports commentator, describing the West Indies cricket captain trying to attract a player's attention

DIVORCE

The difference between divorce and legal separation is that a legal separation gives a husband time to hide his money.
Johnny Carson (1925–2005), American television host and comedian

When a couple decide to divorce, they should inform both sets of parents before having a party and telling all their friends. This is not only courteous but practical. Parents may be very willing to pitch in with comments, criticism and malicious gossip of their own to help the divorce along.
P.J. O'Rourke, American writer and political satirist

You never really know a man until you've divorced him.
Zsa Zsa Gabor, Hungarian-born American socialite

Divorce is the sacrament of adultery.
French proverb

What scares me about divorce is that my children might put me in a home for unwed mothers.
Teressa Skelton

Getting divorced just because you don't love a man is almost as silly as getting married just because you do.
Zsa Zsa Gabor

Fission after fusion.
Rita Mae Brown, American feminist writer

Remarriage is an excellent test of just how amicable your divorce was.
Margo Kaufman (1954–2000), American humorist and broadcaster

In our family we don't divorce our men – we bury them.
Ruth Gordon (1896–1985), American actress and writer

It is he who has broken the bond of marriage – not I. I only break its bondage.
Lady Windermere, in *Lady Windermere's Fan* **by Oscar Wilde (1854–1900), Irish playwright**

My husband and I will soon be celebrating our Golden Anniversary of cloudless separation.
Madame Aubernon de Nerville (1825–1899), French hostess known for her salon, commenting on her husband who left her after only a few days of marriage

A Roman divorced from his wife was highly blamed by his friends, who demanded, 'Was she not chaste? Was she not fair? Was she not faithful?' Holding out his shoe, he asked them whether it was not new and well made. 'Yet,' added he, 'None of you can tell where it pinches me.'
Plutarch (AD 46–120), Greek historian and writer

Caesar's wife must be above suspicion.
Julius Caesar (100–44 BC), Roman emperor

Should a husband be or become of so cold a nature as to be unable to have carnal relations with his wife of the sort proper between husband and wife, then the prelate grants perpetual divorce to the couple and the woman may remarry according to her will and pleasure.
Jean Boutillier (1340–1395), French legal consult, referring to divorce laws in France in the fourteenth century

So many persons think divorce a panacea for every ill, who find out, when they try it, that the remedy is worse than the disease.
Dorothy Dix (Elizabeth Meriwether Gilmer, 1861–1951), American journalist

Judge: You want a divorce on the grounds that your husband is rather careless about his appearance.
Woman: Yes, Your Honour – he hasn't made one for three years.
Anon

Being divorced is like being hit by a Mack truck. If you live through it, you start looking very carefully to the right and to the left.
Jean Kerr (1922–2003), Irish-American playwright

If divorce has increased one thousand per cent, don't blame the women's movement. Blame our obsolete sex roles on which our marriages were based.
Betty Friedan (1921–2006), American feminist, whose book The Feminine Mystique **(1963) was one of the most influential books of the women's movement**

The respondent is unreasonably demanding sex every night from the petitioner, which is causing friction between the parties.
Vanessa Lloyd Platt, divorce lawyer, reporting one of the excuses given for divorce petitions

My divorce came as a complete surprise to me. That will happen when you haven't been home in 18 years.
Lee Trevino, American pro golfer

DOMINATION

In losing a husband, one loses a master who is often an obstacle to the enjoyment of many things.
Madeleine de Scudéry (1607–1701), French writer

I have no wish for a second husband. I had enough of the first. I like to have my own way – to lie down mistress, and get up master.
Susanna Moodie (1803–1885), Canadian writer

DRESS

To attract men, women should dress glamorously in a low-cut dress or short skirt.
Lindi St Clair (aka Miss Whiplash), former madam and dominatrix

A witch and a bitch always dress up for each other, because otherwise the witch would upstage the bitch, or the bitch would upstage the witch, and the result would be havoc.
Tennessee Williams (1911–1983), American playwright

Women dress alike all over the world; they dress to be annoying to other women.
Elsa Schiaparelli (1890–1973), Italian fashion designer

Most women dress as if they had been a mouse in a previous incarnation, or hope to be one in the next.
Edith Sitwell (1887–1964), British writer

The prettiest dresses are worn to be taken off.
Jean Cocteau (1889–1963), French writer and film-maker

As an article of dress for the girl, the corset must be looked upon as distinctly prejudicial to health, and as entirely unnecessary.
Howard A. Kelly (1858–1943), American gynaecologist, in Medical Gynaecology, **1909**

There is no such thing as a moral dress – it's people who are moral or immoral.
Lady Randolph Churchill (1854–1921), American-born mother of Winston Churchill

An after-dinner speech should be like a lady's dress – long enough to cover the subject and short enough to be interesting.
R.A. 'Rab' Butler (1902–1982), British Conservative Party politician

This ad makes me look better than I thought possible.
Nadia Comaneci, Romanian Olympic gold medal gymnast, on her new career modelling underwear

Not only did she wear short tunics, but she dressed herself in tabards and garments open at the sides, besides the matter is notorious since when she was captured she was wearing a surcoat cloak of gold, open on all sides, a cap on her head, and her hair cropped round in man's style. And in general, having cast aside all womanly decency, not only to the scorn of feminine modesty, but also of well-instructed men, she had worn the apparel and garments of most dissolute men, and, in addition, had some weapons of defence.
One of the charges made against Joan of Arc at her trial, quoted in *The Trial of Jeanne d'Arc* **by W.P. Barrett, 1431**

The Republican Party couldn't make up their minds whether I'd be mistaken for a trollop or for the Queen of England. But silly as the request was, I stopped wearing purple.
Elizabeth Taylor (1932–2011), British actress (when Mrs John Warner) on being told by the Republican Party that she could no longer wear purple

All women's dresses are merely variations on the eternal struggle between admitted desire to dress and the unadmitted desire to undress.
Lin Yutang (1895–1976), Chinese writer and inventor

You don't have to signal a social conscience by looking like a frump. Lace knickers won't hasten the holocaust, you can ban the bomb in a feather boa just as well as without, and a mild interest in the length of hemlines doesn't necessarily disqualify you from reading *Das Kapital* and agreeing with every word.
Elizabeth Bibesco (1897–1945), British writer

I dress for women and undress for men.
Angie Dickinson, American actress

You'd be surprised how much it costs to look this cheap.
Dolly Parton, American country music singer

It is difficult to see why lace is so expensive; it is mostly holes.
Mary Wilson Little, American singer in The Supremes

Brevity is the soul of lingerie.
Dorothy Parker (1893–1967), American wit

I only put clothes on so that I'm not naked when I go out shopping.
Julia Roberts, American actress

It was one of the most enjoyable things I've ever done. I wore them around my house.
Sean Bean, British actor, describing wearing women's clothing in preparation for his role as a transsexual

They can have my falsies, pasties, and body stockings any time.
Candice Bergen, American actress

It's a good thing I was born a female, or I'd have been a drag queen.
Dolly Parton, American country music singer

I bet he doesn't put his hand up her dress.
Marilyn Monroe (1926–1962), American actress, on John F. Kennedy's relationship with Jackie Kennedy

I'm just trying to change the world, one sequin at a time.
Lady Gaga, American singer

Judge not a man by his clothes, but by his wife's clothes.
Thomas Dewar (1864–1930), Scottish whisky distiller and founder of Dewar's

At the Billboard Awards my skirt was so tight they had to lift me on stage.
Beyoncé, American singer

DRINK

One more drink and I'll be under the host.
Dorothy Parker (1893–1967), American wit

It provokes the desire, but it takes away the performance. Therefore much drink may be said to be an equivocator with lechery.
Porter, in *Macbeth* by William Shakespeare (1564–1616), British playwright

A man who exposes himself when he is intoxicated has not the art of getting drunk.
Dr Samuel Johnson (1709–1784), British writer and lexicographer

Alcohol is like love: the first kiss is magic, the second is intimate, the third is routine. After that you just take the girl's clothes off.
Raymond Chandler (1888–1959), American novelist

A fuddled woman is a shameful sight, a prey to anyone, and serve her right.
Ovid (43 BC–AD 17), Roman poet

All along the line, physically, mentally, morally, alcohol is a weakening and deadening force, and it is worth a great deal to save women and girls from its influence.
Beatrice Potter Webb (1858–1943), British writer and social reformer

Alcohol was a threat to women, for it released men from the moral control they had learned from a diet of preaching and scolding from ministers and mothers alike.
Alice Rossi, American feminist writer

Nothing equals the joy of the drinker, except the joy of the wine in being drunk.
French proverb

No poems can please for long or live that are written by water-drinkers.
Horace (65–8 BC), Roman poet

I may not here omit those two main plagues, and common dotages of humankind, wine and women, which have infatuated and besotted myriads of people. They go commonly together.
Robert Burton (1577–1640), British philosopher

Wine gives a man nothing . . . it only puts in motion what had been locked up in frost.
Dr Samuel Johnson (1709–1784), British writer and lexicographer

Wine makes a man better pleased with himself; I do not say that it makes him more pleasing to others.
Dr Samuel Johnson

Isadora Duncan probably represents the maximum possible development of emotion at the expense of intellect. She was a creature of impulse and the impulses were usually bad ones. She drank champagne as a thirsty horse drinks water.
London's Weekly, **1933**

I love wine. I probably drink too much for my liver. I used to get pissed in the olden days, but now it goes to my head very quickly. There is just something about that glass cabinet. You forget you've left it open and walk straight into it.
Felicity Kendal, British actress

I have a rare intolerance to herbs which means I can only drink fermented liquids, such as gin.
Julie Walters, British actress, in *Observer* **interview, 1999**

EMOTION

It's scary . . . so personal, giving people the opportunity to see if I'm a good kisser or not. You see, I'm not into sex for the sake of it. I think love scenes are more powerful if it's about communication between two people. It's not about sucking face, it's about emotion.
Patrick Swayze (1952–2009), American actor

All the little hoops were set up for me to jump through, and when you jump, you get a reward – an image. But it's the image they supply . . . You become a perfect couple, or the faded English rose, or the wronged woman, or the rock 'n' roll slut, or whatever.

It has very little to do with real, manageable emotions.
Marianne Faithfull, British singer, referring to her relationship with Mick Jagger, in *City Limits* **magazine, 1981**

I really get inspired by songs. Like, if I hear a thug 'Want to kill ya' song. I'm ready to go out and get crazy. Or if you hear this really sexual, sensual slow song, I want to go have sex. I'm very animalistic when it comes to stuff like that. Very basic emotions.
Channing Tatum, American actor

EQUALITY

It is naive in the extreme for women to expect to be regarded as equals by men . . . so long as they persist in a subhuman (i.e. animal-like) behaviour during sexual intercourse. I'm referring . . . to the outlandish panting, gasping, moaning, sobbing, writhing, scratching, biting, screaming, and the seemingly invariable 'Oh my God!' . . . all so predictably integral to pre-, post-, and orgasmic stages of intercourse.
Terry Southern (1924–1995), American screenwriter

Whatever women do they must do twice as well as men to be thought half as good. Luckily, this is not difficult.
Charlotte Whitton (1896–1975), former Mayor of Ottawa

It's time people stood up and said women are getting too much of the action.
Tina Knight, British businesswoman who insists on no-pregnancy agreements with new recruits

Men seldom make passes at a girl who surpasses.
Franklin P. Jones (1908–1980), American journalist

Once made equal to a man, woman becomes his superior.
Socrates (469–399 BC), Greek philosopher

I refuse to consign the whole male sex to the nursery. I insist on believing that some men are my equals.
Brigid Brophy (1925–1995), British writer and campaigner

Women who want to be equal to men lack ambition.
Marilyn Monroe (1926–1962), American actress

You're used. Used by what you are, eat, believe and who you sleep with. You can't stop it. If you want equality it has to start in bed. If he won't give it to you there, rip him off.
Jane Gallion

There will never be complete equality until women themselves help to make laws and elect lawmakers.
Susan B. Anthony (1820–1906), American writer and feminist, in *The Arena*, **1897**

All this pitting of sex against sex, of quality against quality; all this claiming of superiority and imputing of inferiority belong to the private-school stage of human existence where there are sides, and it is necessary for one side to beat another side.
Virginia Woolf (1882–1941), British writer

A career woman who has survived the hurdle of marriage and maternity encounters a new obstacle: the hostility of men.
Caroline Bird, American writer, in *Born Female*, **1968**

There are very few jobs that actually require a penis or vagina. All other jobs should be open to everybody.
Florynce R. Kennedy, American lawyer and civil-rights activist, 1974

I'm not a believer in equality and my attitude is that women are supposed to be pretty and nice. A woman should be a woman.
Jim Davidson, British comedian

The real theatre of the sex war is the domestic hearth.
Germaine Greer, Australian feminist writer

We have no rage in our bellies against women.
Tim Samuels, British broadcaster and host of Radio 5 Live's *Men's Hour*

Obama, congratulations on being the first sitting President to support marriage equality. Feels like the future, and not the past.
Lady Gaga, American singer

EROTICISM

[He] twisted my nipples as though tuning a radio.
Lisa Alther, American novelist, in *Kinflicks*, **1976**

She has been described as the Maharani of Malice, the Empress of Erotica, the Princess of Pulp, the Pasha of Porn. Despite having received the most spectacularly worst reviews ever written in India, she is the country's best-selling writer.
The Sunday Times Magazine, **on Indian writer Shobhaa De**

I am reading everything she is writing. In one book I am counting seventy-three copulations. I am shocked only. Really – her head is full of perversions.
Mr Satish Lal (who makes carbuncle grinders in Bangalore), on Shobhaa De

He moved his lips about her ears and neck as though in thirsting search of an erogenous zone. A waste of time, he knew from experience. Erogenous zones were either everywhere or nowhere.
Joseph Heller (1923–1999), American novelist, in *Good as Gold*, **1979**

My pictures are not just blatant full-frontals, they are very tasteful. But they tried to insist that women just wanted full-frontal dangly bits.
Nikki Downey, former *Penthouse* **model turned photographer**

There is no difference.
Pablo Picasso (1881–1973), Spanish artist, when asked what the difference was between art and eroticism

The residue of virility in the woman's organism is utilised by nature in order to eroticise her: otherwise the functioning of the maternal apparatus would wholly submerge her in the painful tasks of reproduction and motherhood.
Marie Bonaparte (1882–1962), French psychoanalyst, sexologist and educator

Women have been complaining to us for years that there is nothing like this on the market. They have a right to look at erotic pictures of beautiful men. They want explicit articles about sex. After all,

men have been open and free about their sexuality for a long time.
Isabel Koprowski, the former editor of *Forum,* **on the launch of**
For Women **magazine**

Colette wrote of vegetables as if they were love objects and of sex
as if it were an especially delightful department of gardening.
Brigid Brophy (1925–1995), British writer and campaigner, in *1000*
Makers of the 20th Century

Fishnets at 50 are a no-no. Could somebody please tell Madge.
Mimi Spencer, British journalist, in a *Daily Mail* **article, 2012**

Only the united beat of sex and heart together can create ecstasy.
Anaïs Nin (1903–1977), American writer, in *Delta of Venus,* **1977**

To know the difference between erotica and pornography you must
first know the difference between naked and nude.
Bernard Poulin, Canadian artist

EXCESS

Too much of a good thing can be wonderful.
Mae West (1893–1980), American actress

I have never been afraid of excess. Excess on occasion is exhilarating.
It prevents moderation from acquiring the deadening effect of a
habit.
W. Somerset Maugham (1874–1965), British novelist, in *The*
Summing Up, **1938**

Moderation is a fatal thing. Nothing succeeds like excess.
Lord Illingworth, in *A Woman of No Importance* **by Oscar Wilde**
(1854–1900), Irish playwright

EXPERIENCE

Experience is a good teacher, but her fees are very high.
William Ralph Inge (Dean Inge, 1860–1954), British professor of
Divinity at Cambridge and Dean of St Paul's

You should make a point of trying every experience once – except incest and folk-dancing.
Arnold Bax (1883–1953), British composer and poet, quoted in *The Scotsman*

I know, I should talk with my therapist.
Nancy Dell'Ollio, Italian lawyer and media personality, when asked about her record of dating men with baggage

I have worked with more submarines than leading ladies.
John Mills (1908–2005), British actor, in an interview with *The Times*, **2000**

We accept the love we think we deserve.
Charlie, in *The Perks of Being a Wallflower*, **by Stephen Chbosky, American screenwriter**

Sex: the thing that takes up the least amount of time and causes the most amount of trouble.
John Barrymore (1882–1942), American actor

[Women of my generation], unlike generations before us, have been with several men – or in some cases, many men. I raise the question, Why?
Joni Mitchell, Canadian folk singer, in interview with *Rolling Stone*, **1982**

FAMILY

The fact of the matter is that the prime responsibility of a woman probably is to be on earth long enough to find the best mate possible for herself, and conceive children who will improve the species.
Norman Mailer (1923–2007), American writer and political activist, in *The Presidential Papers*, **1963**

I have a wife, I have sons: all them hostages given to fate.
Lucan (AD 39–65), Roman poet

What a marvellous place to drop one's mother-in-law!
Marshal Ferdinand Foch (1851–1929), French soldier, on visiting the Grand Canyon

He that hath wife and children hath given hostages to fortune, for they are impediments to great enterprises, either of virtue or mischief.
Francis Bacon (1561–1626), British philosopher, in *Of Marriage and Single Life*, **1597**

FANTASY

The times being what they were, if she hadn't existed we would have had to invent her, and we did, in a way. She was the fifties' fiction, the lie that woman has no sexual needs, that she is there to cater to or enhance a man's needs.
Molly Haskell, American film critic, on women in male fantasies, in *From Reverence to Rape*, **1974**

And the crazy part of it was, even if you were clever, even if you spent your adolescence reading John Donne and Shaw, even if you studied history or zoology or physics and hoped to spend your life pursuing some difficult and challenging career, you still had a mind full of all the soupy longings that every high-school girl was awash in . . . underneath it, all you longed to be was annihilated by love, to be swept off your feet, to be filled up by a giant prick spouting sperm, soapsuds, silk and satins and, of course, money.
Erica Jong, American writer

She is every man's fantasy mistress. She gave you the impression that, if your imagination had to sin, it could at least be congratulated on its impeccable taste.
Alistair Cooke (1908–2004), British broadcaster, on actress Greta Garbo

She has made forty films, attempted suicide at least twice, married three men and has shared passion with many more. Her rampant sexuality made her a fantasy figure for men.
TV Times **magazine on Brigitte Bardot**

When I saw him sitting behind his desk in his opulent office, he looked just like Blake Carrington.
Fiona Wright, British columnist and mistress of Sir Ralph Halpern

Harry and me? Why not . . . Sometimes you can find what you want in a very young body. Prince Harry too young for me? No, no.
Nancy Dell'Olio, Italian lawyer and media personality

What turns me on? Tuesday Weld in a dirty slip drinking beer.
Alice Cooper, American singer

There's nothing inherently dirty about sex, but if you try real hard and use your imagination you can overcome that.
Lewis Grizzard (1946–1994), American writer

A girl in a bikini is like having a loaded gun on your coffee table – there's nothing wrong with them, but it's hard to stop thinking about.
Garrison Keillor, American writer and broadcaster

I wouldn't just like to watch her work. Anything. Preferably cleaning things on the floor. Picking stuff on the floor. Anything bending over. She's hot! I mean literally . . . she's so beautiful.
Rihanna, Barbadian singer, of Cheryl Cole, in *The Times of India*, **2012**

FASHION

I dress for women and undress for men.
Angie Dickinson, American actress

You'd be surprised how much it costs to look this cheap.
Dolly Parton, American country music singer

I tend to wear outfits that match the walls.
Debra Winger, American actress

My weakness is wearing too much leopard print.
Jackie Collins, British novelist

It is difficult to see why lace should be so expensive. It is mostly holes.
Mary Wilson Little, American singer in The Supremes

Brevity is the soul of lingerie.
Dorothy Parker (1893–1967), American wit

Statistics are like a bikini. What they reveal is suggestive but what they conceal is vital.
Professor Aaron Levenstein (1911–1986), professor emeritus of Baruch College

I know I was considered by colleagues to be somewhat of a card. Even with the narcissistic, claustrophobic, perfumed field of haute couture right through to the tatty commercialism of Carnaby Street and beyond, I was not considered the norm. My eye and judgment were influenced too easily by the pulling power of clothing. I couldn't endorse the sexually unappealing. Nor push the visually drab, designed to dampen in a puritan fashion the joyous animal urges.
Molly Parkin, British writer and artist

Girls who wear zippers shouldn't live alone.
John Van Druten, British theatre director

Where's a man who could case a heart like a satin gown?
Dorothy Parker (1893–1967), American wit

Clothes by a man who doesn't know women, never had one, and dreams of being one.
Coco Chanel **(1883–1971), French fashion designer, on Dior's new look**

I'm usually all about the tight jeans and little T-shirt, but sometimes I want to put on a black sequined dress and be a freaking girl.
Britney Spears, American singer

FAUX PAS

Chris Tarrant: I'll give you a clue. His name sounds like something hard that tastes good when you suck it.
Contestant: Ah, it must be Dickie Davies.
Chris Tarrant, British game-show host, trying to help a contestant name a famous motor-racing commentator; the answer was Murray Walker

Forty seconds on the cock.
Henry Kelly, British game-show host, to a female contestant on *Going for Gold*

Does your friend always give you one before you appear on TV?
Bob Holness (1928–2012), British host of quiz show *Blockbusters,* **asking about a contestant's mascot which had been given to her by a friend**

They get the size they want you to be.
Carol McGiffin, British television personality, on how men buy underwear for women

FEMINISM

If you catch a man throw him back.
Australian women's liberation slogan, 1970s

Adam was a rough draft.
Women's Liberation Movement slogan, 1970s

A liberated woman is one who has sex before marriage and a job after.
Gloria Steinem, American feminist writer

No man is as anti-feminist as a really feminine woman.
Frank O'Connor (1903–1966), Irish writer

Remember, Ginger Rogers did everything Fred Astaire did, but backwards and in high heels.
Faith Whittlesey, former Republican politician and White House Senior Staff member under President Reagan

But if God wanted us to think with our wombs, why did he give us a brain?
Clare Boothe Luce (1903–1987), American writer and politician

If men could get pregnant, abortion would be a sacrament.
Florynce R. Kennedy (1916–2000), American lawyer and civil-rights activist

Take your secretary to lunch. He'll appreciate it.
Anon

Sometimes the best man for the job isn't.
Anon

Women's liberation is just a lot of foolishness. It's men who are discriminated against. They can't bear children. And no one's likely to do anything about that.
Golda Meir (1898–1978), fourth Prime Minister of Israel from 1969 to 1974

Whatever women do they must do twice as well as men to be thought half as good. Luckily, this is not difficult.
Charlotte Whitton (1896–1975), on becoming Mayor of Ottawa

I would rather lie on the sofa than sweep beneath it.
Shirley Conran, British novelist and journalist

Beware of the man who praises women's liberation; he is about to quit his job.
Erica Jong, American writer

Scratch most feminists and underneath there is a woman who longs to be a sex object. The difference is, that is not all she longs to be.
Betty Rollin, American news correspondent and author

The major concrete achievement of the Women's Movement of the 1970s was the Dutch Treat.
Nora Ephron (1941–2012), American screenwriter and director

I'm furious with women's liberationists. They keep getting up on soapboxes and proclaiming that women are brighter than men. That's

true, but it should be kept very quiet or it ruins the whole racket.
Anita Loos (1893–1981), American screenwriter of *Gentlemen Prefer Blondes*, **1953**

Women are the only exploited group in history to have been idealised into powerlessness.
Erica Jong, American writer

No one should have to dance backward all of their lives.
Jill Ruckelshaus, American government official and lecturer

Despite a lifetime of service to the cause of sexual liberation, I have never caught venereal disease, which makes me feel rather like an Arctic explorer who has never had frostbite.
Germaine Greer, **Australian feminist writer**

If you want to know, I'm really tired of feminists, sick of them. They've really dug themselves into their own grave. Any man would be a fool who didn't agree with equal rights and pay, but some women now, juggling with career, lover, children, wifehood, have spread themselves too thin and are very unhappy.
Michael Douglas, American actor

Wife: Cooking! Cleaning! Why should women do it?
Husband: You're right – let's get an au pair girl.
Mel Calman (1931–1994), British cartoonist, in a 'Couples' cartoon, 1972

We had taken the first step along the tortuous road that led to the sex war, sado-masochism, and ultimately to the whole contemporary snarl-up, to prostitution, prudery, Casanova, John Knox, Marie Stopes, white slavery, Women's Liberation, *Playboy* magazine, *crimes passionnels*, censorship, strip clubs, alimony, pornography, and a dozen different brands of mania. This was the Fall. It had nothing to do with apples.
Elaine Morgan (1920–2013), Welsh writer, in *The Descent of Woman*, **1972**

The Women's Movement hasn't changed my sex life at all. It wouldn't dare.
Zsa Zsa Gabor, Hungarian-American socialite

Never go to bed mad. Stay up and fight.
Phyllis Diller (1917–2012), American actress

To me, the important task of modern feminism is to accept and proclaim sex: to bury for ever the lie that the body is a hindrance to the mind, and sex is a necessary evil to be endured for the perpetuation of our race.
Dora Russell (1894–1986), British socialist campaigner and writer

When a woman behaves like a man, why can't she behave like a nice man?
Edith Evans (1888–1976), British actress

I'm the most liberated woman in the world. Any woman can be liberated if she wants to be. First, she has to convince her husband.
Martha Mitchell (1918–1976), wife of US Attorney General John N. Mitchell

I'm not afraid of my femininity and I'm not afraid of my sexuality.
Goldie Hawn, American actress

Leaving sex to the feminists is like letting your dog vacation at the taxidermist.
Camille Paglia, American professor at the University of the Arts in Philadelphia, and self-proclaimed dissident feminist

FLIRT

Flirt: a woman who thinks it's every man for herself.
Anon

My heart is a bargain today. Will you take it?
W.C. Fields (1880–1946), American actor and comedian

She'll be on more laps than a napkin.
Walter Winchell (1897–1972), American gossip columnist

No matter how happily a woman may be married, it always pleases her to discover that there is a nice man who wishes that she were not.
H.L. Mencken (1880–1956), American writer and humorist

Ah, beautiful passionate body that has never ached with a heart!
A.C. Swinburne (1837–1909), British writer

What attracts us in a woman rarely binds us to her.
John Churton Collins (1848–1909), British literary critic

Men do make passes at girls who wear glasses – but it all depends on their frames.
Optician, 1964

In order to avoid being called a flirt, she always yielded easily.
Charles Maurice de Talleyrand (1754–1838), former Prime Minister of the French Republic

We start with a close embrace and I have to ignore the guilt that my husband is in LA with the grandchildren.
Pamela Stephenson, Australian celebrity psychologist, on learning new dance craze Zouk Lambada in 2012

It's sexier when a girl is flirty but she doesn't do anything.
Paris Hilton, American socialite and heiress to the Hilton fortune, in interview with *The Guardian*, **2006**

FOLLY

When lovely woman stoops to folly, and finds too late that men betray, what charm can soothe her melancholy, what art can wash her guilt away?
Oliver Goldsmith (1730–1774), Anglo-Irish writer, in *The Vicar of Wakefield*, **1766**

Man should be trained for war and women for recreation of the warrior: all else is folly.
Friedrich Nietzsche (1844–1900), German philosopher, in *Thus Spake Zarathustra*, **1883**

Anyone who says he can see through women is missing a lot.
Groucho Marx (1880–1977), American comedian

It's steamy, scintillating, and one of the things that makes this lumbering old world go round. When combined with age,

however, there's a very real risk that you'll wind up looking like an ancient madame holed up in the corner of a bar nursing a port and lemon.
Mimi Spencer, British journalist, describing the folly of older women wearing fishnet stockings, in a *Daily Mail* **article, 2012**

The follies which man regrets most in his life are those which he didn't commit when he had the opportunity.
Helen Rowland (1875–1950), American writer and humorist

FOOD

A gourmet who thinks of calories is like a tart who looks at her watch.
James Beard (1903–1985), American chef and food writer, quoted beneath his picture in Charlie O's Bar, New York City

Too many cooks spoil the brothel.
Pearl 'Polly' Adler (1900–1962), American madam and author, in *A House is not a Home*, **1953**

Great food is like great sex – the more you have the more you want.
Gael Greene, **American food critic**

Cooking is like love. It should be entered into with abandon or not at all.
Harriet Van Horne (1920–1998), American critic and writer

Large naked raw carrots are acceptable as food only to those who live in hutches eagerly awaiting Easter.
Fran Lebowitz, American writer

There is no spectacle on earth more appealing than that of a beautiful woman in the act of cooking dinner for someone she loves.
Thomas Wolfe (1900–1938), American writer

Unnecessary dieting is because everything from television to fashion ads has made it seem wicked to cast a shadow. This wild, emaciated look appeals to some women, though not to many men, who are

seldom seen pinning up a *Vogue* illustration in a machine shop.
Peg Bracken (1918–2007), American writer

The right diet directs sexual energy into the parts that matter.
Barbara Cartland (1901–2000), British novelist

I don't get sent anything strange like underwear. I get sent cookies.
Jennifer Aniston, American actress

As they get on, after five or six years, in most married couples, the old feeling begins to dissipate. Food often takes the place of sex in a relationship.
Alfred Hitchcock (1899–1980), British film director

It's absolutely unfair for women to say that guys only want one thing: sex. We also want food.
Jarod Kintz, American writer

There are two things I like stiff, and one of them's Jell-O.
Nellie Melba (1861–1931), Australian operatic soprano

Food has it over sex for variety. Hedonistically, gustatory possibilities are much broader than copulatory ones.
Joseph Epstein, American writer

Remember, sex is like a Chinese dinner. It ain't over 'til you both get your cookie.
Alec Baldwin, American actor

Sex is as important as eating or drinking and we ought to allow the one appetite to be satisfied with as little restraint or false modesty as the other.
Marquis de Sade (1740–1814), French aristocrat, known for his erotic writing

FOREPLAY

How a man must hug, and dandle, and kittle, and play a hundred little tricks with his bedfellow when he is disposed to make that use of her that nature designed her for.
Erasmus (1466–1536), Dutch Catholic priest, humanist and writer, in *The Praise of Folly*, 1509

Girls like to be played with and rumpled a little too, sometimes.
Oliver Goldsmith (1730–1774), Anglo-Irish writer

The 1950s were ten years of foreplay.
Germaine Greer, Australian feminist writer

Half the time, if you really want to know the truth, when I'm horsing around and with a girl, I have a helluva lot of trouble just finding what I'm looking for, for God's sake, if you know what I mean. Take this girl that I just mentioned having sexual intercourse with, that I told you about. It took me about an hour just to get her Goddam brassiere off, she was about ready to spit in my eye.
Holden Caulfield, in *The Catcher in the Rye*, by J.D. Salinger (1919–2010), American writer

There is no petting . . . Modern couples just strip their clothes and go at it . . . [B]lame must . . . be placed on ex-President Nixon's decision to let the US dollar float in relation to other western currencies. More than a decade of monetary instability has conditioned people to utilise their assets immediately. If the sex urge is not spent forthwith, it might degenerate into something less valuable – affection, for instance.
P.J. O'Rourke, American writer and political satirist, in *Modern Manners*, 1983

She tried to pull me once. Her thing was to hang from my minstrel gallery and swing like some great bat, while murmuring sexy things at me. This was supposed to turn me on but the effect it actually had was to make me run upstairs and lock the darkroom door . . . These were very big ladies. It made me feel inadequate.
Keith Morris (1938–2005), British photographer, describing his relationship with Germaine Greer in the 1960s

Nell Gwynn, lover and patron of Charles II, discovering a rival had been invited to the King's bed, entertained the woman at a pre-coital dinner where she doctored her meal with 'physical ingredients' . . . The effect thereof had such an operation upon the harlot, when the King was caressing her in bed with amorous sports of Venus, that a violent and sudden looseness obliging her ladyship to discharge her artillery, she made the King, as well as herself in a most lamentable pickle.

Reported by **Captain Alexander Smith**, in *The School of Venus: A History of Cuckolds and Cuckold Makers*, **published in 1716**

Kissing, fondling and foreplay are regarded as the height of bad behaviour among the tribe and its culture contains not one romantic song or story. There is no Manuan word for 'love'.
Margaret Mead (1901–1978), American anthropologist and writer, describing the Manus tribe of the Admiralty Islands

Don't stint on the foreplay. Be inventive.
Dr Ruth Westheimer, German-American sex therapist

You men have no idea what we're dealing with down there. Teeth placement, and jaw stress, and suction, and gag reflex, and all the while bobbing up and down and moaning and trying to breathe through our noses. Easy? Honey, they don't call it a job for nothing.
Samantha Jones, played by American actress Kim Cattrall, in *Sex and the City*

Once the buttons are undone, you know how it'll all end. It's all in the game, there are no miracles.
Gao Xingjian, Chinese Nobel Prize-winning writer

I'm a foreplay junkie.
Richard Dreyfuss, American actor

FRIENDSHIP

Friendship is a disinterested commerce between equals; love, an abject intercourse between tyrants and slaves.
Oliver Goldsmith (1730–1774), Anglo-Irish writer

He's the kind of man who picks his friends – to pieces.
Mae West (1893–1980), American actress

Platonic friendship – the interval between the introduction and the first kiss.
Sophie Irene Loeb (1876–1929), American journalist and social welfare advocate

Most friendship is feigning, most loving mere folly.
Amiens, in *As You Like It* by William Shakespeare (1564–1616)

Her friendships were flames of extravagant passion ending in aversion.
Sarah Churchill (1914–1982), British actress, on Queen Anne

Friendship between men and women can be a tricky business because a pretty face all too easily attracts a weak soul, and visual temptation kindles carnal lust, often to produce a defiled mind and body. Familiarity between men and women is apt to turn to virtue's disadvantage.
Richard Rolle (*c.*1290–1349), British writer, in *The Fire of Love*, *c.*1343

I have always detested the belief that sex is the chief bond between man and woman. Friendship is far more human.
Agnes Smedley (*c.*1892–1950), American writer, in *Battle Hymn of China*, 1943

It's a bit like being friends with a woman in a good looking man's body.
Jackie Brambles, British television presenter, on having gay friends

There is not enough celebration of companionship. Relationships aren't just about eroticism and sexuality.
Francesca Annis, British actress

FUN

Most of the time I don't have much fun. The rest of the time I don't have any fun at all.
Woody Allen, American actor and film-maker

The game women play is men.
Adam Smith (1720–1790), British political economist

People must not do things for fun. We are not here for fun. There is no reference to fun in any Act of Parliament.
A.P. Herbert (1890–1971), British writer

Eric: It was a gay nineties party. It was terrible.
Ernie: Why was that?
Eric: All the men were gay and all the women were ninety.
The Morecambe and Wise Joke Book, **by Eric Morecambe, Ernie
Wise and Eddie Braben, 1979**

The proliferation of massage establishments in London in the last
few years appears to indicate a dramatic increase in muscular
disorders amongst the male population.
Anonymous Environmental Health officer quoted in the *New
Statesman* **magazine, 1980**

Setting a good example for your children takes all the fun out of
middle age.
William Feather (1889–1981), American publisher and writer, in
The Business of Life, **1949**

Jealousy is all the fun you think they had.
Erica Jong, American writer, in *How to Save Your Own Life*

Let's just say I've gotten laughs in bed.
Steve Martin, American actor, when asked about his sex life

Most girls blush at dirty scenes in a movie. I laugh, because I know
that I can do it better.
Anon

I like being sexy. It's fun, and I have had a nice little career off it.
Carmen Electra, American glamour model

GOSSIP

If you haven't got anything nice to say about anybody, come sit
next to me.
**Alice Roosevelt Longworth (1884–1980), daughter of President
Theodore Roosevelt**

She'll wear the pants in that marriage.
Harvey Smith, British show-jumping champion, on Princess Anne

Men have always detested women's gossip because they suspect the truth about their measurements being taken and compared.
Erica Jong, American writer

I am not some sort of sexpot or randy masseuse.
Carole Caplin, lifestyle coach to Cherie Blair, denying she ever had sex with Tony, 2011

HABIT

Teenagers and old people may know how to dance, but real people who go to real parties haven't the slightest. The only dances they even half-remember how to do are the ones they learned 20 years ago. This is what the old Supremes tape is for: still and overweight versions of the Jerk, the Mashed Potato, the Pony, the Swim, and the Watusi. And after six drinks everyone will revert to the Twist.
P.J. O'Rourke, American writer and political satirist, in *Modern Manners*, **1983**

Like so many substantial Americans, he had married young and kept on marrying, stringing from blonde to blonde like the chamois of the Alps leaping from crag to crag.
P.G. Wodehouse (1881–1975), British writer

Just as old habits die hard, old hards die habits.
Kenneth Tynan (1927–1980), British theatre critic, on pornography, in *Esquire* **magazine, 1968**

Oh my God, what are you doing down there? Get off! Get off!
Michael Curtiz (1886–1962), Hungarian-born film director best known for *Casablanca*, **interrupted by his cast and crew in an 'unbuttoned moment' with one of the make-up girls**

I don't believe in vitamin pills, I swear by men, darling – and as many as possible.
Joan Collins, British actress, in *The Independent*, **2000**

We'll engage in pretty extreme violence in the world but, you know, the one thing that comes to humans as easily as eating or breathing or sleeping, is sex.
Mark Ruffalo, American actor

HAPPINESS

The happiness of man is: I will. The happiness of women is: he wills.
Friedrich Nietzsche (1844–1900), German philosopher

When I was a small child . . . I thought that success spelled happiness. I was wrong. Happiness is like a butterfly which appears and delights us for one brief moment, but soon flits away.
Anna Pavlova (1881–1931), Russian ballerina

It is only possible to live happily ever after on a day-to-day basis.
Margaret Bonnano, American science-fiction writer

I feel like a kid in the world's biggest candy store.
Hugh Hefner, American founder of *Playboy* magazine, referring to his *Playboy* empire

I'm getting a divorce and dating a much younger woman. There's no way I can keep my wife and my girlfriend happy at the same time.
Ted Turner, American media mogul and founder of CNN

HATE

I never hated a man enough to give him his diamonds back.
Zsa Zsa Gabor, Hungarian-American socialite

Malice is like a game of poker or tennis; you don't play it with anyone who is manifestly inferior to you.
Hilde Spiel (1911–1990), Austrian writer and cultural historian

HOLLYWOOD

You can seduce a man's wife there, attack his daughter and wipe your hands on his canary, but if you don't like his movie, you're dead.
Josef von Sternberg (1894–1969), Austrian-American film director

Hollywood's a place where they'll pay you a thousand dollars for a kiss, and fifty cents for your soul.
Marilyn Monroe (1926–1962), American actress

If we have to kiss Hollywood goodbye, it may be with one of those tender, old-fashioned, seven-second kisses as exchanged between two people of the opposite sex with all their clothes on.
Anita Loos (1893–1981), American screenwriter of *Gentlemen Prefer Blondes*, **1953**

Sometimes I feel like an old hooker
Cher, American singer

Can you imagine anybody wanting to look this way for real?
Dolly Parton, American country music singer, on her appearance

My breasts are beautiful, and I've got to tell you, they've gotten a lot of attention for what is relatively short screen time.
Jamie Lee Curtis, American actress

I remained Ryan's companion in the Hollywood party circuit, growing inured to sex and drugs before I was in my teens.
Tatum O'Neal, American actress and daughter of actor Ryan O'Neal

I think any girl who comes to Hollywood with sex symbol or bombshell hanging over her has a rough road.
Kim Basinger, American actress

HOMOSEXUALITY

It was out of the closet and into the streets for the nation's homosexuals in the 1970s. This didn't do much for the streets but, on the other hand, your average closet was improved immeasurably.
Rick Meyerowitz, American artist, and John Weidman, American librettist, writing in *National Lampoon* **magazine, 1980**

If homosexuality were the normal way, God would have made Adam and Bruce.
Anita Bryant, American anti-gay rights campaigner

I became one of the stately homos of England.
Quentin Crisp (1908–1999), British writer, in *The Naked Civil Servant*, **1968**

Homosexuality is a sickness, just as are baby-rape or wanting to become the head of General Motors.
Eldridge Cleaver (1935–1998), American writer and leader of the Black Panther Party, in *Soul on Ice*, **1968**

This sort of thing may be tolerated by the French – but we are British, thank God.
Viscount Montgomery (1887–1976), British Army officer

There is probably no sensitive heterosexual alive who is not preoccupied with his latent homosexuality.
Norman Mailer (1923–2007), American writer and political activist

Postumus, are you really taking a wife? . . . Isn't it better to sleep with a pretty boy? Boys don't quarrel all night, or nag you for little presents while they're on the job, or complain that you don't come up to their expectations, or demand more gasping passion.
Juvenal (AD 60–130), Roman poet, in *Satires VI*

Texas Woman: Are you a homosexual? We don't have homosexuals in Texas – live ones, anyway.
From *Soap* **(1978) by Susan Harris, American screenwriter**

I'd rather be black than gay because when you're black you don't have to tell your mother.
Charles Pierce (1926–1999), American female impersonator

My favourite city is San Francisco because it's gay. They teach the kids in school: AC . . . DC . . . EFG . . .
Joan Rivers, American comedienne

As a mother, I know that homosexuals cannot biologically produce children, therefore they must recruit our children.
Anita Bryant, American anti-gay rights campaigner

Homosexuals have the time for everybody . . . every detail of lives of real people, however mundane it may be, seems romantic to them.
Quentin Crisp (1908–1999), British writer, in *The Naked Civil Servant*, **1968**

We didn't go for the gay concept when we put the show together. We went for a totally male, masculine celebration – that men can get up there and feel their tits and do bumps and grinds and still remain men. Narcissism is a good thing. Everybody does it, I don't care what they say. Everyone gets off on mirror tripping.
David 'Scar' Hodo, construction work character in the American disco group The Village People

I was too polite to ask.
Gore Vidal (1925–2012), American writer and wit, when asked whether his first sexual experience had been heterosexual or homosexual

I cover the waterfront.
Tennessee Williams (1911–1983), American playwright, on being asked by David Frost if he was homosexual

This is a celebration of individual freedom, not of homosexuality. No government has the right to tell its citizens when or whom to love. The only queer people are those who don't love anybody.
Rita Mae Brown, American feminist writer

People who have low self-esteem . . . have a tendency to cling to their own sex because it is less frightening.
Clara Thompson (1893–1958), American physician

A lot of my friends are gay. It makes sense to hang around with gay men if you're single, because they're the same as you. They haven't got kids and as a result have money to spend.
Carole McGiffin, British television personality, in interview

My mother made me a homosexual.
If I send her the wool will she make me one?
Famous graffiti from the 1980s

I started to be really proud of the fact I was gay even though I wasn't.
Kurt Cobain (1967–1994), American lead singer of Nirvana

I spent years growing up being told what my sexuality was.
George Michael, British singer

I was certainly open for something being on the edge of a nervous breakdown, perplexed by my own sexuality. I was gay.
Rabbi Lionel Blue, British Reform Rabbi and the first to publicly declare his homosexuality

All men are homosexual, some turn straight. It must be very odd to be a straight man because your sexuality is hopelessly defensive. It's like an ideal of racial purity.
Derek Jarman (1942–1994), British film-maker and gay activist

People already think I'm that way – homo – because of my voice, and I'm not.
Michael Jackson (1958–2009), American singer

HUMOUR

Do you come here often? Only in the mating season.
Spike Milligan (1918–2002), British comedian, in *The Goon Show*

My father told me all about the birds and the bees, the liar – I went steady with a woodpecker till I was 21.
Bob Hope (1903–2003), American comedian

Those hotpants of hers were so damned tight, I could hardly breathe.
Benny Hill (1924–1992), British comedian

He looks like he's got a cheese danish stuffed in his pants!
Tom Wolfe, American writer, in *Bonfire of the Vanities*, **1987**

A one-time US Ambassador in Europe, astonishing in view of his age, is said to have approached all problems with a closed mind and an open fly.
John Kenneth Galbraith (1908–2006), Canadian economist

Please, Sir John, does that apply to those of us who only have small parts?
An *actor* to Sir John Gielgud, who had told them that all the men must wear jock-straps under their leotards

Comedy, like sodomy, is an unnatural act.
Marty Feldman (1934–1982), American actor and comedian, in *The Times,* **1969**

I'm never vulgar. I kid sex. I take it out in the open and laugh at it.
Mae West (1893–1980), American actress

Wit in women is apt to have bad consequences; like a sword without a scabbard, it wounds the wearer and provokes assailants. I am sorry to say the generality of women who have excelled in wit have failed in chastity.
Elizabeth Montagu (1720–1800), British social reformer

I thought coq au vin was love in a lorry.
Victoria Wood, British comedienne, in *Talent,* **1979**

I am not interested in an inanimate statue of a little bald man. I like something with long blonde curls.
Woody Allen, American actor and film-maker, refusing to attend the Oscars ceremony, 1978

She sleeps alone at last.
Robert Benchley (1889–1945), American humorist, suggesting an epitaph for a certain actress

Women find men who have a sense of humour extremely sexy. You don't have to look like Robert Redford. All you have to do is tickle her funny bone, and she'll follow you anywhere. If you can make her laugh, you've got it made!
Man: One to call her dad and the other to open her Diet Pepsi!
Woman: Oh, stop! You're killing me! Take off your clothes, quick!
Mimi Pond, American cartoonist, in *Mimi Pond's Secrets of the Powder Room,* **1983**

Martina was so far in the closet she was in danger of being a garment bag.
Rita Mae Brown, American feminist writer, on her relationship with Martina Navratilova

I'd rather laugh in bed than do it . . . If I went to a lady of the night, I'd probably pay her to tell me jokes. Would that be perverted?
Billy Joel, American singer

You have to have a sense of humour about sex. When you look at it, it's all pretty ridiculous, isn't it?
Cat Deeley, British television presenter

If someone had told me years ago that sharing a sense of humour was so vital to partnerships, I could have avoided a lot of sex.
Kate Beckinsale, British actress

HUSBANDS

I've been asked to say a couple of words about my husband Fang. How about 'short' and 'cheap'.
Phyllis Diller (1917–2012), American actress

He tells you when you've got too much lipstick
And helps you with your girdle when your hips stick.
Ogden Nash (1902–1971), American poet, in 'The Perfect Husband,' 1949

A woman usually respects her father, but her view of her husband is mingled with contempt, for she is of course privy to the transparent devices by which she snared him.
H.L. Mencken (1880–1956), American writer and humorist

No one asks how his marriage survives if he's away.
Angela Rippon, British television presenter, in reply to interviewer who asked if living apart puts a strain on a relationship

A small band of men armed only with wallets, besieged by a horde of wives and children.
National Lampoon, **1979**

The way to hold a husband is to keep him a little jealous; the way to lose him is to keep him a little more jealous.
H.L. Mencken

American husbands are the best in the world; no other husbands are so generous to their wives, or can be so easily divorced.
Elinor Glyn (1864–1943), British writer

Husbands think we should know where everything is – like the uterus is the tracking device. He asks me, 'Roseanne, do we have any Cheetos left?' Like he can't go over to that sofa cushion and lift it himself.
Roseanne Barr, American comedienne

One exists with one's husband – one lives with one's lover.
Honoré de Balzac (1799–1850), French writer

I think every woman is entitled to a middle husband she can forget.
Adela Rogers St Johns (1894–1988), American journalist and screenwriter

A husband is what is left of the lover after the nerve is extracted.
Helen Rowland (1875–1950), American writer and humorist

There is so little difference between husbands you might as well keep the first.
Adela Rogers St Johns

Before I met him, I wasn't used to the fact that buying the wrong length shoelaces would be the reason to contemplate suicide.
Sarah Woods, estranged wife of actor James Woods, talking about his moodiness

I have three pets at home which answer to the same purpose as a husband: I have a dog which growls every morning, a parrot which swears all afternoon and a cat that comes home late at night.
Marie Corelli (1855–1924), British novelist

An archaeologist is the best husband any woman can have; the older she gets, the more interested he is in her.
Agatha Christie (1890–1976), British crime writer

Husbands are like fire. They go out if unattended.
Zsa Zsa Gabor, Hungarian-American socialite

If you cannot have your dear husband for a comfort and a delight, for a breadwinner and a cross-patch, for a sofa chair or hot water bottle, one can use him as a cross to be borne.
Stevie Smith (1902–1971), British poet

The divine right of husbands, like the divine right of kings, may, it is hoped in this enlightened age, be contested without danger.
Mary Wollstonecraft (1759–1797), British feminist writer, in *A Vindication of the Rights of Women,* 1792

I began as a passion and ended as a habit, like all husbands.
George Bernard Shaw (1856–1950), **Irish playwright**

I know many married men, I even know a few happily married men, but I don't know one who wouldn't fall down the first open coal hole running after the first pretty girl who gave him a wink.
George Jean Nathan (1882–1958), **American theatre critic**

Being a husband is a whole-time job. That is why so many husbands fail. They cannot give their entire attention to it.
Arnold Bennett (1867–1931), British novelist

The majority of husbands remind me of an orang-utan trying to play the violin.
Honoré de Balzac (1799–1850), French writer

A good husband makes a good wife.
Robert Burton (1577–1640), British philosopher

Husbands never become good. They merely become proficient.
H.L. Mencken (1880–1956), American writer and humorist

Nothing flatters a man as much as the happiness of his wife; he is always proud of himself as the source of it.
Dr Samuel Johnson (1709–1784), British writer and lexicographer

Every man who is high up likes to think he has done it all himself, and the wife smiles and lets it go at that.
J.M. Barrie (1860–1937), British writer

The concern that some women show at the absence of their husbands does not arise from their not seeing them and being with them, but from the apprehension that their husbands are enjoying pleasures in which they do not participate, and which, from their being at a distance, they have not the power of interrupting.
Michel de Montaigne (1533–1592), French writer

The most popular labour-saving device today is still a husband with money.
Joey Adams (1911–1999), American comedian

Celibacy is the better stake, since the best husband is not worth a fig.
Duchess of Orléans (1652–1722), sister-in-law to Louis XIV

When two people marry they become in the eyes of the law one person, and that one person is the husband.
Shana Alexander (1925–2005), American journalist, in *State-by-State Guide to Women's Legal Rights,* **1975**

I do, and I also wash and iron them.
Denis Thatcher (1915–2003), husband of Margaret Thatcher, replying to the question, 'Who wears the pants in your house?', in *Los Angeles Times,* **1981**

I have no wish for a second husband. I had enough of the first. I like to have my own way, to lie down mistress and get up master.
Susanna Moodie (1803–1885), Canadian writer

The husband who decides to surprise his wife is often very much surprised himself.
Voltaire (François-Marie Arouet, 1694–1778), French writer and philosopher

He is always dealing with beautiful women but it must be like being in a chocolate shop – after a while, you don't notice the goodies any more.
Barbara Taylor Bradford, British novelist, of her husband

Bigamy is having one husband too many. Monogomy is the same.
Erica Jong, American writer, in *Fear of Flying*

Husband and dog missing . . . reward for dog.
Della Bovey, posting a sign outside her home after her husband, Grant, left her for television presenter Anthea Turner, as reported in the *Mail on Sunday*

Johnny can't write about sex. He knows very little about it.
Renée Grisham, wife of bestselling American author John Grisham

IMAGINATION

Were it not for imagination, Sir, a man would be as happy in the arms of a chambermaid as of a duchess.
Dr Samuel Johnson (1709–1784), British writer and lexicographer, in *Life of Johnson*, **vol. III, 1778**

A lady's imagination is very rapid; it lumps from admiration to love, from love to matrimony in a moment.
Jane Austen (1775–1817), British novelist

Sex is more exciting on the screen and between the pages than between the sheets.
Andy Warhol (1928–1987), American artist

IMPOTENCE

Thou treacherous, base deserter of my flame, false to my passion, fatal to my fame, through what mistaken magic dost thou prove so true to lewdness, so untrue to love?
John Wilmot, 2nd Earl of Rochester (1647–1680), British poet and courtier

IMPRESSIONS

Hubert Humphrey talks so fast that listening to him is like trying to read *Playboy* magazine with your wife turning the pages.
Barry Goldwater (1909–1998), American businessman and Senator

Along comes Christina Aguilera wearing fishnets (and little else) on stage, looking as if her bottom had got itself trapped in a Tesco trolley. You can almost hear her buttocks screaming through those little net windows: 'Please help.'
Mimi Spencer, British journalist, in *First Word*

He was just trying to be cool. I bet he couldn't name a single song of ours.
Cheryl Cole, British singer, on meeting David Cameron, who admitted he fancied her, 2006

INFATUATION

Many a man in love with a dimple makes the mistake of marrying the wrong girl.
Stephen Leacock (1869–1944), Canadian political scientist and writer, in *Literary Lapses*, **1910**

Infatuation is when you think that he's as sexy as Robert Redford, as smart as Henry Kissinger, as noble as Ralph Nader, as funny as Woody Allen and as athletic as Jimmy Connors. Love is when you realise that he's as sexy as Woody Allen, as smart as Jimmy Connors, as funny as Ralph Nader, as athletic as Henry Kissinger and nothing like Robert Redford – but you'll take him anyway.
Judith Viorst, American writer, in *Redbook*, **1975**

INFIDELITY

I have always held that it was a very good thing for a young girl to fall hopelessly in love with a married man so that, later on and in the opposite predicament, she could remember what an unassailable citadel a marriage can be.
Katharine Whitehorn, British journalist

A man does not look behind the door unless he has stood there himself.
Henri Dubois (1859–1930), French sculptor

When a man steals your wife, there is no better revenge than to let him keep her.
Sacha Guitry (1885–1957), French writer and director

Husbands are chiefly good lovers when they are betraying their wives.
Marilyn Monroe (1926–1962), American actress

It is better to be unfaithful than to be faithful without wanting to be.
Brigitte Bardot, French actress turned animal-rights campaigner

If your home burns down, rescue the dogs. At least they'll be faithful to you.
Lee Marvin (1924–1987), American actor

Never tell. Not if you love your wife . . . In fact, if your old lady walks in on you deny it. Yeah. Just flat out she'll believe it: 'I'm tellin' ya. This chick came downstairs with a sign around her neck: "Lay On Top Of Me Or I'll Die." I didn't know what I was gonna do . . . '
Lenny Bruce (1925–1966), American comedian

One man's folly is another man's wife.
Helen Rowland (1875–1950), American writer and humorist

I didn't want to upset my marriage. The best way I could satisfy a man's urge was to pick on somebody who would not be a threat to my wife.
Sir Ralph Halpern, British businessman, on his much-publicised affair with model Fiona Wright

I Could Never Have Sex With Any Man Who Has So Little Regard For My Husband.
Title of 1973 film by American film-maker Dan Greenburg

I said to the wife, guess what I heard in the pub? They reckon the milkman has made love to every woman in this road except one. And she said, I'll bet it's that stuck-up Phyllis at number 23.
Max Kauffman, American writer and wit

There is one thing I would break up over, and that is if she caught me with another woman. I won't stand for that.
Steve Martin, American actor

Your idea of fidelity is not having more than one man in bed at the same time.
Robert Gold, played by Dirk Bogarde in *Darling,* **a 1965 film by Frederic Raphael**

Accursed from their birth they be
Who seek to find monogamy
Pursuing it from bed to bed –
I think they would be better dead.
Dorothy Parker (1893–1967), American wit

Sara could commit adultery at one end and weep for her sins at the other, and enjoy both operations at once.
Joyce Cary (1888–1957), Irish novelist, in *The Horse's Mouth,* **1944**

Benchley and I had an office in the old *Life* magazine that was so tiny, if it were an inch smaller it would have been adultery.
Dorothy Parker (1893–1967), American wit

I have looked on a lot of women with lust. I've committed adultery in my heart many times. God recognises I will do this and forgives me.
Jimmy Carter, 39th President of the United States

What men call Gallantry, and the Gods adultery,
Is much more common when the climate's sultry.
Lord Byron (1788–1824), British Romantic poet, in *Don Juan*

Thou shall not commit adultery . . . unless in the mood.
W.C. Fields (1880–1946), American actor and comedian

Eric: She's a lovely girl . . . I'd like to marry her, but her family objects.
Ernie: Her family?
Eric: Yes, her husband and four kids.
The Morecambe and Wise Joke Book, **by Eric Morecambe, Ernie Wise and Eddie Braben, 1979**

A father will have compassion on his son. A mother will never forget her child. A brother will cover the sin of his sister. But what husband ever forgave the faithlessness of his wife?
Marguerite de Navarre (1492–1549), French Renaissance poet, in *Mirror of the Sinful Soul*

Of course I've known for years our marriage has been a mockery. My body lying there night after night in the wasted moonlight. I know now how the Taj Mahal must feel.
Mrs Wicksteed, in *Habeas Corpus* **by Alan Bennett, British playwright**

I was a very good husband, I was just not faithful.
Peter Stringfellow, British nightclub owner, in an interview in *The Observer*

I think we explored the further reaches of 'for better or for worse', more than some other married couples.
Mary Archer, wife of Jeffrey Archer, at his trial for perjury in 2001

INNUENDO

Never do with your hands what you could do better with your mouth.
Cherry Vanilla, American publicist for group Vangelis

Nudge, nudge, wink, wink, say no more, know what I mean . . .
Catchphrase of a character played by Eric Idle in a sketch from
Monty Python's Flying Circus

If Miss means respectfully unmarried and Mrs respectfully married, then Ms means nudge, nudge, wink, wink.
Angela Carter (1940–1992), British writer, in 'The Language of Sisterhood', *The State of the Language,* **1980, by Michaels & Richs**

The only thing about a joke with a double meaning is that it can only mean one thing.
Ronnie Barker (1929–2005), British comedian

She was pleased to have him come and never sorry to see him go.
Dorothy Parker (1893–1967), American wit

INSULTS

If there's a worse insult, I don't know it. I have just been told by my friend Gladys that she'd trust her husband to spend an evening alone with me.
Marjorie Proops (1911–1996), British agony aunt with the *Daily Mirror*

With a head like yours I am surprised you don't get it circumcised.
Pamela Armstrong, former British TV presenter, in reply to a heckler during a speech she was making at Cambridge University Union

Eric: Who was that lady I seen you with last night?
Ernie: You mean, 'I saw'.
Eric: Sorry. Who was that eyesore I seen you with last night?
The Morecambe and Wise Joke Book, **by Eric Morecambe, Ernie Wise and Eddie Braben, 1979**

Firefly: Oh, er, I suppose you'll think me a sentimental old fluff, but, er, would you mind giving me a lock of your hair?
Mrs Teasdale: A lock of my hair? Why I had no idea . . .
Firefly: I'm letting you off easy. I was going to ask for the whole wig.
From the Marx Brothers' film *Duck Soup*, **1933**

I missed the naughtiness, the pigtail pulling and the laugh that you have when Simon's around. He's wicked – I don't mean in the cool sense, but in the evil sense. I used to call him Darth Vader, but this year I've changed to Voldermort as he is particularly evil.
Amanda Holden, British actress and *Britain's Got Talent* **judge, of Simon Cowell**

If I am one of Blair's babes – well, I've been called a damn sight worse.
Glenda Jackson, British Labour Party politician and former actress, referring to the nickname given to the women MPs in PM Tony Blair's Labour government

You look like an Easter Island statue with an arse full of razor blades.
Paul Keating, Australian Labour leader, to Malcolm Fraser in Parliament, 1983

They don't have a page that broad.
Gennifer Flowers, American model and actress, on why Hillary Clinton couldn't pose nude in *Penthouse*

Those guys from KISS couldn't wipe their ass by themselves.
Alan Lanier, American musician, describing rock group KISS

INTIMACY

If ever a man and his wife, or a man and his mistress, who pass nights as well as days together, absolutely lay aside all good breeding, their intimacy will soon degenerate into a coarse familiarity.
Philip Stanhope, 4th Earl of Chesterfield (1694–1773)

To really know someone is to have loved and hated him in turn.
Marcel Jouhandeau (1888–1979), French writer

I regret to say that we of the FBI are powerless to act in cases of oral-genital intimacy, unless it has in some way obstructed interstate commerce.
J. Edgar Hoover (1895–1972), first Director of the FBI, issuing an edict concerning homosexuality and the possible negative effects on commerce

IRONY

Woman is: finally screwing and your groin and buttocks and thighs ache like hell and you're all wet and bloody and it wasn't like a Hollywood movie at all, but Jesus, at least you're not a virgin any more – but is that what it's all about? And meanwhile he's asking, 'Did you come?'
Robin Morgan, American poet and feminist

A fox is a wolf who sends flowers.
Ruth Weston (1906–1955), American actress

He sleeps fastest who sleeps alone.
Richard Avedon (1923–2004), American photographer

A 25-year-old virgin is like the man who was set upon by thieves – everyone passes by.
Charlotte Bingham, British novelist

Everyone has experienced that truth: that love, like a running brook, is disregarded, taken for granted; but when the brook freezes over, then people begin to remember how it was when it ran, and they want it to run again.
Kahil Gibran (1833–1931), Lebanese poet, in *Beloved Prophet,* **c.1930**

Love, so-called, is based upon a view of women that is impossible to those who have had any experience with them.
H.L. Mencken (1880–1956), American writer and humorist

Literature is mostly about having sex and not much about having children; life is the other way round.
David Lodge, British writer and critic, in *The British Museum is Falling Down,* **1965**

Remember that no matter how critical you may be, how loathsome you may find your body, someone out there will always fancy you.
Janet Street-Porter, British journalist

It's only horny people who shoot people. I mean, you never feel aggressive just after you've gotten laid.
Ted Turner, American media mogul and founder of CNN

I have found men who didn't know how to kiss. I've always found time to teach them.
Mae West (1893–1980), American actress

Fighting for peace is like screwing for virginity.
George Carlin (1937–2008), **American comedian**

People equate sexy with promiscuity. They think that because I'm shaped this way, I must be scandalous. But it's just the opposite.
Jennifer Lopez, American singer and actress

JEALOUSY

Jealousy is the fear of losing the thing you love most. It's very normal. Suspicion is the thing that's abnormal.
Jerry Hall, American model and former girlfriend of Mick Jagger

People may go on talking for ever of the jealousies of pretty women; but for real genuine hard-working envy, there is nothing like an ugly woman with a taste for admiration.
Emily Eden (1797–1869), British writer

I think the only jealousy worth having is sexual jealousy. If I find something out, I go. I'm not a masochist. I don't hang around.
Jean Marsh, British actress

KINKY

Business lady and gentleman would like to rent ground-floor rooms or flat in North London in order to breed a litter of wire fox-terriers, very careful tenants, no children.
Advertisement placed in *Our Dogs* **magazine**

I gave her a sheer negligee and she let me put it on. But I don't look good in a sheer negligee.
Anon

Are you fond of nuts? Is this a proposal?
Anon

Kinky as a very old dancing pump.
Clive James, Australian broadcaster

It's always been my ambition to have a baby elephant.
Elephant keeper, London Zoo

Danny DeVito went a little crazy after he put his make-up on. He would become the Penguin. Once he had his beak on, we had to stop him biting anybody who came near him.
Tim Burton, British director of *Batman Returns*

I only used to bite one person, and that was Michelle Pfeiffer. And every guy would like to do that.
Danny DeVito, American actor, denying Burton's allegation

Corrie: There isn't the least bit of adventure in you. You're a watcher. There are watchers in this world and there are do-ers. And the watchers sit around watching the do-ers do. Well, tonight you watched and I did.
Paul: Yeah . . . well, it was harder to watch what you did than it was for you to do what I was watching.
From *Barefoot in the Park* **(1967) by Neil Simon, American playwright**

I get letters, sometimes scores of them a week, asking if I am available, available on my own. Available with wardrobe. Available with my husband. Available back, front, side and arse-ways up. In short – do I swing? I don't know, that's the trouble, I speak a lot instead.
Molly Parkin, British writer and artist, in *Good Golly Miss Molly*

If you are looking for a really fascinating, out-of-the-ordinary pet, may we suggest you visit the speciality section and ask to see our Miss Mortimore?
Reported in the *Manchester Evening News*

Y-Fronts wanted. No questions asked. Interesting career possibilities.
Reported in the *Henley Standard*

Sex means spank and beautiful means bottom and always will.
Kenneth Tynan (1927–1980), British theatre critic

See that couple over there – they're looking at you, behave.
John Betjeman (1906–1984), British poet laureate, to his teddy bear, Archie, while on the London Underground

I had to give up masochism – I was enjoying it too much.
Mel Calman (1931–1994), British cartoonist, in *Dr Calman's Dictionary of Psychoanalysis,* **1979**

After all: one man's tuna-and-sweetcorn casserole is another woman's vintage Klingon costume.
Dylan Jones, British editor of *GQ*

I'm not kinky, but occasionally I like to put on a robe and stand in front of a tennis-ball machine.
Garry Shandling, American comedian

It's been so long since I made love, I can't remember who gets tied up.
Joan Rivers, American comedienne

A dame that knows the ropes isn't likely to get tied up.
Mae West (1893–1980), American actress

I could serve coffee using my rear as a ledge.
Jennifer Lopez, American singer and actress

My wife wants sex in the back of the car and she wants me to drive.
Rodney Dangerfield (1921–2004), American comedian

KISSING

It takes a lot of experience for a girl to kiss like a beginner.
Reported in Ladies Home Journal, **1948**

Lord! I wonder what fool it was that first invented kissing.
Jonathan Swift (1667–1745), Anglo-Irish writer

I'd love to kiss you, but I just washed my hair.
Bette Davis (1908–1989), American actress, in the film The Cabin in the Cotton, 1932

I wasn't kissing her; I was whispering in her mouth.
Chico Marx (1887–1961), explaining to his wife after being caught in a compromising position with a chorus girl, in the Marx Brothers Scrapbook, 1973

I kissed my first girl and smoked my first cigarette on the same day. I haven't had time for tobacco since.
Arturo Toscanini (1867–1957), Italian conductor

When women kiss it always reminds one of prizefighters shaking hands.
H.L. Mencken (1880–1956), American writer and humorist

In love there is always one who kisses and one who offers the cheek.
French proverb

To a woman the first kiss is just the end of the beginning, but to a man it is the beginning of the end.
Helen Rowland (1875–1950), American writer and humorist

The sound of a kiss is not so loud as that of a cannon, but its echo lasts a great deal longer.
Dr Oliver Wendell Holmes (1809–1894), American physician

But his kiss was so sweet, and so closely he pressed, that I languished and pined till I granted the rest.
John Gay (1685–1732), British poet and playwright

The kiss originated when the first male reptile licked the first female reptile, implying in a subtle, complimentary way that she was as succulent as the small reptile he had for dinner the night before.
F. Scott Fitzgerald (1896–1940), American novelist

Everybody winds up kissing the wrong person goodnight.
Andy Warhol (1928–1987), American artist

I'll scream if you touch me – explained a pert miss, when her lover attempted an innocent kiss. But when he gave up and made ready to go, the damsel cried louder – I'll scream till you do.
Martial (AD 40–c.102), Spanish poet

We did one of those quick, awkward kisses where each of you gets a nose in the eye.
Clive James, Australian broadcaster, in *Unreliable Memoirs*

An office party is not, as is sometimes supposed, the managing director's chance to kiss the tea-girl. It is the tea-girl's chance to kiss the managing director (however bizarre an ambition this may seem to anyone who has seen the managing director face on).
Katharine Whitehorn, British journalist, in *Roundabout*

A young woman who allows herself to be kissed and caressed goes the rest of the way too.
Duchess of Orléans (1622–1752), sister-in-law to Louis XIV

A man who spent the last eight years working with Franciscan monks punched a woman and hit another when they refused to kiss him on the Edinburgh–Glasgow train.
Report in the *Glasgow Evening Times*

Wherever one wants to be kissed.
Coco Chanel **(1883–1971), French fashion designer, on being asked where one should wear perfume**

Always remember this: A kiss will never miss, and after many kisses, a miss becomes a misses.
John Lennon (1940–1980), British singer with The Beatles

Never delay kissing a pretty girl or opening a bottle of whisky.
Ernest Hemingway (1899–1961), American writer

People who throw kisses are hopelessly lazy.
Bob Hope (1903–2003), American comedian

I married the first man I ever kissed. When I tell my children that, they just about throw up.
Barbara Bush, wife of President George Bush

Kissing – and I mean like, yummy, smacking kissing – is the most delicious, most beautiful and passionate thing that two people can do, bar none. Better than sex, hands down.
Drew Barrymore, American actress

One is obliged to do a great deal of kissing in my line of work: air kissing, butt kissing, kissing up, and of course actual kissing. Much like hookers, actors have to do it with people we may not like or even know.
Meryl Streep, American actress

LADY

I have bursts of being a lady, but it doesn't last long. I'm the modern, intelligent, independent-type of woman. In other words, a girl who can't get a man.
Shelley Winters (1920–2006), American actress

A lady is nothing very specific. One man's lady is another man's woman; sometimes, one man's lady's another man's wife. Definitions overlap but they almost never coincide.
Russell Lynes (1910–1991), American editor of *Harper's* magazine

A lady is one who never shows her underwear unintentionally.
Lillian Day, American writer

LAW

There are only about 20 murders a year in London and many not at all serious – some are just husbands killing their wives.
Commander G.H. Hatherill of Scotland Yard, 1954

Legislation and case law still exist in some parts of the United States permitting the 'passion shooting by husband of a wife'; the reverse, of course, is known as homicide.
Diane Schulder, American lawyer, in *Sisterhood is Powerful* **by Robin Morgan, 1970**

He would stand the chance of violent sexual abuse and becoming a homosexual if sent to a state prison.
Judge Robert C. Abel (c.1932–2000), explaining why be had given a sentence of only 120 days to a man found guilty of raping and beating a woman

I am not saying that a girl hitching home late at night should not be protected by the law, but she was guilty of a great deal of contributory negligence.
Bertrand Richards, British judge, during a rape case, 1982

LESBIANISM

My lesbianism is an act of Christian charity. All those women out there are praying for a man, and I'm giving them my share.
Rita Mae Brown, American feminist writer

Our sexuality is used only when film-makers want to spice up the plot . . . we're never shown in a realistic light.
Lesbian activist protesting about Hollywood's unfair representation of gay people

Male heckler: Are you a lesbian?
Florynce: Are you my alternative?
Florynce R. Kennedy (1916–2000), American lawyer and civil-rights activist

Girls who put out are tramps. Girls who don't are ladies. This is, however, a rather archaic usage of the word. Should one of you boys happen upon a girl who doesn't put out, do not jump to the conclusion that you have found a lady. What you have probably found is a lesbian.
Fran Lebowitz, American writer

Once you know what women are like, men get kind of boring. I'm

not trying to put them down, I mean I like them sometimes as people, but sexually they're dull.
Rita Mae Brown, American feminist writer

Lesbianism has always seemed to me an extremely inventive response to the shortage of men but otherwise not worth the trouble.
Nora Ephron (1941–2012), American screenwriter and director, in Heartburn, **1983**

The Well of Loneliness, a novel by Radclyffe Hall, which treats of intimate relationships between women, was withdrawn on the advice of the Home Secretary, to whom the publishers submitted it for an opinion. But this was not before it had been condemned by the editor of the Sunday Express, who declared he 'would sooner give a healthy boy or girl a dose of prussic acid than a copy of it'.
Report in the Daily Telegraph, **1928**

Refusal to make herself the object is not always what turns women to homosexuality: most lesbians, on the contrary, seek to cultivate the treasures of their femininity.
Simone de Beauvoir (1908–1986), French writer, in The Second Sex, **1949**

I discarded the whole book because the leading character wasn't on my wavelength. She was a lesbian with doubts about her masculinity.
Peter de Vries (1910–1993), American editor and writer, in the New York Times, **1967**

Don't say we are here because we get sexual gratification from seeing these women playing.
Lesbian attending the Pilkington Glass Ladies Tennis Championships 1992, in which Martina Navratilova was playing

What's the point of being a lesbian if a woman is going to look and act like an imitation man?
Rita Mae Brown, American feminist writer

I never said I was a dyke even to a dyke because there wasn't a dyke in the land who thought she should be a dyke or even thought she was a dyke so how could we talk about it.
Jill Johnston (1929–2010), American feminist writer, in Lesbian Nation, **1973**

My sexuality has never been a problem to me but I think it has been for other people.
Dusty Springfield (1939–1999), British singer

LIES

By the time you say you're his
Shivering and sighing
And he vows his passion is
Infinite, undying –
Lady, make a note of this
One of you is lying.
Dorothy Parker (1893–1967), American wit

The tombstone is about the only thing that can stand upright and lie on its face at the same time.
Mary Wilson Little, American singer in The Supremes

He led a double life. Did that make him a liar? He did not feel a liar. He was a man of two truths.
Iris Murdoch (1919–1999), British novelist, in *The Sacred and Profane Love Machine*

Only lies and evil come from letting people off.
Iris Murdoch, in *A Severed Head*

Sex is full of lies. The body tries to tell the truth. But it's usually too battered with rules to be heard, and bound with pretences so it can hardly move. We cripple ourselves with lies.
Jim Morrison (1943–1971), American lead singer of The Doors

Clinton lied. A man might forget where he parks or where he lives, but he never forgets oral sex, no matter how bad it is.
Barbara Bush, wife of President George Bush, on the inquiry into President Clinton's sexual exploits

LIFE

If I had my life to live again, I'd make the same mistakes – only sooner.
Tallulah Bankhead (1902–1968), American actress

A lot of love-making and a little abuse; a little fame and more abuse; a real man and great happiness; the love of children and seventh heaven; an early death and a crowded memorial service.
Margot Asquith (1865–1945), wife of Prime Minister Herbert Henry Asquith (1864–1945), summing up her life

I was raised to feel that doing nothing was a sin. I had to learn to do nothing.
Jenny Joseph, British poet

Life is too short to dissect the nitty-gritty of your love life.
Janet Street-Porter, British journalist

A life is more valuable than a penis.
Lisa Kemler, defence attorney for Lorena Bobbitt, who cut off her husband's penis on discovering his infidelity

Serendipity is looking in a haystack for a needle and discovering a farmer's daughter.
Julius H. Comroe, Jr (1911–1984), American surgeon, in *What Does That Mean? Exploring Mind, Meaning and Mysteries* **by Eldon Taylor, 2010**

It doesn't bother me to talk about my private life, it doesn't bother me to talk about anything. My life is like a glass of water, transparent.
Shakira, Colombian singer

You can live to be a hundred if you give up all the things that make you want to live to be a hundred.
Woody Allen, American actor and film-maker

I feel like I'm too old to just have sex. I mean, I want to have sex, but with somebody who loves me.
Teri Hatcher, American actress

LOOKS

She wore far too much rouge last night and not quite enough clothes. That is always a sign of despair in a woman.
Lord Goring in *An Ideal Husband* **by Oscar Wilde (1854–1900), Irish playwright**

She wore a short skirt and a tight sweater and her figure described a set of parabolas that could cause cardiac arrest in a yak.
Woody Allen, American actor and film-maker, in *Getting Even,* **1973**

It was a blonde. A blonde to make a bishop kick a hole in a stained-glass window.
Raymond Chandler (1888–1959), American novelist, in *Farewell, My Lovely,* **1940**

She was a vivacious girl, not pretty by any accepted standards, if anything ugly by any accepted standards, but she could speak Latin and foot a quadrille and sometimes the two simultaneously if the tempo was right.
Denis Norden, British comedy writer, in *Upon My Word,* **1974**

She got her looks from her father – he's a plastic surgeon.
Groucho Marx (1880–1977), American comedian

The less I behave like Whistler's Mother the night before, the more I look like her the morning after.
Tallulah Bankhead (1902–1968), American actress

Just like Winnie; like a barracks in a pinny, gave up food for Lent, weight loss was fantastic, but her skin was not elastic, like an inefficient camper in a creased pink tent.
Victoria Wood, British comedienne

. . . so dreadfully dowdy that she reminded one of a badly bound hymn-book.
Oscar Wilde (1854–1900), Irish playwright, in *The Picture of Dorian Gray*

Wearing very tight striped pants, he looked like a bifurcated marrow . . . like a pensionable cherub.
Clive James, Australian broadcaster, on Rod Stewart

Young and handsome . . . looks like his teeth will stay in all night.
Victoria Wood, British comedienne, describing an ideal man

A woman with cut hair is a filthy spectacle, and much like a monster; and all repute it a very great absurdity for a woman to walk abroad with shorn hair; for this is all one as if she should take upon her the form or person of a man, to whom short cut hair is proper.
William Prynne (1600–1669), British lawyer and polemicist, in *Histriomastix*, **1669**

I've got saggy breasts and a low-slung ass . . . but I can still get men.
Édith Piaf (1915–1963), French singer

A plumber's idea of Cleopatra.
W.C. Fields (1880–1946), American actor and comedian, describing Mae West

Good girls come in wee bulk.
Helen Liddell, British Labour Party politician, describing her height

Sex keeps me fit and healthy. What can be better than that? It's not about crazy diets or gym workouts.
Kelly Brook, British model and actress

Heart throbs are a dime a dozen.
Brad Pitt, American actor

LOVE

Just another four-letter word.
Tennessee Williams (1911–1983), American playwright

If two people love each other, there can be no happy end to it.
Ernest Hemingway (1899–1961), American writer

Love is like quicksilver in the hand. Leave the fingers open and it stays. Clutch it, and it darts away.
Dorothy Parker (1893–1967), American wit

To fall in love you have to be in a state of mind for it to take, like a disease.
Nancy Mitford (1904–1973), British writer and one of the Mitford sisters

I could follow him around the world in my shift.
Mary, Queen of Scots (1542–1587), on James Hepburn, Earl of Bothwell

If it is your time, love will track you down like a Cruise missile. If you say 'No! I don't want it right now', that's when you'll get it for sure. Love will make a way out of no way. Love is an exploding cigar which we willingly smoke.
Lynda Barry, American cartoonist and writer

Love is so much better when you are not married.
Maria Callas (1923–1977), American-born Greek soprano

Everything we do in life is based on fear, especially love.
Mel Brooks, American film-maker

Fantasy love is much better than reality love. Never doing it is exciting. The most exciting attractions are between two opposites that never meet.
Andy Warhol (1928–1987), American artist

People in love, it is well known, suffer extreme conceptual delusions; the most common of these being that other people find your condition as thrilling and eye-watering as you do yourselves.
Julian Barnes, British novelist

I can see from your utter misery, from your eagerness to misunderstand each other, and from your thoroughly bad temper, that this is the real thing.
Peter Ustinov (1921–2004), British writer and actor, in *Romanoff & Juliet*, 1957

Love is much nicer to be in than an automobile accident, a tight girdle, a higher tax bracket or a holding pattern over Philadelphia.
Judith Viorst, American writer, in *Redbook*, 1975

I can understand companionship. I can understand bought sex in the afternoon. I cannot understand the love affair.
Gore Vidal (1925–2012), American writer and wit

I have never loved anyone for love's sake, except perhaps Josephine – a little.
Napoleon Bonaparte (1769–1821), French military leader

I love Mickey Mouse more than any woman I've ever known.
Walt Disney (1901–1966), American animator and business magnate

Desperate madness.
John Ford (1894–1973), American film director

Romantic love is mental illness. But it's a pleasurable one. It's a drug. It distorts reality, and that's the point of it. It would be impossible to fall in love with someone that you really saw.
Fran Lebowitz, American writer

Love has no great influences upon the sum of life.
Dr Samuel Johnson (1709–1784), British writer and lexicographer

If the rustle of a woman's petticoat has ever stirred my blood, of what matter is that to any reader?
Anthony Trollope (1815–1882), British novelist, on being asked why no reference to love appeared in his two-volume autobiography

Love: woman's eternal spring and man's eternal fall.
Helen Rowland (1875–1950), American writer and humorist

If love be good, from whence cometh my woe?
Geoffrey Chaucer (1343–1400), British poet, known as the Father of English Literature

Love is what you feel for a dog or a pussycat. It doesn't apply to humans.
Johnny Rotten (aka John Lydon), British singer and former member of the Sex Pistols

You need someone to love you, while you're looking for someone to love.
Shelagh Delaney, British playwright, in *A Taste of Honey*, **1958**

'Yes,' I answered you last night; 'No,' this morning, 'Sir,' I say.
Colours seen by candlelight will not look the same by day.
Elizabeth Barrett Browning (1806–1861), British poet

A grave mental disease.
Plato (427–347 BC), Greek philosopher

It's the nature of women not to love when we love them, and to
love when we love them not.
Miguel de Cervantes (1547–1616), Spanish writer

Had we never lov'd sae kindly,
Had we never lov'd sae blindly,
Never met – or never parted,
We had ne'er been broken hearted.
Robert Burns (1759–1796), Scottish poet, in 'Ae Fond Kiss'

Love is an ocean of emotions entirely surrounded by expenses.
**Lord Arthur Dewar (1860–1917), British politician and Liberal MP
for Edinburgh South**

Night of love descend!
Make me forget that I am alive.
Richard Wagner (1813–1883), German composer, in *Tristan und
Isolde*, **1865**

The heart can do anything.
Molière (1622–1673), French playwright

Love is often a consequence of marriage.
Molière, in *Sganarelle*

The whole pleasure of love lies in the variety.
Molière, in *Don Juan*

The heaviest object in the world is the body of the woman you
have ceased to love.
**Luc de Clapiers, Marquis de Vauvenargues (1715–1747), French
writer and close friend of Voltaire**

A man can be happy with any woman as long as he does not love
her.

Lord Henry, in *The Picture of Dorian Gray* **by Oscar Wilde (1854–1900), Irish playwright**

I sold my memoirs of my love life to Parker Brothers and they are going to make a game out of it.
Woody Allen, American actor and film-maker

In literature as in love we are astonished at what is chosen by others.
André Maurois (1885–1967), French novelist and writer

Never forget that the most powerful force on earth is love.
Nelson Rockefeller (1908–1979), American businessman and philanthropist, to Henry Kissinger

Love doesn't make the world go round. Love is what makes the ride worthwhile.
Franklin P. Jones (1908–1980), American journalist

Platonic love is love from the neck up.
Thyra Samter Winslow (1885–1961), American writer

Let there be spaces in your togetherness.
Kahil Gibran (1883–1931), Lebanese poet

Religion has done love a great service by making it a sin.
Anatole France (1844–1924), French writer

Take away love and our earth is a tomb.
Robert Browning (1812–1889), British poet

I had a lover's quarrel with the world.
Robert Frost (1874–1963), American poet

The good life is one inspired by love and guided by knowledge.
Bertrand Russell (1872–1970), British philosopher

Faults are thick where love is thin.
James Howell (1594–c.1666), British writer and historian

The head is always the dupe of the heart.
François, Duc de La Rochefoucauld (1613–1680), French writer

If love makes the world go round, why are we going to outer space?
Margaret Gilman

Love your enemy – it will drive him nuts.
Eleanor Doan, British children's author

How absurd and delicious it is to be in love with someone younger than yourself. Everyone should try it.
Barbara Pym (1913–1980), British novelist

A narcissism shared by two.
Rita Mae Brown, American feminist writer

Something you have to make . . . It's all work, work.
Joyce Cary (1888–1957), Irish novelist

The drug which makes sexuality palatable in popular mythology.
Germaine Greer, Australian feminist writer

Love is the wisdom of the fool and the folly of the wise.
Dr Samuel Johnson (1709–1784), British writer and lexicographer, in *Johnsonian Miscellanies*, **1784**

Such ever was love's way; to rise, it stoops.
Robert Browning (1812–1889), British poet, in *A Death in the Desert*, **1864**

Love means never having to say you're sorry.
Erich Segal (1937–2010), American writer, in *Love Story*, **1970**

Love will never be ideal until man recovers from the illusion that he can be just a little bit faithful or a little bit married.
Helen Rowland (1875–1950), American writer and humorist

Some women and men seem to need each other.
Gloria Steinem, American feminist writer

Falling out of love is very enlightening; for a short while you see the world with new eyes.
Iris Murdoch (1919–1999), British novelist

If you can stay in love for more than two years, you're on something.
Fran Lebowitz, American writer

Security is when I'm very much in love with somebody extraordinary who loves me back.
Shelley Winters (1920–2006), American actress

A woman that loves to be at the windows is like a bunch of grapes in the highway.
American proverb

I have had two great loves in my life. Mike Todd was the first.
Elizabeth Taylor (1932–2011), British actress

A woman despises a man for loving her, unless she returns his love.
Elizabeth Drew Stoddard (1823–1902), American writer

We don't believe in rheumatism and true love until after the first attack.
Marie Von Ebner-Eschenbach (1830–1916), Austrian writer

Love is moral without legal marriage, but marriage is immoral without love.
Ellen Key (1849–1926), Swedish writer, in *The Morality of Women*, **1911**

It seems to me that he has never loved, that he has only imagined that he has loved, that there has been no real love on his part. I even think that he is incapable of love; he is too much occupied with other thoughts and ideas to become strongly attached to anyone earthly.
Anna Dostoevsky (1846–1918), Russian diarist, on her husband, Fyodor Dostoevsky

True love is like ghosts, which everyone talks about and few have seen.
François, Duc de La Rochefoucauld (1613–1680), French writer

People who are not in love fail to understand how an intelligent man can suffer because of a very ordinary woman. This is like being surprised that anyone should be stricken with cholera because of a creature so insignificant as the common bacillus.
Marcél Proust (1871–1922), French writer

Love is a disease that fills you with a desire to be desired.
Henri de Toulouse-Lautrec (1864–1901), French painter

The woman one loves always smells good.
Remy de Gourmont (1858–1915), French writer and critic

Nuptial love maketh mankind; friendly love perfecteth it; but wanton love corrupteth and embaseth it.
Francis Bacon (1561–1626), British philosopher, in his essay *Of Love*, **1597**

Love is the self-delusion we manufacture to justify the trouble we take to have sex.
Dan Greenburg, American film-maker

Love is so different with men!
Robert Browning (1812–1889), British poet, in 'In a Year, IX'

Rick: I mean, what am I supposed to call you? My girlfriend? My companion? My room-mate? Nothing sounds quite right.
Joanie: How about your reason for living?
Rick: No, no, I need something I can use around the office.
Garry Trudeau, American cartoonist and creator of the Doonesbury cartoons

By the end of those six weeks, you are either in love or you can't stand the sight of each other. But for us, it worked out. I have such great expectations of our future together. I have never been so happy.
David Bowie, British singer, on a cruise he took with his new wife Iman, in *Hello!* **magazine, 1992**

You've got to love something enough to kill it.
Martin Scorsese, American film director

Love is what you've been through with somebody.
James Thurber (1894–1961), American writer and cartoonist, quoted in *Life* **magazine, 1960**

Love, though a very acute disorder in Andalusia, puts on a very chronic shape in these high northern latitudes; for first the lover must prove metaphysically that he ought to; and then in the fifth

or sixth year of courtship, or rather argument, if the summer is tolerable warm, and oat meal plenty, the fair one yields.
Sydney Smith (1771–1845), British writer and Anglican cleric, in a letter to Lady Holland

Love is 2 minutes 52 seconds of squishing noises. It shows your mind isn't clicking right.
Johnny Rotten (aka John Lydon), British singer and former member of the Sex Pistols

Love, love, love – all the wretched cant of it, masking egotism, lust, masochism, fantasy under a mythology of sentimental postures, a welter of self-induced miseries and joys, blinding and masking the essential personalities in the frozen gestures of courtship, in the kissing and the dating and the desire, the compliments and the quarrels which vivify its barrenness.
Germaine Greer, Australian feminist writer, in *The Female Eunuch*, **1970**

Once a woman has given you her heart, you can never get rid of the rest of her.
Sir John Vanbrugh (1664–1726), British playwright, in *The Relapse*, **1696**

Because women can do nothing except love, they've given it a ridiculous importance.
W. Somerset Maugham (1874–1965), British novelist, in *The Moon and Sixpence*, **1919**

Between women love is contemplative . . . there is no struggle, no victory, no defeat; in exact reciprocity, each is at once subject and object, sovereign and slave; duality becomes mutuality.
Simone de Beauvoir (1908–1986), French writer, in *The Second Sex*, **1949**

Now what is Love, I pray thee, tell?
. . .
It is a pretty kind of sporting fray,
It is a thing will soon away;
. . .
It is also a toothache or like pain;
It is a game where none doth gain.
Sir Walter Raleigh (1552–1618), British explorer

I want the deepest, darkest, sickest parts of you that you are afraid to share with anyone, because I love you that much.
Lady Gaga, American singer, clarifying the meaning of her lyrics in interview with Alexa Chung in 2009

Americans make love worse than any other race on earth.
Walt Whitman (1819–1892), American poet

The one you love and the one who loves you are never ever the same person.
Chuck Palahniuk, American writer, in *Invisible Monsters*

To me love is being able to go to bed with someone and feel better about them when you wake up the next morning.
Sylvester Stallone, American actor

Before I met my husband, I'd never fallen in love, though I've stepped in it a few times.
Rita Rudner, American actress and comedienne

I love that feeling of being in love, the effect of having butterflies when you wake up in the morning. That's special.
Jennifer Aniston, American actress

LOVE IS BLIND

If Jack's in love, he's no judge of Jill's beauty.
Benjamin Franklin (1706–1790), one of the Founding Fathers of the United States

Many a man has fallen in love with a girl in a light so dim he would not have chosen a suit by it.
Maurice Chevalier (1888–1972), French singer and actor

LOVE LETTERS

Be so good as to tell me . . . who is against my having any shirts. You can deny clean linen to the inmates of a hospital; but I do not intend to go without it. How your meanness, that of your origin and that of your parents, shines forth in your every act! My dove,

the day I so far forgot what I was that I could be willing to sell you what I am, it may have been to get you under the covers – but it wasn't to go uncovered.
Marquis de Sade (1740–1814), French aristocrat, known for his erotic writing, speaking to his wife

I will marry you so gladly with the old marriage service: for better or worse, in sickness and in health, and forsaking all others – until death do us part, Ha! Ha!
Dorothy Thompson (1893–1961), American journalist and radio broadcaster, to her intended, Sinclair Lewis

Loving you is like loving a red-hot poker, which is a worse bedfellow than even Lytton's umbrella; every caress brings on agony.
Bertrand Russell (1872–1970), British philosopher, to Ottoline Morrell

I could not love thee, dear, so much if I did not love my freedom more.
Johannes Brahms (1833–1897), German composer, to soprano Agatha Von Siebold, breaking their engagement

You must make a serious effort to change, my dear Clara . . . passions are not a natural adjunct to human nature, they are always exceptional or aberrant . . . look on yourself as ill, dear Clara, seriously ill.
Johannes Brahms, to German pianist Clara Schumann

If we love we must not live as other men and women do. I cannot brook the wolfsbane of fashion and foppery and tattle. You must be mine to die upon the rack if I want you . . . Goodbye! I kiss you – O the torments!
John Keats (1795–1821), British poet, to Fanny Brawne, to whom he was engaged until his death

Almost everything you have asked for – with the exception of a mink coat – I have given you. But you show no appreciation – only boredom, discontent. You can't bear to remain at home of an evening. If you do, it is only to cut your toenails.
Henry Miller (1891–1980), American writer, to his fifth wife

I will not meet you at the pier, as it will probably be chilly.
Anton Chekhov (1860–1904), Russian playwright, to Olga Knipper

LOVERS

I wouldn't give up one minute of my time with Richard Burton . . .
We were like magnets, alternating pulling towards each other and
inexorably pushing away.
Elizabeth Taylor (1932–2011), British actress

All mankind loves a lover.
Ralph Waldo Emerson (1803–1882), American writer, in *Love*

My life was better before I knew you.
**Edith Wharton (1862–1937), American writer, to Morton Fullerton,
a correspondent for** *The Times*, **with whom she had a long affair**

I am so anxious for you not to abdicate and I think the fact that
you do is going to put me in the wrong light to the entire world
because they will say that I could have prevented it.
Wallis Simpson, Duchess of Windsor (1896–1986), to Edward VIII

Please bring my flute.
**Percy Bysshe Shelley (1792–1822), British poet, to his wife,
informing her that he had eloped with Mary Godwin and asking
her to join them**

I hope you have lost your good looks, for while they last any fool
can adore you, and the adoration of fools is bad for the soul. No,
give me a ruined complexion and a lost figure and sixteen chins
on a farmyard of crow's feet and an obvious wig. Then you shall
see me coming out strong.
George Bernard Shaw (1856–1950), **Irish playwright, to Mrs Patrick
Campbell, an actress with whom he had an amusing correspondence**

I love the bitch to death.
Keith Richards, British musician with The Rolling Stones, on his wife

Darling Laura, sweet whiskers, do try to write me better letters.
Your last, dated 19 December received today, so eagerly
expected, was a bitter disappointment. Do realise that a letter
need not be a bald chronicle of events; I know you lead a dull
life now, my heart bleeds for it, though I believe you could
make it more interesting if you had the will. But that is no
reason to make your letters as dull as your life. I simply am not

interested in Bridget's children, do grasp that.
Evelyn Waugh (1903–1966), British novelist, to his wife

Dear United States Army:
My husband asked me to write a recommend that he supports his family. He cannot read, so don't tell him. Just take him. He ain't no good to me. He ain't done nothing but raise hell and drink lemon essence since I married him eight years ago, and I got to feed seven kids of his. Maybe you can get him to carry a gun. He's good on squirrels and eating. Take him and welcome. I need the grub and his bed for the kids. Don't tell him this, but just take him.
Anonymous letter hand-delivered in 1943 by an Arkansas man to his draft board

I've always been interested in lust, and everybody has lusted for someone at some time in their lives. It's human nature. The fact is, whether they acted it out or not, there's a carnal chemical reaction that's fascinating – especially if someone acted on it and then lost control of their life after their animal side took over.
Michael Douglas, American actor

It is very Victorian of the council to think that the ladies of Darlington will lose control at the sight of a few male bodies.
Rita Fishwick (1942–2002), American former Mayor of Darlington, on a decision to ban a male strip show

No, not too old at fifty-three a worn defeated fool like me. Still the tickling lust devours long stretches of my waking hours. Busty girls in flowered scanties hitching down St Michael panties. Easing off their wet-look boots, to step into their birthday suits.
Wicksteed, in *Habeas Corpus* by Alan Bennett, British playwright

Thunder and lightning, wars, fires, plagues, have not done that mischief to mankind as this burning lust.
Robert Burton (1577–1640), British philosopher, in *Anatomy of Melancholy*, 1621

It is even possible, quite often, to spot women on the pill from a certain deadness about their flesh, lustiness about their eyes and lifelessness in their movements.
Malcolm Muggeridge (1903–1990), British writer and satirist, speaking on BBC television, 1965

They are much more amorous than men, and as sparrows do not live long, because they are too hot and too susceptible to love, so women last less time; because they have a devouring heat, that consumes them by degrees.
Nicolas Venette (1633–1698), French physician, explaining why women have a shorter life expectancy than men

Dancing is the perpendicular expression of a horizontal desire.
George Bernard Shaw **(1856–1950), Irish playwright**

I doubt a girl would ever be satisfied with her lover's mind if she knew the whole of it.
Anthony Trollope (1815–1882), British novelist, in *The Small House at Allington,* **1864**

'Tis strange what a man may do, and a woman yet think him an angel.
William Makepeace Thackeray (1811–1863), British novelist

I haven't had sex with enough Americans to generalise. You'd have to have sex with somebody from every state, and the last time I checked, I've missed North and South Dakota, Maine and Alaska. I did screw an Eskimo once, but she wasn't an American citizen. Ever try to make love in a kayak?
Lewis Grizzard (1946–1994), American writer, on being asked if Americans were good lovers

Here is a sad slaughter at Windsor, the young men taking your leaves and going to France, and, although they are none of my lovers, yet I am loath to part with the men.
Nell Gwynn (1650–1687), British actress and mistress of King Charles II, in a letter to Madam Jennings

All really great lovers are articulate, and verbal seduction is the surest road to actual seduction.
Marya Mannes (1904–1990), American author

All of my sexual experiences when I was young were with girls. I mean we didn't have those sleepovers for nothing. I think that's really normal; same sex experimentation.
Madonna, American singer

Remember, if you smoke after sex you're doing it too fast.
Woody Allen, American actor and film-maker

Man and woman, love, what is it? A cork and a bottle.
James Joyce (1882–1941), Irish writer, in *Ulysses*

LUST

License my roving hands, and let them go
Before, behind, between, above, below.
John Donne (1572–1631), British poet

All witchcraft comes from carnal lust which, in women, is insatiable.
Heinrich Kramer (c.1430–1505) and Jakob Sprenger (c.1436–1495), German Catholic clergymen

Females are naturally libidinous, incite the males to copulation, and cry out during the act of coition.
Aristotle (384–322 BC), Greek philosopher, in *Historia Animalium*

To leap into a great vessel of cold water, or to put nettles in the codpiece.
Andrew Boorde (1490–1549), British physician, describing a cure for lust

Marriage is an adventure, like going to war.
G.K. Chesterton (1874–1936), British writer

No married man is genuinely happy if he has to drink worse whisky than he used to drink when he was single.
H.L. Mencken (1880–1956), American writer and humorist

I hate to be a failure. I hate and regret the failure of my marriages. I would gladly give all my millions for just one lasting marital success.
J. Paul Getty (1892–1976), American philanthropist

Marriage is an alliance entered into by a man who can't sleep with the window shut, and a woman who can't sleep with the window open.
George Bernard Shaw (1856–1950), Irish playwright

Marriage, a market which has nothing free but the entrance.
Michel de Montaigne (1533–1592), French writer

The chief cause of unhappiness in married life is that people think that marriage is sex attraction which takes the form of promises and hopes and happiness – a view supported by public opinion and by literature. But marriage cannot cause happiness. Instead, it is always torture, which man has to pay for satisfying his sex urge.
Leo Tolstoy (1828–1910), Russian novelist

Spouses are impediments to great enterprises.
Francis Bacon (1561–1626), British philosopher

By all means marry; if you get a good wife, you'll be happy. If you get a bad one, you'll become a philosopher.
Socrates (469–399 BC), Greek philosopher

If you are afraid of loneliness, do not marry.
Anton Chekhov (1860–1904), Russian playwright

If they only married when they fell in love, most people would die unwed.
Robert Louis Stevenson (1850–1894), British writer

David and I ate Dover sole, Kimberley ate Mr Blunkett.
Petronella Wyatt, British journalist, describing the lunch when she was introduced to David Blunkett, Labour politician, and Kimberley Quinn, with whom he had an affair

Lust will curdle like milk if you don't keep using it up.
Anon

You know that look that women have when they want to have sex? Me neither.
Steve Martin, American actor

I felt like an animal, and animals don't know sin, do they?
Jess C. Scott, American novelist

Let's face it, when an attractive but aloof man comes along, there are some of us who offer to shine his shoes with our underpants.
Lynda Barry, American cartoonist and writer

My schoolmates would make love to anything that moved, but I never saw any reason to limit myself.
Emo Philips, American comedian

MARRIAGE

It destroys one's nerves to be amiable every day to the same human being.
Benjamin Disraeli (1804–1881), former Conservative Prime Minister of Britain

Don't marry a man to reform him – that's what reform schools are for.
Mae West (1893–1980), American actress

It is a truth universally acknowledged, that a single man in possession of a good fortune, must be in want of a wife.
Jane Austen (1775–1817), British novelist

It's a funny thing that when a man hasn't anything on earth to worry about, he goes off and gets married.
Robert Frost (1874–1963), American poet

Someone asked me why women don't gamble as much as men do, and I gave the commonsensical reply that we don't have as much money. That was a true and incomplete answer. In fact, women's total instinct for gambling is satisfied by marriage.
Gloria Steinem, American feminist writer

Putting one's hand into a bag of snakes on the chance of drawing out an eel.
Leonardo da Vinci (1452–1519), leading figure of the Italian Renaissance

Nobody else could sleep with Dick. He wakes up during the night, switches on the lights, speaks into his tape recorder, or takes notes – it's impossible.
Pat Nixon (1912–1993), wife of President Richard Nixon

A man can be a fool and not know it – but not if he is married.
H.L. Mencken (1880–1956), American writer and humorist

Marriage is a bribe to make the housekeeper think she's a householder.
Thornton Wilder (1897–1975), American playwright

One wishes marriage for one's daughter and, for one's descendants, better luck.
Fay Weldon, British writer

Politics doesn't make strange bedfellows – marriage does.
Groucho Marx (1880–1977), American comedian

Most of the time in married life is taken up by talk.
Friedrich Nietzsche (1844–1900), German philosopher

No man is regular in his attendance at the House of Commons until he is married.
Benjamin Disraeli (1804–1881), former Conservative Prime Minister of Britain

In olden times sacrifices were made at the altar – a practice which is still continued.
Helen Rowland (1875–1950), American writer and humorist

My Nellie knows that the front door to the back is hers, and the outside world's mine. She's even quite good at changing plugs and all those little things you have to train women to do.
Lord Gormley (1917–1993), President of the National Union of Mineworkers, on his wife

Bad enough to make mistakes, without going ahead and marrying them.
Craig Rice (1908–1957), American novelist

You, poor and obscure, and small and plain as you are – I entreat you to accept me as a husband.
Mr Rochester in *Jane Eyre* by Charlotte Brontë (1816–1855), British novelist

I've married a few people I shouldn't have, but haven't we all?
Mamie Van Doren, American actress who modelled herself on Marilyn Monroe

Do you take sugar?
Sir Ian MacGregor (1912–1998), former Chairman of British Coal, to his wife, despite having being married to her for 45 years

It is true that I never should have married, but I didn't want to live without a man. Brought up to respect the conventions, love had to end in marriage. I'm afraid it did.
Bette Davis (1908–1989), American actress

I always say a girl must get married for love – and keep on getting married until she finds it.
Zsa Zsa Gabor, Hungarian-American socialite, who is currently on her eighth marriage

He's the kind of man a woman would have to marry to get rid of.
Mae West (1893–1980), American actress

The only solid and lasting peace between a man and his wife is doubtless a separation.
Philip Stanhope, 4th Earl of Chesterfield (1694–1773)

Marriage is not a word but a sentence.
Oscar Wilde (1854–1900), Irish playwright

My mother-in-law broke up my marriage. One day my wife came home early from work and found us in bed together.
Lenny Bruce (1925–1966), American comedian

Marry money.
Max Schulman (1919–1988), American writer and creator of Dobie Gillis, giving advice to aspiring authors

An optimist is one who believes marriage is a gamble.
Laurence J. Peter (1919–1990), Canadian professor and founder of the Peter Principle

A working girl is one who quit her job to get married.
E.J. Kiefer, American businessman

A man marries to have a home, but also because he doesn't want to be bothered with sex and all that sort of thing.
W. Somerset Maugham (1874–1965), British novelist

Marriage is a mistake every man should make.
George Jessel (1898–1981), **American actor and producer**

Dora and I are married, but just as happy as we were before.
Bertrand Russell (1872–1970), British philosopher

All marriages are happy. It's the living together afterward that causes all the trouble.
Raymond Hull (1919–1985), Canadian playwright

Matrimony is a process by which a grocer acquires an account the florist had.
Frances Rodman

One was never married, and that's his hell; another is, and that's his plague.
Robert Burton (1577–1640), British philosopher

I shall marry in haste and repent at leisure.
James Branch Cabell (1879–1958), American writer

Marriage is a feast where the grace is sometimes better than the dinner.
Charles Caleb Colton (1780–1832), British cleric and writer

Marriage is a community consisting of a master, a mistress, and two slaves – making in all two.
Ambrose Bierce (1842–1914), American writer

Marriage is the deep, deep peace of the double bed after the hurly-burly of the chaise longue.
Mrs Patrick Campbell (1865–1940), British actress

God, for two people to be able to live together for the rest of their lives is almost unnatural.
Jane Fonda, American actress

Happiness in marriage is entirely a matter of chance.
Jane Austen (1775–1817), British novelist

Marriage is a bargain, and somebody has to get the worst end of the bargain.
Helen Rowland (1875–1950), American writer and humorist

Any intelligent woman who reads the marriage contract, and then goes into it, deserves all the consequences.
Isadora Duncan (1878–1927), American dancer

It is always incomprehensible to a man that a woman should refuse an offer of marriage.
Jane Austen (1775–1817), British novelist

Love-matches are made by people who are content, for a month of honey, to condemn themselves to a life of vinegar.
Marguerite, Countess of Blessington (1789–1849), Irish writer

People who haven't spoken to each other for years are on speaking terms again today – including the bride and groom.
Dorothy Parker (1893–1967), American wit, on marrying Alan Campbell for the second time

When you see what some girls marry, you realise how they must hate to work for a living.
Helen Rowland

When a girl marries, she exchanges the attentions of many men for the inattention of one.
Helen Rowland

Almost all married people fight, although many are ashamed to admit it. Actually, a marriage in which no quarrelling at all takes place may well be one that is dead or dying from emotional undernourishment. If you care, you probably fight.
Flora Davis

A man in love is incomplete until he has married. Then he's finished.
Zsa Zsa Gabor, Hungarian-American socialite

Marriage always demands the greatest understanding of the art of insincerity possible between two human beings.
Vicki Baum (1888–1960), Austro-American writer

Marriage is a great institution, but I'm not ready for an institution.
Mae West (1893–1980), American actress

It was so cold I almost got married.
Shelley Winters (1920–2006), American actress

Before marriage, a man declares that he would lay down his life for you; after marriage, he won't even lay down his newspaper to talk to you.
Helen Rowland

Intelligent women always marry fools.
Anatole France (1844–1924), French writer

Marrying a man is like buying something you've been admiring for a long time in a shop window. You may love it when you get it home, but it doesn't always go with everything else in the house.
Jean Kerr (1922–2003), Irish-American playwright

I'd marry again if I found a man who had $15 million and would sign over half of it to me before the marriage, and guarantee he'd be dead within the year.
Bette Davis (1908–1989), American actress

A book of which the first chapter is written in poetry and the remaining chapters in prose.
Beverley Nichols (1898–1983), British writer

I feel sure that no girl could go to the altar, and would probably refuse, if she knew all . . .
Queen Victoria (1819–1901)

Writing is like getting married. One should never commit oneself until one is amazed at one's luck.
Iris Murdoch (1919–1999), British novelist

In no country, I believe, are the marriage laws so iniquitous as in England, and the conjugal relation, in consequence, so impaired.
Harriet Martineau (1802–1876), British writer, in *Society in America,* **1837**

The early marriages of silly children . . . where . . . every woman is married before she well knows how serious a matter human life is.
Harriet Martineau

Each coming together of man and wife, even if they have been mated for many years, should be a fresh adventure; each winning should necessitate a fresh wooing.
Marie Stopes (1880–1958), British birth-control campaigner, in her best-selling manual *Married Love,* **1918**

Why should marriage bring only tears? All I wanted was a man with a single heart and we would stay together as our hair turned white, not somebody always after wriggling fish with his big bamboo rod.
Chuo Wen-Chun (c. second century BC), Chinese poet

Courtship is to marriage as a very witty prologue is to a very dull play.
Belinda, in *The Old Bachelor* **by William Congreve (1670–1729), British playwright**

Remember it is as easy to marry a rich woman as a poor woman.
William Makepeace Thackeray (1811–1863), British novelist, in *Pendennis,* **1848**

No man should marry until he has studied anatomy and dissected at least one woman.
Honoré de Balzac (1799–1850), French writer, in *La Physiologie du Marriage*

The most happy marriage I can picture or imagine to myself would be the union of a deaf man to a blind woman.
Samuel Taylor Coleridge (1772–1834), British poet

Lastly (and this is, perhaps, the golden rule), no woman should marry a teetotaller, or a man who does not smoke.
Robert Louis Stevenson (1850–1894), British writer

If I had my choice, I would marry Roger Moore but have Sean Connery as my lover. He has a cross between menace and humour in his eyes. And a very chewable bottom lip.
Lois Maxwell (1927–2007), British actress who played Miss Moneypenny in the James Bond films

Never feel remorse for what you have thought about your wife; she has thought much worse things about you.
Jean Rostand (1894–1977), French biologist and writer, in Le Marriage, **1927**

You can measure the social caste of a person by the distance between the husband's and wife's apartments.
King Alfonso XIII of Spain (1886–1941)

Marriage is a wonderful invention, but then again so is a bicycle repair kit.
Billy Connolly, British comedian

The triumph of hope over experience.
Dr Samuel Johnson (1709–1784), British writer and lexicographer, on the hasty remarriage of a friend after the death of his first wife, with whom he had been very unhappy

Marrying merely to be married, to manage her own affairs, and have her own way – so childish! – or marrying merely to get an establishment – so base! How women, and such young creatures, can bring themselves to make these venal matches.
Maria Edgeworth (1768–1849), Irish writer, in Ormond, **1817**

Every woman should marry – and no man.
Benjamin Disraeli (1804–1881), former Conservative Prime Minister of Britain

Marriage is far and away the most sanitary and least harmful of all the impossible forms of the man–woman relationship, though I would sooner jump off the Brooklyn Bridge than be married.
H.L. Mencken (1880–1956), American writer and humorist

A word which should be pronounced 'mirage'.
Herbert Spencer (1820–1903), British philosopher and anthropologist

Why did he not marry? Could the answer be that Jesus was not by nature the marrying sort?
The Right Reverend Hugh Montefiore (1920–2005), when vicar of St Mary's, Cambridge

I totally disagree with you. By any other arrangement four people would have been unhappy instead of two.
Alfred, Lord Tennyson (1809–1892), British poet laureate, in reply to a statement that the marriage of Jane and Thomas Carlyle had been a mistake; it had been suggested that with anyone but each other they might have been perfectly happy

We sleep in separate rooms, we have dinner apart, we take separate vacations – we're doing everything we can to keep our marriage together.
Rodney Dangerfield (1921–2004), American comedian

If I ever marry, it will be on a sudden impulse – as a man shoots himself.
H.L. Mencken (1880–1956), American writer and humorist

Zsa Zsa Gabor got married as a one-off and it was so successful she turned it into a series.
Bob Hope (1903–2003), American comedian

Wife: Mr Watt next door blows his wife a kiss every morning as he leaves the house. I wish you'd do that.
Husband: But I hardly know the woman.
Alfred McFote

Some people ask the secret of our long marriage. We take time to go to a restaurant two times a week. A little candlelight dinner, soft music and dancing. She goes Tuesdays, I go Fridays.
Henny Youngman (1906–1998), British-American violinist and comedian

I belong to Bridegrooms Anonymous. Whenever I feel like getting married, they send over a lady in a house coat and hair curlers to burn my toast for me.
Dick Martin (1922–2008), American comedian, quoted in _Playboy_ magazine, 1969

She was another of his near Mrs.
Alfred McFote

The other night I said to my wife Ruth: 'Do you feel that the sex and excitement has gone out of our marriage?' Ruth said: 'I'll discuss it with you during the next commercial.'
Milton Berle (1908–2002), American comedian and actor, in *Variety*

The whole point of marriage is to stop you getting anywhere near real life. You think it's a great struggle with the mystery of being. It's more like . . . being smothered in warm cocoa. There's sex, but it's not what you think. Marvellous for the first fortnight. Then every Wednesday, if there isn't a good late-night concert on the Third. Meanwhile you become a biological functionary, an agent of the great female womb, spawning away, dumping its goods on your lap for succour: Daddy, Daddy, we're here and we're expensive.
Malcolm Bradbury (1932–2000), British academic, in *Love on a Gunboat*

EXCUSE ME COULD YOU PLEASE SAY THAT AGAIN I DON'T BELIEVE I HEARD YOU CORRECTLY LISTEN JUST WHO THE HELL DO YOU THINK YOU ARE FOR GOD'S SAKE WHAT AM I SUPPOSED TO BE YOUR SERVANT DON'T YOU DARE TALK TO ME IN THAT TONE OF VOICE I GUESS WE JUST AREN'T MEANT TO BE TOGETHER THAT'S ALL I'VE HAD IT UP TO HERE WITH YOU THAT'S RIGHT YOU HEARD ME THAT'S NOT MEANT TO BE A THREAT WE'RE JUST IN DIFFERENT TIMES IN OUR LIFE OK GO AHEAD THEN LEAVE I'LL HELP YOU PACK YOUR BAGS I GUESS I DON'T HAVE TO STAND.
Suzanne O'Malley (1980–1998), American writer, and Dan Greenburg, American writer's wallpaper design for the marital bedroom, in *How to Avoid Love and Marriage*, **1983**

I never knew what real happiness was until I got married. And by then it was too late.
Max Kauffman, American writer and wit

There is nothing in the world like the devotion of a married woman. It's a thing no married man knows anything about.
Cecil Graham, in *Lady Windermere's Fan* **by Oscar Wilde (1854–1900), Irish playwright**

The first part of our marriage was very happy. But then, on the way back from the ceremony . . .
Henny Youngman (1906–1998), British-American violinist and comedian

There were one hundred and seventeen psychoanalysts on the Pan Am flight to Vienna and I'd been treated by at least six of them, and married a seventh.
Erica Jong, American writer

Marriage is not just spirited communion and passionate embraces; marriage is also three meals a day and remembering to carry out the trash.
Joyce Brothers (1927–2013), American psychologist and advice columnist, in *Good Housekeeping*, **1972**

Marriage, I am convinced, is going to be the last subject to be effectively computerised.
Drusilla Beyfus, British writer

It has been discovered experimentally that you can draw laughter from an audience anywhere in the world, of any class or race, simply by walking onto a stage and uttering the words: 'I am a married man.'
Ted Kavanagh (1892–1958), British radio scriptwriter

'We stay together, but we distrust one another.'
'Ah, yes . . . but isn't that a definition of marriage?'
Malcolm Bradbury (1932–2000), British academic, in *The History Man*, **1975**

If you do not consent to be awakened your husband will be deeply disappointed . . . He will not call it purity, he will call it prudery; and he will be right . . . He will know that you have not fully given yourself in marriage: and married joys are for those who give with royal generosity.
Introduction to *The Sex Factor in Marriage* **by Dr Helena Wright (1887–1982), British family-planning pioneer**

Married women are kept women, and they are beginning to find it out.
Logan Pearsall Smith (1865–1946), American writer

He that gets a wench with child and marry her afterwards is as if a man should shit in his hat and then clap it on his head.
Samuel Pepys (1633–1703), British diarist

Marry Prince William? I'd love that. Who wouldn't want to be a princess?
Britney Spears, American singer

They say all marriages are made in heaven, but so are thunder and lightning.
Clint Eastwood, American actor and director

It's simple, you don't get divorced.
Olivia Harrison (née Olivia Trinidad Arias), widow of Beatle George Harrison, when asked the secret of a long marriage

Marriage 2001 style, as I know to my cost, is entirely expendable, more easily disposable than a McDonald's wrapper.
Vanessa Feltz, British writer and broadcaster

I want to wait to have sex until I'm married.
Britney Spears

Some people claim that marriage interferes with romance. There's no doubt about it. Anytime you have a romance, your wife is bound to interfere.
Groucho Marx (1880–1977), American comedian

If sex is supposed to be satisfying and anxiety-free once we are safely ensconced in marriage, how come that's when many of us stop wanting it?
David Morris Schnarch, American psychologist, in *Passionate Marriage,* **1997**

The chain of wedlock is so heavy that it takes two to carry it – sometimes three.
Alexandre Dumas (1802–1870), French novelist

Wonder if the fucking you get is worth the fucking you get.
Humphrey Bogart (1899–1957), American actor, on his fourth marriage

My favourite hobby? I married them all.
Stan Laurel (1890–1965), American actor and one half of Laurel & Hardy

We were happily married for eight months. Unfortunately we were married for four and a half years.
Nick Faldo, British professional golfer

The trouble with some women is that they get all excited about nothing; and then they marry him.
Cher, American singer

Being married means I can break wind and eat ice cream in bed.
Brad Pitt, American actor

I think same-sex couples should be able to get married.
Barack Obama, 44th President of the United States

MASTURBATION

A woman occasionally is quite a serviceable substitute for masturbation.
Karl Kraus (1874–1936), Austrian writer

A niggling feeling of discomfort and unease follows masturbation, even in those who do not feel guilty about it.
Dr Charlotte Wolff (1897–1996), German-born British psychologist, in Love Between Women, **1971**

Don't knock it, it's sex with someone you love.
Woody Allen, American actor and film-maker

You are throwing away the seed that has been handed down to you as a trust instead of keeping it and ripening it for bringing a son to you later.
Lord Robert Baden-Powell (1857–1941), founder of the Scout Movement, arguing against masturbation in Rovering to Success, **1922**

Masturbation the primary sexual activity of mankind. In the nineteenth century it was a disease; in the twentieth, it's a cure.
Thomas Szasz (1920–2012), Hungarian psychiatrist

Writers are the most masturbatory of creatures. Ask any writer – they're like monkeys.
Anthony Burgess (1917–1993), British writer

Masturbation is like procrastination, it's all good and fun until you realise you are only fucking yourself.
Anon

We have reason to believe that man first walked upright to free his hands for masturbation.
Lily Tomlin, American actress and comedienne

My first sex scene – and it was with myself.
Judge Reinhold, American actor

The first time I masturbated . . . it flew across the room and hit the far wall.
Jack Lemmon (1925–2007), American actor

MATING RITUAL

I don't believe we've met. I'm Mr Right.
If National Security were at stake, would you spend the night with a man whose name you don't even know?
I'm glad you don't recognise me. I'd rather have you like me for myself.
I don't dance. But I'd love to hold you while you do.
Four tested opening lines, in *Playboy* magazine, 1969

Roseberry to his lady says, 'My Hinnie and my succour,
O shall we do the thing ye ken, or shall we take our supper?'
Wi' modest face, sae fu' o' grace, replied the bonny lady;
'My noble Lord do as you please, but supper is na ready.'
Anon, quoted by Robert Burns (1759–1796), British poet, in 'The Merry Muses of Caledonia'

Good underwear is essential. Any help you can get underneath the outfit is always handy, but make sure you get time to whip it off before your husband or boyfriend sees it, because it looks vile.
Coleen Nolan, British singer and television presenter, on *Loose Women*, **2009**

MEN

A man is by nature a sexual animal. I've always had my special pets.
Mae West (1893–1980), American actress

Men are but children too: though they have grey hairs; they are only a larger size.
Seneca (*c*.4 BC–AD 65), Roman philsopher

Male sexual response is far brisker and more automatic. It is triggered easily by things – like putting a quarter in a vending machine.
Dr Alex Comfort (1920–2000), British psychologist and author of *The Joy of Sex*, **1972**

A man running after a hat is not half so ridiculous as a man running after a woman.
G.K. Chesterton (1874–1936), British writer

If man is only a little lower than the angels, the angels should reform.
Mary Wilson Little, American singer in The Supremes

There's nineteen men livin' in my neighbourhood, eighteen of them are fools and the one ain't no doggone good.
Bessie Smith (1894–1937), American blues singer

It's a man's world and you men can have it.
Katherine Ann Porter (1890–1980), American writer

The only really masterful noise a man ever makes in a house is the noise of his key, when he is still on the landing, fumbling for the lock.
Colette (Sidonie-Gabrielle, 1873–1954), French writer

His mother should have thrown him away and kept the stork.
Mae West (1893–1980), American actress

A man's home may seem to be his castle on the outside; inside, it is more often his nursery.
Clare Boothe Luce (1903–1987), American writer and politician

If men had more up top we'd need less up front.
Jaci Stephen, British journalist

The natural thing is to grab hold of someone and go wallop! That's what we've been born to, us blokes.
Ian Dury (1942–2000), British lead singer of Ian Dury and The Blockheads

There are two things no man will admit he can't do well: drive and make love.
Stirling Moss, British Formula One racing driver

All men are rapists and that's all they are. They rape us with their laws and their codes.
Marilyn French (1929–2009), American writer

I require only three things in a man: he must be handsome, ruthless and stupid.
Dorothy Parker (1893–1967), American wit

Never accept rides from strange men, and remember that all men are as strange as hell.
Robin Morgan, American poet and feminist

The male sex still constitutes in many ways the most obstinate vested interests one can find.
Frank Pakenham, 7th Earl of Longford (1905–2001), Labour peer

Men are beasts and even beasts don't behave as they do.
Brigitte Bardot, French actress turned animal-rights campaigner

The more I see of men, the more I like dogs.
Madame de Staël (1766–1817), French writer

Giving a man space is like giving a dog a computer: the chances are he will not use it wisely.
Bette-Jane Raphael, American writer

It's not the men in my life that count – it's the life in my men.
Mae West (1893–1980), American actress

Give a man a free hand and he'll run it all over you.
Mae West

None of you [men] ask for anything – except everything, but just for so long as you need it.
Doris Lessing, Zimbabwean-British writer

I'd never seen men hold each other. I thought the only thing they were allowed to do was shake hands or fight.
Rita Mae Brown, American feminist writer

I only like two kinds of men: domestic and imported.
Mae West

Probably the only place where a man can feel really secure is in a maximum-security prison, except for the imminent threat of release.
Germaine Greer, Australian feminist writer

I love men like some people like good food or wine.
Germaine Greer

The first time you buy a house you see how pretty the paint is and buy it. The second time you look to see if the basement has termites. It's the same with men.
Lupe Velez (1908–1944), Mexican actress

I want a man who's kind and understanding. Is that too much to ask of a millionaire?
Zsa Zsa Gabor, Hungarian-American socialite

The male sex, as a sex, does not universally appeal to me. I find the men today less manly; but a woman of my age is not in a position to know exactly how manly they are.
Katharine Hepburn (1907–2003), American actress

A man in the house is worth two in the street.
Mae West

I like men to behave like men – strong and childish.
Françoise Sagan (1935–2004), French writer

I did not sleep; I never do when I am over happy, over unhappy, or in bed with a strange man.
Edna O'Brien, Irish novelist, in *The Love Nest,* **1963**

To a smart girl, men are no problem – they're the answer.
Zsa Zsa Gabor

He's the kind of bore who's here today and here tomorrow.
Binnie Barnes (1903–1998), British actress

Sometimes I think if there was a third sex men wouldn't get so much as a second glance from me.
Amanda Vail (1921–1966), American writer

The rule in the women's colleges was that after 7 p.m. all men were beasts. Up until 7 p.m. they were all angels, and the girls simply had to learn to live with that routine and practise love in the afternoon.
Harry G. Johnson (1923–1977), Canadian economist, on Cambridge in the 1950s

There are a lot of men who will ask me out just to be with a celebrity.
Elizabeth Taylor (1932–2011), British actress

I truly believe I can be content only with a man who's a little crazy.
Elizabeth Taylor

Happy is a man with a wife to tell him what to do and a secretary to do it.
Stormont Mancroft, 2nd Baron Mancroft (1917–1987), British businessman and writer

You know the problem with men? After the birth, we're irrelevant.
Dustin Hoffman, American actor

However much men say sex is not on their minds all the time, it is – most of the time.
Jackie Collins, British novelist

American men are all mixed up today . . . There was a time when this was a nation of Ernest Hemingways, real men. The kind of men who could defoliate an entire forest to make a breakfast fire – and then wipe out an endangered species while hunting for lunch. But not any more. We've become a nation of wimps. Pansies. Alan Alda types who cook and clean and 'relate' to their wives. Phil Donahue clones who are 'sensitive' and 'vulnerable' and understanding of their children. And where's it gotten us? I'll tell you where. The Japanese make better cars. The Israelis better soldiers. And the rest of the world is using our embassies for target practice.
Bruce Feirstein, American screenwriter, in 'Real Men Don't Eat Quiche', *Playboy* magazine, 1982

It's no news to anyone that nice guys finish last. Almost every female I know has had the uncomfortable experience of going out with the 'nice man', spelled, 'N-E-R-D'. How many times has your girlfriend said, 'He's so sweet and so cute, so why don't I like him?' Let's face it, when an attractive but aloof ('cool') man comes along, there are some of us who offer to shine his shoes with our underpants. If he has a mean streak, somehow this is 'attractive'. There are thousands of scientific concepts as to why this is so, and yes, yes, it's very sick – but none of this helps.
Lynda Barry, American cartoonist and author, in Big Ideas cartoon, 1987

No nice men are good at getting taxis.
Katharine Whitehorn, British journalist, *The Observer*, 1977

There is nothing about which men lie so much as their sexual powers. In this at least every man is, what in his heart he would like to be, a Casanova.
W. Somerset Maugham (1874–1965), British novelist, in *A Writer's Notebook*, 1941

Is it too much to ask that women be spared the daily struggle for superhuman beauty in order to offer it to the caresses of a subhumanly ugly mate?
Germaine Greer, Australian feminist writer, in *The Female Eunuch*, **1970**

On such a basis, one can't call a man ugly.
Caroline 'La Belle' Otero (1868–1965), Spanish actress and courtesan, on receiving a priceless jewel from a hideous lover

He must be a creature who makes me feel that I am a woman.
Elinor Glyn (1864–1943), British writer, giving her definition of a man

Men are like wine – some turn to vinegar, but the best improve with age.
Pope John XXIII (1881–1963), quoted in *Thoughts in a Dry Season* **by Gerald Brenan, 1978**

About sex especially men are born unbalanced; we might almost say men are born mad. They scarcely reach sanity till they reach sanctity.
G.K. Chesterton (1874–1936), British writer

Whenever I date a guy, I think, is this the man I want my children to spend their weekends with?
Rita Rudner, American actress and comedienne

Women want mediocre men, and men are working to be as mediocre as possible.
Margaret Mead (1901–1978), American anthropologist and writer

Some of my best leading men have been horses and gods.
Elizabeth Taylor (1932–2011), British actress

Men are creatures with two legs and eight hands.
Jayne Mansfield (1933–1967), American actress

I never hated a man enough to give him his diamonds back.
Zsa Zsa Gabor, Hungarian-American socialite

One hell of an outlay for a very small return with most of them.
Glenda Jackson, British Labour Party politician and former actress

A hard man is a good find
Mae West (1893–1980), American actress

MEN AND WOMEN

The sad lesson in life is that you treat a girl like that with respect, and the next guy comes along and he's banging the hell out of her.
Art Buchwald (1925–2007), American humorist and *Washington Post* **columnist**

Men play the game; women know the score.
Roger Woddis (1917–1993), British writer

I judge how much a man cares for a woman by the space he allots her under a jointly-shared umbrella.
Jimmy Cannon (1909–1973), American sports commentator

The most interesting women characters in a picture are whores, and every man in love is a sex pervert at heart.
Billy Wilder (1906–2002), Austrian-born American film director

Men want a woman whom they can turn on and off like a light switch.
Ian Fleming (1908–1964), British writer of the James Bond novels

If a woman wants to hold a man, she has merely to appeal to the worst of him.
Lady Windermere, in *Lady Windermere's Fan* **by Oscar Wilde (1854–1900), Irish playwright**

A man who is honest with himself wants a woman to be soft and feminine, careful of what she's saying and talk like a man.
Ann-Margret, Swedish-American actress

Boy meets girl, girl gets boy into pickle; boy gets pickle into girl.
Jack Woodford (1894–1971), American writer

Men look at themselves in mirrors. Women look for themselves.
Elissa Melamed, feminist writer

The average man is more interested in a woman who is interested in him than he is in a woman with beautiful legs.
Marlene Dietrich (1901–1992), German-American actress and singer

A man's heart may have a secret sanctuary where only one woman may enter, but it is full of little anterooms that are seldom vacant.
Helen Rowland (1875–1950), American writer and humorist

A man thinks he knows, but a woman knows better.
Chinese proverb

Plain women know more about men than beautiful ones do.
Katharine Hepburn (1907–2003), American actress

Men have been trained and conditioned by women, not unlike the way Pavlov conditioned his dogs, into becoming their slaves. As compensation for their labours men are given periodic use of a woman's vagina.
Esther Vilar, Argentinian-German writer

Woman serves as a looking-glass possessing the magic powers of reflecting the figure of man at twice its natural size.
Virginia Woolf (1882–1941), British writer

A woman is a woman until the day she dies, but a man's a man only as long as he can.
Moms Mabley (1894–1975), American comedienne

I don't mind living in a man's world as long as I can be a woman in it.
Marilyn Monroe (1926–1962), American actress

Why does a woman work ten years to change a man's habits and then complain that he's not the man she married?
Barbra Streisand, American actress and singer

Men always fall for frigid women because they put on the best show.
Fanny Brice (1891–1951), American comedienne

A woman has to be twice as good as a man to go half as far.
Fannie Hurst (1889–1968), American novelist

Women prefer men who have something tender about them – especially the legal kind.
Kay Ingram

Whether women are better than men I cannot say – but I can say they are certainly no worse.
Golda Meir (1898–1978), fourth Prime Minister of Israel from 1969 to 1974

A romantic man often feels more uplifted with two women than with one; his love seems to hit the ideal mark somewhere between the two different faces.
Elizabeth Bowen (1899–1973), Irish novelist

Woman's life must be wrapped up in a man, and the cleverest woman on earth is the biggest fool with a man.
Dorothy Parker (1893–1967), American wit

Girls are so queer you never know what they mean. They say no when they mean yes, and drive a man out of his wits for the fun of it.
Louisa May Alcott (1832–1888), American novelist, in *Little Women*, **1868**

Men know that women are an overmatch for them, and therefore they choose the weakest or the most ignorant. If they did not think so, they never could be afraid of women knowing as much as themselves.
Dr Samuel Johnson (1709–1784), British writer and lexicographer

When Eve ate this particular apple, she became aware of her own womanhood, mentally. And mentally she began to experiment with it. She has been experimenting ever since. So has man. To the rage and horror of both of them.
D.H. Lawrence (1885–1930), British writer, in *Fantasia of the Unconscious*, **1922**

There is a vast difference between the savage and the civilised man, but it is never apparent to their wives until after breakfast.
Helen Rowland (1875–1950), American writer and humorist

The man who gets on best with women is the one who knows best how to get on without them.
Charles Baudelaire (1821–1867), French poet

There are two things a real man likes – danger and play; and he likes woman because she is the most dangerous of playthings.
Friedrich Nietzsche (1844–1900), German philosopher

Most men who run down women are only running down a certain woman.
Remy de Gourmont (1858–1915), French writer and critic

Women love men for their defects; if men have enough of them women will forgive them everything, even their gigantic intellects.
Oscar Wilde (1854–1900), Irish playwright

More and more it appears that, biologically, men are designed for short, brutal lives and women for long, miserable ones.
Dr Estelle Ramey (1917–2006), physiology professor, Georgetown University

Men have a much better time of it than women. For one thing, they marry later; for another thing, they die earlier.
H.L. Mencken (1880–1956), American writer and humorist

Men make gods, and women worship them.
James G. Frazer (1854–1941), British social anthropologist

Sure men were born to lie, and women to believe them.
John Gay (1685–1732), British poet and playwright

A man is as good as he has to be, and a woman as bad as she dares.
Elbert Hubbard (1856–1915), American writer and philosopher

Men lose more conquests by their own awkwardness than by any virtue in the woman.
Ninon de Lenclos (1620–1705), French author and courtesan

Women represent the triumph of matter over mind, just as men represent the triumph of mind over morals.
Oscar Wilde in *The Picture of Dorian Gray*, **1890**

It is rare that one can see in a little boy the promise of a man, but one can almost always see in a little girl the threat of a woman.
Alexandre Dumas, fils (1824–1895), French writer

All women become like their mothers. That is their tragedy. No man does. That's his.
Algernon, in The Importance of Being Earnest **by Oscar Wilde (1854–1900), Irish playwright**

Women who love the same man have a kind of bitter freemasonry.
Max Beerbohm (1872–1956), British writer and satirist

A woman can become a man's friend only in the following stages – first an acquaintance, next a mistress, and only then a friend.
Astrov in Uncle Vanya, **by Anton Chekhov (1860–1904), Russian playwright**

We study ourselves three weeks, we love each other three months, we squabble three years, we tolerate each other thirty years, and then the children start all over again.
Hippolyte Taine (1828–1893), French historian

She was so glad to see me go, that I have almost a mind to come again, that she may again have the same pleasure.
Dr Samuel Johnson (1709–1784), British writer and lexicographer

You see, dear, it is not true that woman was made from man's rib; she was really made from his funny bone.
J.M. Barrie (1860–1937), British writer, in What Every Woman Knows, **1908**

While man has a sex, woman is a sex.
Elizabeth Belfort Bax (1854–1926), British journalist and philosopher

Men and women do not have the faintest idea of what to do with one another. Each sex looks at the other with suspicion. The slightest gesture (scratching an ear), the most casual remark (how are your tomatoes?) are seen as hostile acts. Now that women are equal, they feel awful about it and wonder if they should have pushed so hard. Men would like to reach out and help but are afraid they will be smashed in the head.
Bruce Jay Friedman, American novelist and screenwriter, The Lonely Guy's Book of Life, **extracted in** Esquire **magazine, 1977**

We can call each other girls, chicks, broads, birds and dames with equanimity. Many of us prefer to do so since the word 'woman', being two syllables, is long, unwieldy and earnest. But a man must watch his ass. Never may a man be permitted to call any female a 'chick'. He may call you a 'broad' or a 'dame' only if he is a close friend and fond of John Garfield movies. The term 'bird', generally used by fatuous Englishmen, is always frowned upon.
Cynthia Heimel, American feminist writer, in *Sex Tips for Girls*, **1983**

The hardest task in a girl's life is to prove to a man that his intentions are serious.
Helen Rowland (1875–1950), American writer and humorist, *Reflections of a Bachelor Girl*, **1903**

The only place men want depth in a woman is in her décolletage.
Zsa Zsa Gabor, Hungarian-American socialite

There are three things a man can do with women: love them, suffer for them, or turn them into literature.
Stephen Stills, Canadian musician and member of Crosby, Stills & Nash

It is a mark of civilised men that they defend their women.
Taki (aka Taki Theodoracopulos), British gossip columnist and author, in 'High Life', *Spectator* **magazine, 1980**

'What do you call a bad man?'
'The sort of man who admires innocence.'
'And a bad woman?'
'Oh, the sort of woman a man never gets tired of.'
Conversation between Lord Illingworth and Mrs Allonby, in *A Woman of No Importance* **by Oscar Wilde (1854–1900), Irish playwright**

I am a woman meant for a man, but I never found a man who could compete.
Bette Davis (1908–1989), American actress, speaking about her five marriages

Men shall always be what the women make them; if, therefore, you would have men great and virtuous, impress upon the minds of women what greatness and virtues are.
Jean-Jacques Rousseau (1712–1778), Swiss philosopher

Since God chose his spouse from among women, most excellent Lady, because of your honour, not only should men refrain from reproaching women, but should also hold them in great reverence.
Christine de Pisan (c.1364–1430), **Italian-French writer, in** *La Vite des Dames*, **1405**

Men, some to business, some to pleasure take;
But every woman is at heart a rake.
Alexander Pope (1688–1744), British poet, in *Moral Essays*, *c.*1731–1735

God made woman for the man, and for the good and increase of the world.
Alfred, Lord Tennyson (1809–1892), British poet laureate, in 'Edwin Morris', 1860

When a man gives his opinion, he's a man. When a woman gives her opinion, she's a bitch.
Bette Davis

Most men tell me that they prefer the woman to get out of bed in the middle of the night so that they don't have to look at her.
Soraya Khashoggi, ex-wife of billionaire Adnan Khashoggi, founder of Mr Fixit

Nymphomaniac: A woman as obsessed with sex as an average man.
Mignon McLaughlin (1913–1983), American writer, in *The Neurotic's Notebook*, **1960**

Man may have discovered fire, but women discovered how to play with it.
Candace Bushnell, American writer and creator of *Sex and the City*

I babysit his girlfriends.
Jamie Lee Curtis, American actress, of her father Tony

When you really don't like a guy, they're all over you, and as soon as you act like you like them, they're no longer interested.
Beyoncé, American singer

MISTRESSES

Music is my mistress and she plays second fiddle to no one.
Duke Ellington (1899–1974), American jazz pianist

She sleeps with others because she loves them, but for money, only
with me!
**Ferenc Molnár (1878–1952), Hungarian playwright, on being told
that his mistress had been unfaithful to him while he was out of
town**

Who is she? The executive mistress, that important figure standing
behind so many top executives and kneeling in front of still more.
A national survey conducted by *Off the Wall Street Journal* shows
that 86 per cent of senior officers in 65 per cent of the Fortune
500 companies keep a mistress currently, and have kept a mistress
in the past or intend to find one as soon as they finish reading this
article.
Article in *Off the Wall Street Journal*, **1982**

My advice is to keep two mistresses. Few men have the stamina
for more.
Ovid (43 BC–AD 17), Roman poet, in *Cures for Love*

Next to the pleasures of taking a new mistress is that of being rid
of an old one.
William Wycherley (1640–1716), British playwright, in *The Country
Wife*, **1675**

My executive often arrives at the apartment exhausted and
emotionally detached after a hard day of corporate manipulation
and chancery, says Karen (not her real name). He depends on me
to raise his lowered interest rate and stimulate his private sector.
Article in *Off the Wall Street Journal*, **1982**

I have lost my mistress, horse and wife,
And when I think of human life,
Cry mercy 'twas no worse.
My mistress sickly, poor and old,
My wife damn'd ugly and a scold,
I am sorry for my horse.
Anonymous epigraph, 1784

That shouldn't hamper your marrying.
Queen Caroline (Caroline of Anspach, 1683–1737), urging her husband, King George II, to marry again after her death; he had replied that he would have mistresses

When a man marries his mistress it creates a job opportunity.
Sir James Goldsmith (1933–1997), French billionaire financier

Buy Old Masters. They fetch a better price than old mistresses.
Max Aitken, Lord Beaverbrook (1879–1964), Canadian press magnate

O sire, it were better to be your mistress than your wife.
Catherine Parr (1512–1548), sixth wife of Henry VIII

She is the only woman in France who makes me forget I am a sexagenarian.
Louis XV (1710–1774), on his mistress, Madame du Barry

I need several mistresses; if I had only one, she'd be dead inside eight days.
Alexandre Dumas (1802–1870), French novelist

MODERN TIMES

In these days when royalties vanish, when children turn against their parents, when husbands turn on wives and uncles on nieces, one thing stands unshaken – the love of a woman for her gynaecologist.
Arthur Dickson Wright (1897–1976), British royal surgeon and father of chef Clarissa Dickson Wright

Modern man isn't as virile as he used to be. Instead of making things happen, he waits for things to happen to him. He goes with the current. Something . . . has led him to stop swimming upstream.
Marcello Mastroianni (1924–1996), Italian actor, quoted in *Playboy* magazine, 1965

We have to compete with newspapers which have double-page spreads of pubic hair.
Rupert Murdoch, Australian-born media tycoon, justifying pin-ups in his newspapers

The so-called 'new morality' is too often the old immorality condoned.
Lord Shawcross (1902–2003), British politician and barrister

Sex has become one of the most discussed subjects of modern times. The Victorians pretended it did not exist; the moderns pretend that nothing else exists.
Fulton J. Sheen (1895–1979), American Archbishop of the Catholic church

This is true.
Nancy Dell'Olio, Italian lawyer and media personality, when asked if her toilet stays cleaner without men around

Having one child makes you a parent; having two makes you a referee.
David Frost (1936–2013), British television broadcaster

The feminist movement seems to have beaten the manners out of me, but I didn't see them put up a lot of resistance.
Clarissa Dickson Wright, British television chef

Hacking is like sex. You get in, you get out, and hope that you didn't leave something that can be traced back to you.
Anon

Sex is a slot machine.
John Dos Passos (1896–1970), American writer and artist

MODESTY

I wasn't really naked. I simply didn't have any clothes on.
Josephine Baker (1906–1975), American-born French dancer and singer

In some remote regions of Islam it is said a woman caught unveiled by a stranger will raise her skirt to cover her face.
Raymond Mortimer (1895–1980), British literary critic

Put off your shame with your clothes when you go in to your husband, and put it on again when you come out.
Theano (c.420 BC), Greek priestess

Age will bring all things, and everyone knows, Madame, that twenty is no age to be a prude.
Molière (1622–1673), French playwright, in *The Misanthrope*, **1666**

The perfect hostess will see to it that the works of male and female authors be properly separated on her bookshelves. Their proximity, unless they happen to be married, should not be tolerated.
From *Lady Gough's Book of Etiquette*, **1863**

She just wore enough for modesty – no more.
Robert Williams Buchanan (1841–1901), British poet and writer, in *White Rose and Red*, **1871**

It serves me right for putting all my eggs in one bastard.
Dorothy Parker (1893–1967), American wit, on going to hospital to have an abortion

It's not what you'd call a figure, is it?
Twiggy, British model and icon of the 1960s, on herself

Little girls think it's necessary to put all their business on MySpace and Facebook, and I think it's a shame . . . I'm all about mystery.
Stevie Nicks, American singer with Fleetwood Mac

MONEY

When you don't have any money, the problem is food. When you have money, it's sex. When you have both, it's health. If everything is simply jake, then you're frightened of death.
J.P. Donleavy, Irish-American writer

No woman marries for money; they are all clever enough, before marrying a millionaire, to fall in love with him first.
Cesare Pavese (1908–1950), Italian writer

Money is the sinews of love, as of war.
George Farquhar (1677–1707), Irish playwright

The big difference between sex for money and sex for free is that sex for money usually costs less.
Brendan Behan (1923–1964), Irish poet

When a man talks dirty to a woman, it's sexual harassment. When a woman talks dirty to a man, it's £5 a minute.
Anon

Money, it turned out, was exactly like sex, you thought of nothing else if you didn't have it and thought of other things if you did.
James A. Baldwin (1924–1987), American writer

Sex: the pleasure is momentary, the position ridiculous, and the expense damnable.
Philip Stanhope, 4th Earl of Chesterfield (1694–1773)

MORALS

My mom is going to kill me for talking about sleeping with people. But I don't want to put myself in the position where I'm in a monogamous relationship right now. I'm not dating just one person. *Sex and the City* changed everything for me because those girls would sleep with so many people.
Lindsay Lohan, American actress

Morality consists in suspecting other people of not being legally married.
Louis, in *The Doctor's Dilemma* **by George Bernard Shaw (1856–1950), Irish playwright**

We are told by moralists with the plainest faces that immorality will spoil our looks.
Logan Pearsall Smith (1865–1946), American writer

Morality comes with the sad wisdom of age, when the sense of curiosity has withered.
Graham Greene (1904–1991), British novelist

The Englishman thinks he is moral when he is only uncomfortable.
The Devil, in *Man and Superman* **by George Bernard Shaw**

Morality is simply the attitude we adopt towards people we personally dislike.
Oscar Wilde (1854–1900), Irish playwright

About morals, I know only that what is moral is what you feel good after and what is immoral is what you feel bad after.
Ernest Hemingway (1899–1961), American writer

I did not use paint, I made myself up morally.
Eleonora Duse (1858–1924), Italian actress, in Le Gaulois**, 1922**

An erection at will is the moral equivalent of a valid credit card.
Dr Alex Comfort (1920–2000), British sexologist and author of The Joy of Sex**, 1972**

It still strikes me as strange that anyone could have any moral objection to someone else's sexuality. It's like telling someone else how to clean their house.
River Phoenix (1970–1993), American actor

Nothing one does in bed is immoral if it helps to perpetuate love.
Gabriel García Márquez, Colombian novelist, in Love in the Time of Cholera

Where I live, nobody who's 14 is having sex and doing major drugs. And I think if you see it in the movies, you may be influenced by it. I think it's so important to preserve your innocence.
Natalie Portman, American actress

MOTHERS AND MOTHERHOOD

Motherhood is the most emotional experience of one's life. One joins a kind of women's mafia.
Janet Suzman, British actress and director

I'm not against mothers. I am against the ideology which expects every woman to have children, and I'm against the circumstances under which mothers have to have their children.
Simone de Beauvoir (1908–1986), French writer

I always thought they'd become more independent as they got older. But it doesn't work like that. I think that all new mothers imagine their baby can't survive without them, but in fact someone else can look after the baby unless you're breast-feeding. It's when they get older that the parents assume a more special role. Other people can't really help with growing-up problems, homework or giving your children the continuity and stability they need in their lives.
Carol Barnes (1944–2008), British newsreader

If I was the Virgin Mary, I would have said no.
Stevie Smith (1902–1971), British poet

Mothers are fonder than fathers of their children because they are more certain they are their own.
Aristotle (384–322 BC), Greek philosopher

Women who miscalculate are called mothers.
Abigail Van Buren (Pauline Phillips, 1918–2003), American journalist and 'Dear Abby' advice columnist

Instant availability without continuous presence is probably the best role a mother can play.
Lotte Bailyn, American professor at the MIT Sloan School of Management

My relationship with my mother was unhealthily close. She was very supportive but wanted to fulfil her ambitions through me and was very reluctant to let go. She also hated my homosexuality.
David Starkey, British historian, in an interview in *The Observer,* **2012**

I'm convinced my mother only had sex eight times.
Linda Fiorentino, American actress

MUSIC

Love is not the dying moan of a distant violin – it's the triumphant twang of a bedspring.
S.J. Perelman (1904–1979), American screenwriter

Music helps set a romantic mood. Some men believe the only good music is live music. Imagine her surprise when you say, 'I don't

need a stereo – I have an accordion!' Then imagine the sound of the door slamming.
Martin Mull, American actor, quoted in *Playboy* **magazine, 1978**

When I first glimpse the backs of women's knees I seem to hear the first movement of Beethoven's Pastoral Symphony.
Anon

Seeing unhappiness in the marriage of friends, I was content to have chosen music and laughter as a substitute for a husband.
Elsa Maxwell (1883–1963), American gossip columnist and hostess

She's a gay man trapped in a woman's body.
Boy George, British singer, of Madonna, in *Take It Like a Man*, **1995**

It's no good pretending that any relationship has a future if your record collections disagree violently or if your favourite films wouldn't even speak to each other if they met at a party.
Nick Hornby, British novelist

To a certain extent, this tour is a celebration of individuality and that you can invent and reinvent yourself. You should have the power to be able to do that. Sexuality is a part of that. It should release you. It doesn't have to be an issue. It shouldn't box you in.
Neil Tennant, British lead singer of the Pet Shop Boys

I don't make music for eyes. I make music for ears.
Adele, British singer

Sexuality is the lyricism of the masses.
Charles Baudelaire (1821–1867), French poet

I really want to call this album Teenage Wet Dreams.
Katy Perry, American singer

My music is supposed to make you wanna fuck.
Janis Joplin (1943–1970), American singer

My team and I have reunited two elements that coexist with difficulty: respect and affection. Because when they love you they don't respect you, and when they respect you they don't love you.
Shakira, Colombian singer

We feel like the girls in *Sex and the City*, but without the sex.
Cheryl Cole, British singer

MYTHS

I think women are basically quite lazy. Marriage is still a woman's best investment, because she can con some man into supporting her for the rest of her life.
Alan Whicker (1925–2013), British travel journalist

We consider first that the promiscuous assemblage of the sexes in the same class is a dangerous innovation . . . that the presence of young females as passive spectators in the operating theatre is an outrage to our natural instincts and feelings, and calculated to destroy those sentiments of respect and admiration with which the opposite sex is regarded by all right-minded men, such feelings being a mark of civilisation and refinement.
Report from the Medical School committee, Middlesex Hospital, 1861

Were it not for gold and women, there would be no damnation.
Vindici, in *The Revenger's Tragedy*, by Thomas Middleton (1580–1627), British playwright

People in the States used to think that if girls were good at sports their sexuality would be affected.
Martina Navratilova, Czech-American tennis champion

There is nothing safe about sex. There never will be.
Norman Mailer (1923–2007), American writer and political activist

NUDITY

I have seen three emperors in their nakedness and the sight was not inspiring.
Prince Otto Von Bismarck (1815–1898), German statesman and Prime Minister of Prussia

Whew, what a bony butt.
Michael Douglas, American actor, on seeing himself naked on screen

Don't miss our show! Six beautiful dancing girls! Five beautiful costumes!
Poster outside a London nightclub

The trouble with nude dancing is that not everything stops when the music does.
Robert Helpmann (1909–1986), Australian dancer and choreographer

I'm not against naked girls – not as often as I'd like to be.
Benny Hill (1924–1992), British comedian

Full frontal nudity . . . has now become accepted by every branch of the theatrical profession with the possible exception of the lady accordion players.
Denis Norden, British comedy writer, in *You Can't Have Your Kayak and Heat It*, **1973**

I didn't pay three pounds fifty just to see half a dozen acorns and a chipolata.
Noël Coward (1899–1973), British playwright, after watching male nude scenes in David Storey's *The Changing Room*, **1971**

Actually, nude bathing at seaside resorts is nothing new to this country, or at least certain parts of it.
Mr E. Bareham, editor of *British Naturism* **magazine**

Scores of artistically selected teams of traditional dancers from various parts of Kenya exposed themselves to the world Scouts delegates in a grand performance on Saturday night.
From Kenyan newspaper *Daily Nation*, **quoted in** *Private Eye* **magazine**

I'm an interesting, shy and vulnerable woman. My husband has never seen me naked. Nor has he expressed the least desire to do so.
Dame Edna Everage (aka Barry Humphries), Australian comedian

To an artist a husband named Bicket
Said 'Turn your backside and I'll kick it.
You have painted my wife
In the nude to the life,
Do you think for a moment that's cricket?'
John Galsworthy (1867–1933), British writer

People who live in glass houses should pull the blinds when removing their trousers.
Spike Milligan (1918–2002), British comedian, in *The Little Pot Boiler,* **1963**

It was nice to see your private parts anyway.
David Frost (1939–2013), British television broadcaster, to Lord Montagu, who explained that part of his stately home was open to the public

If one wants to see people naked one doesn't go to the theatre, one goes to a Turkish bath.
Noël Coward, in *The Observer,* **1971**

Oh yes, I had the radio on.
Marilyn Monroe (1926–1962), American actress, discussing a nude photograph of herself, with a journalist who asked whether she had anything on

I think naked people are very nice. Posing in the nude is perhaps the best way of reaching people.
Stella Stevens, American actress

This is 'in the raw' theatre. There have been objections on moral grounds. But the main worry is hygiene. People fear AIDS. However, the nudists will be screened off from the rest of the audience and individual washable seat covers will be supplied.
Spokesman for the Brewhouse Theatre in Taunton, after there were protests when the management agreed that a group of nudists should be allowed to enjoy the play *Steaming* **stark naked**

My way probably won't work for most people, but the more I got naked the more comfortable I felt.
Rihanna, Barbadian singer

I admire a person who, for the love of art, is able to take off their clothes in front of a camera. But I'm not capable, I'm too cowardly for that.
Shakira, Colombian singer

We've been asked to do *Playboy* together, me and Victoria, as a pair. I don't think I'll ever go naked, but I'll never say never.
David Beckham, British footballer

OBESITY

A big man has no time really to do anything but just sit and be big.
F. Scott Fitzgerald (1896–1940), American novelist

OBSCENITY

Obscenity is whatever happens to shock some elderly and ignorant magistrate.
Bertrand Russell (1872–1970), British philosopher, in *Look*, 1954

I just want to go and be obscene in private with my friends.
Richard Neville, Australian journalist, on his release after the *Oz* magazine obscenity trial, 1971

Obscenity is whatever gives the Judge an erection.
Anon

OPINIONS

A society in which women are taught anything but the management of a family, the care of men, and the creation of the future generation, is a society which is on the way out.
L. Ron Hubbard (1911–1986), American science-fiction writer and founder of the Church of Scientology

Women should remain at home, sit still, keep house, and bring up children.
Martin Luther (1483–1546), German Catholic priest and seminal figure in the Reformation

I think making love is the best form of exercise.
Cary Grant (1904–1986), British actor

Sex is the consolation you have when you can't have love.
Gabriel García Márquez, Colombian novelist

ORGASM

Is there a way to accept the concept of the female orgasm and still command the respect of your foreign auto-mechanic?
Bruce Feirstein, American screenwriter, in 'Real Men Don't Eat Quiche', *Playboy* magazine, 1982

I finally had an orgasm . . . and my doctor told me it was the wrong kind.
Character in *Manhattan*, a 1979 film by Woody Allen, American actor and film-maker

In the case of some women, orgasms take a bit of time. Before signing on with a partner, make sure you are willing to lay aside, say, the month of June, with sandwiches having to be bought in.
Bruce Jay Friedman, American novelist and screenwriter, in *The Lonely Guy's Book of Life*, extracted in *Esquire* magazine, 1977

The orgasm has replaced the cross as the focus of longing and the image of fulfilment.
Malcolm Muggeridge (1903–1990), British writer and satirist

An orgasm is just a reflex like a sneeze.
Dr Ruth Westheimer, German-American sex therapist

As women have known since the dawn of our time, the primary site for stimulation to orgasm centres on the clitoris. The revolution unleashed by The Kinsey Report of 1953 has, by now, made this information available to men who, for whatever reason, had not figured it out for themselves by the more obvious routes of experience and sensitivity.
Stephen Jay Gould (1941–2002), American paleontologist and writer, in *Bully for Brontosaurus*, 1991

When the ecstatic body grips its heaven, with little sobbing cries.
E.R. Dodds (1893–1979), British classical scholar

The soil is fertile, Sir, because it is full of micro-orgasms.
Thirteen-year-old pupil at Cranleigh School, Surrey

So female orgasm is simply a nervous climax to sex relations . . .
It may be thought of as a sort of pleasure prize like a prize that
comes with a box of cereal. It is all to the good if the prize is there
but the cereal is valuable and nourishing if it is not.
Madeline Gray, American writer, in *The Normal Woman*, **1967**

When modern woman discovered the orgasm it was (combined
with modern birth control) perhaps the biggest single nail in the
coffin of male dominance.
Eva Diges, British writer

At 70 I find orgasmic sex quite dispensible.
Tennessee Williams (1911–1983), American playwright

No woman gets an orgasm from shining the kitchen floor.
Betty Friedan (1921–2006), American feminist, whose book *The
Feminine Mystique* **(1963) was one of the most influential books
of the women's movement**

Seen through the glow of a building orgasm, a woman seems to
blaze with angelic glory.
Larry Niven, American science-fiction writer, in *Ringworld*, **1970**

Electric flesh-arrows traversing the body. A rainbow of colour strikes
the eyelids. A foam of music falls over the ears. It is the gong of
the orgasm.
Anaïs Nin, American writer

ORGIES

You get a better class of person at orgies, because people have to
keep in trim more. There is an awful lot of going round holding in
your stomach, you know. Everybody is very polite to each other.
The conversation isn't very good but you can't have everything.
Gore Vidal (1925–2012), American writer and wit

Once, a philosopher; twice, a pervert!
Voltaire (François-Marie Arouet, 1694–1778), French writer and philosopher, after participating in an orgy and declining an invitation to go back the very next night

If God meant us to have group sex, I guess he'd have given us all more organs.
Malcolm Bradbury (1932–2000), British academic

All right, ladies, any girl who doesn't want to fuck can leave right now.
Babe Ruth (1895–1948), American baseball player, on entering a party

PARENTS

The first half of our lives is ruined by our parents, and the second half by our children.
Clarence Darrow (1857–1938), American lawyer and leading member of the American Civil Liberties Union

To lose one parent may be regarded as a misfortune; to lose both looks like carelessness.
Lady Bracknell, in *The Importance of Being Earnest* **by Oscar Wilde (1854–1900), Irish playwright**

The thing that impresses me most about America is the way parents obey their children.
Edward VIII, Duke of Windsor (1894–1972)

If you have never been hated by your child, you have never been a parent.
Bette Davis (1908–1989), American actress

I want some day to be able to love with the same intensity and unselfishness that parents love their children with.
Shakira, Colombian singer

PASSIONS

Great passions don't exist, they are liars' fantasies. What do exist

are little loves that may last for a short or longer while.
Anna Magnani (1918–1973), Italian actress

I've always admitted that I'm ruled by my passions.
Elizabeth Taylor (1932–2011), British actress

Men are often blind to the passions of women; but every woman is as quick-sighted as a hawk on these occasions.
Henry Fielding (1707–1754), British novelist, in *Amelia*, **1751**

The natural man has only two primal passions – to get and to beget.
Sir William Osler (1849–1919), Canadian physician

Be a good animal, true to your animal instincts.
D.H. Lawrence (1885–1930), British writer

Some people lose control of their sluice gates of passion.
Reported in the *Beijing Workers Daily*, **1981**

If we resist our passions, it is more because of their weakness than because of our strength.
François, Duc de La Rochefoucauld (1613–1680), French writer

Passion, though a hard regulator, is a powerful spring.
Ralph Waldo Emerson (1803–1882), American writer

The passions are the only orators which always persuade.
François, Duc de La Rochefoucauld

A really grand passion is comparatively rare nowadays. It is the privilege of people who have nothing to do. That is the one use of the idle classes in the country.
Lord Ilingworth in *A Woman of No Importance*; **also spoken by Lord Henry in** *The Picture of Dorian Gray* **by Oscar Wilde (1854–1900), Irish playwright**

The passion and starry-eyed joys of the honeymoon are but callow experiments in a search for the magnificent which lies beyond the horizon.
Barbara Cartland (1901–2000), British novelist

Nobody on earth loves more than I, because I love without being ashamed of the reason why I love.
George Sand (Amantine Lucile Dupin, 1804–1876), French writer

You had forgotten, then, that I loved you to distraction, and that I was your husband? One or the other can drive a man to extremities – how much more so the two together.
Marie de La Fayette (1634–1693), French writer, in *The Princess of Cleves,* **1678**

We must act out passion before we can feel it.
Jean-Paul Sartre (1905–1980), French writer, in *The Words,* **1964**

Why not put up that pane of glass called passion between us? It may distort things at times, but it's wonderfully convenient. But no, we were two of a kind, allies and accomplices. In terms of grammar, I could not become the object, or the subject. He had neither the capacity nor the desire to define our roles in any such way.
Françoise Sagan (1935–2004), French writer, in *A Certain Smile,* **1956**

For me it's part of falling madly, passionately in love as opposed to, let's have an affair. Although I did live through some raving times.
Felicity Kendal, British actress, talking about falling in love

PAST

If someone with whom one is having an affair keeps on mentioning some woman whom he knew in the past, however long ago it is since they separated, one is always irritated.
Sei Shōnagon (c.966–1017), Japanese writer, in *The Pillow Book of Sei Shonagon*

Whatever happened to the days when sex was Celia Johnston and Rachmaninov on the piano?
Imogen Stubbs, British actress

I adore football players. Their passes are so forward.
Mae West (1893–1980), American actress

I once went to one of those parties where everyone threw their car keys into the middle of the room. I don't know who got my moped, but I've been driving that Peugeot for years.
Victoria Wood, British comedienne

PATERNITY

There was a young man in Rome that was very like Augustus Caesar; Augustus took knowledge of it and sent for the man, and asked him: 'Was your mother ever at Rome?' He answered, 'No, Sir; but my father was.'
Francis Bacon (1561–1626), British philosopher

He that bulls the cow must keep the calf.
Sixteenth-century proverb

Maternity is a matter of fact; paternity is a matter of opinion.
Anon

I've got more paternity suits than leisure suits.
Engelbert Humperdinck, British singer

PENIS

He is proud that he has the biggest brain of all the primates, but he attempts to conceal that he also has the biggest penis.
Desmond Morris, British zoologist

One night I was sitting with friends at a table in a crowded Key West bar. At a nearby table, there was a mildly drunk woman with a very drunk husband. Presently, the woman approached us and asked me to sign a paper napkin. All this seemed to anger her husband; he staggered over to the table and, after unzipping his trousers and hauling out his equipment, said: 'Since you're autographing things, why don't you autograph this?' The tables surrounding us had grown silent, so a great many people heard my reply, which was: 'I don't know if I can autograph it, but perhaps I can initial it.'
Truman Capote (1924–1984), American writer

A man is two people, himself and his cock. A man always takes his friend to the party. Of the two, the friend is the nicer, being more able to show his feelings.
Beryl Bainbridge (1932–2010), British writer

I wonder why men get serious at all. They have this delicate, long thing hanging outside their bodies which goes up and down by its own will. If I were a man I would always be laughing at myself.
Yoko Ono, Japanese artist and widow of John Lennon

The penis is obviously going the way of the veriform appendix.
Jill Johnston (1929–2010), American feminist writer

He put it back into his pants as if he were folding a dead octopus tentacle into his shorts.
Richard Brautigan (1935–1984), American writer

During the feminist revolution, the battle lines were again simple. It was easy to tell the enemy, he was the one with the penis. This is no longer strictly true. Some men are okay now, we're allowed to like them again. We still have to keep them in line, of course, but we no longer have to shoot them on sight.
Cynthia Heimel, American feminist writer, in *Sex Tips for Girls*, **1983**

When his cock wouldn't stand up, he blew his head off. He sold himself a line of bullshit and he bought it.
Germaine Greer, Australian feminist writer, on Ernest Hemingway

No woman except for so-called 'deviants' seriously wishes to be male and have a penis. But most women would like to have the privileges and opportunities that go with it.
Elena G. Bellotti, Italian feminist writer, in *What Are Little Girls Made Of?*, **1973**

An erection at will is the moral equivalent of a valid credit card.
Dr Alex Comfort (1920–2000), British sexologist and author of *The Joy of Sex*, **1972**

An erection is a mysterious thing. There's always that fear, each time one goes, that you won't be seeing it again.
Kirk Douglas, American actor, in his autobiography, *The Ragman's Son*, **1990**

Generally speaking, it is in love as it is in war, where the longest weapon carries it.
John Leland (1503–1552), British poet, in *Fanny Hill*

Keithley Miller (an American lady) asked a Scotsman whether it was true that they wore nothing under their kilts. Lifting up his kilt, the somewhat inebriated Scot revealed all and asked, 'What do you think of that?' She replied, 'Well, it looks like a penis . . . only smaller.'
Anon

Every Prime Minister needs a Willie.
Margaret Thatcher (1925–2013), first female British Prime Minister, at the farewell dinner for William Whitelaw

The penis confers with human intelligence and has intelligence itself . . . and takes its own course . . . without license of thought by man.
Leonardo da Vinci (1452–1519), leading figure of the Italian Renaissance

A stiff cock is nothing to be ashamed of.
Linda Lovelace (1949–2002), American pornographic actress

I'm going to Iowa for an award, Carnegie Hall, to France to be honoured. I'd give it all up for one erection.
Groucho Marx (1880–1977), American comedian

I just wanted to see what it looked like in the spotlight.
Jim Morrison (1943–1971), American lead singer of The Doors, explaining why he exposed himself on stage

I want a woman to love me for me and not just for my piggly diggly . . . You catch my drift?
Bruno Mars, American singer

God would have been merciful if He had given him a little tiny penis so that he could get on with his life.
Sean Young, American actress, referring to actor James Woods

How do you know it's time to wash the dishes and clean your house? Look inside your pants. If you find a penis in there, it's not time.
Jo Brand, British comedienne

PLASTIC SURGERY

If you have a psychotic fixation and you go to the doctor and you want these two fingers amputated, he will not cut them off. But he will remove your genitals. I have more trouble getting a prescription for Valium than I do having my uterus lowered and made into a penis.
Lily Tomlin, American actress and comedienne, quoted in *Rolling Stone* **magazine, 1974**

You have gone through all that and nothing has changed. It's the same old you, except you're now swollen like a distressed turnip.
Sherrie Hewson, British actress

After I had my eyes done, I looked at myself and thought, Did I fall off the trolley?
Jane McDonald, British singer and television presenter

I can't stand to touch those plastic breasts.
Donald Trump, American business magnate, on ex-wife Ivana's cosmetic surgery

I did not have implants, I just had a growth spurt.
Britney Spears, American singer

PLEASURE

Pleasure is the only thing to live for. Nothing ages like happiness.
Lord Goring, in *An Ideal Husband* **by Oscar Wilde (1854–1900), Irish playwright**

You wear yourself out in the pursuit of wealth or love or freedom, you do everything to gain some right, and once it's gained, you take no pleasure in it.
Oriana Fallaci (1930–2006), Italian journalist

All the things I really like to do are either immoral, illegal or fattening.
Alexander Woollcott (1887–1943), American columnist with *The New Yorker*

If I had no duties, and no reference to futurity, I would spend my life in driving briskly in a post-chaise with a pretty woman.
Dr Samuel Johnson (1709–1784), British writer and lexicographer

Scratching is one of nature's sweetest gratifications, and the one nearest at hand.
Michel de Montaigne (1533–1592), French writer

Going overseas? Emigration, business or lust pleasure. Immediate passages available.
Misprint in the *Liverpool Echo*

Nine out of ten women would rather have a man who would surreptitiously caress their thighs under a nightclub table than a good, rugged chap who'll slap them heartily on the back at a Saturday football game.
Marjorie Proops (1911–1996), British agony aunt with the *Daily Mirror*

In diving to the bottom of pleasure we bring up more gravel than pearls.
Honoré de Balzac (1799–1850), French writer

Men may experience an erection while on horseback, or driving in a carriage or travelling by train; more rarely perhaps while motoring or bicycling.
Theodoor Hendrik van de Velde (1873–1937), Dutch gynaecologist, in *Ideal Marriage: Its Physiology and Technique,* **1926**

All the young ladies I took advantage of.
Harry Belafonte, American singer, when asked his guiltiest pleasure, in *The Guardian,* **2012**

There is nothing like a good bong.
Prince Charles, Prince of Wales, on being the first to test the Royal Jubilee Bells, 2012

I wouldn't recommend sex, drugs or insanity for everyone, but they've always worked for me.
Hunter S. Thompson (1937–2005), American writer

I enjoyed sex and indulged in it when I fancied the men.
Christine Keeler, British former model, famous for being involved in the Profumo Affair

POLITICS

My choice in life was either to be a piano player in a whorehouse or a politician. And to tell you the truth, there's hardly any difference.
Harry S. Truman (1884–1972), 33rd President of the United States

If presidents don't do it to their wives, they do it to the country.
Mel Brooks, American film-maker

I still love you, but in politics there is no heart, only head.
Napoleon Bonaparte (1769–1821), French military leader, referring to his divorce, for reasons of state, from the Empress Josephine, 1800

She has the eyes of Caligula but the mouth of Marilyn Monroe.
François Mitterrand (1916–1996), former President of France, of Margaret Thatcher, in *The Observer*

Don't vote for that fucking Bush.
Bruce Springsteen, American singer

Well, did you do any fornicating this weekend?
Richard Nixon (1913–1994), 37th President of the United States, to David Frost before an interview

Anyone who knows Dan Quayle knows he would rather play golf than have sex any day.
Marilyn Quayle, American lawyer and wife of the former US Vice President, of her husband

One of the things being in politics has taught me is that men are not a reasoned or reasonable sex.
Margaret Thatcher (1925–2013), first female British Prime Minister

Run for office? No. I've slept with too many women, I've done too many drugs, and I've been to too many parties.
George Clooney, American actor

PORNOGRAPHY

The worst that can be said about pornography is that it leads not to anti-social acts but to the reading of more pornography.
Gore Vidal (1925–2012), American writer and wit, in *Reflections Upon a Sinking Ship*, **1969**

It's red hot, mate. I hate to think of this sort of book getting into the wrong hands. As soon as I've finished this, I shall recommend they ban it.
Tony Hancock (1924–1968), British comedian

The citizens' committee to clean up New York's porn-infested areas continued its series of rallies today, as a huge, throbbing, pulsating crowd sprang erect from nowhere and forced its way into the steaming nether regions surrounding the glistening, sweating intersection of Eighth Avenue and Forty-Second Street. Thrusting, driving, pushing its way into the usually receptive neighbourhood, the excited throng, now grown to five times its original size, rammed itself again and again and again into the quivering, perspiring, musty dankness, fluctuating between eager anticipation and trembling revulsion. Now suddenly the tumescent crowd and the irresistible area were one heaving, alternately melting and thawing turgid entity, ascending to heights heretofore unexperienced. Then, with a gigantic, soulsearching, heart-stopping series of eruptions, it was over. Afterwards the crowd had a cigarette and went home.
'Weekend Update', on *Saturday Night Live*, **NBC TV**

Immediately before dashing to the airport to fly home, the Prime Minister engaged in some personal and highly unorthodox garden-party diplomacy. I did not see him myself but he is reported to have done some business behind a tree with General Gowon, the Nigerian Leader.
Reported in the *London Evening Standard*

I would like to see all people who read pornography, or have anything to do with it, put in a mental hospital for observation so we could find out what we have done to them.
Linda Lovelace (1949–2002), American pornographic actress

Obscenity is such a tiny kingdom that a single tour covers it completely.
Heywood Broun (1888–1939), American journalist

Pornography is the attempt to insult sex, to do dirt on it.
D.H. Lawrence (1885–1930), British writer

It'll be a sad day for sexual liberation when the pornography addict has to settle for the real thing
Brendan Behan (1923–1964), Irish poet

Pornography is in the groin of the beholder.
Charles Rembar (1915–2000), American lawyer and literary agent

Nine-tenths of the appeal of pornography is due to the indecent feelings concerning sex which moralists inculcate in the young; the other tenth is physiological, and will occur in one way or another, whatever the state of the law may be.
Bertrand Russell (1872–1970), British philosopher

The fact remains that, no matter how disturbing violent fantasies are, as long as they stay within the world of pornography they are still only fantasies. The man masturbating in a theatre showing a snuff film is still only watching a movie, not actually raping and murdering.
Deidre English, American former editor of Mother Jones

She is the pin-up, the centrefold, the poster, the postcard, the dirty picture, naked, half-dressed, laid out, legs spread, breast or ass protruding. She is the thing she is supposed to be; the thing that makes him erect.
Andrea Dworkin (1946–2005), American feminist writer, in Pornography: Men Possessing Women, **1981**

Women, for centuries not having access to pornography and unable to bear looking . . . are astonished. Women do not believe that men believe what pornography says about women. But they do From the worst to the best of them, they do.
Andrea Dworkin

A word about pornography. You'll need it. Lots of it . . . The dirty filthy degrading kind. But keep it well hidden. Don't discount secre

wall panels, trick drawers, holes in the yard, etc. Especially if you have teenage boys or a Baptist wife with a housekeeping obsession. Also keep in mind that you could die at any moment and nothing puts a crimp in the funeral worse than having the bereaved family wonder what kind of sick, perverted beast you were under that kind and genteel exterior.
John Hughes (1950–2009), American film-maker, in 'Very Married Sex', National Lampoon, 1979

I got paid less for my pictures than the male photographers – it is the most sexually discriminating magazine of its kind. The editor is a man and many of the staff are male. They are imposing their values about what is sexy onto women.
Nikki Downey, former Penthouse model turned photographer

Pornography is any matter or thing exhibiting or visually representing persons or animals performing the sexual act whether normal or abnormal.
From To the Pure, by M.L. Ernst and W. Seagle, 1929

Let's say, I think a man is more likely to make love to his wife after coming to the revue bar than on any other night of the year.
Paul Raymond (Geoffrey Anthony Quinn, 1925–2008), British publisher and nightclub owner

Real pornography is movies starring Doris Day or any picture of big-breasted girls to illustrate stories on lung cancer.
Al Alvarez, British writer

That's films where the plot doesn't thicken.
Sean Lock, British comedian, performing at the Edinburgh Festival Fringe, 2000

I think there's a place for the old Frankie Vaughan, as the people at work call it. A healthy interest in it is fine.
Denise Welch, British actress, on Loose Women

My first time I jacked off, I thought I'd invented it. I looked down at my sloppy, handful of junk and thought: This is going to make me rich.
Chuck Palahniuk, American writer, in Choke, 2002

My reaction to porn films is as follows: after the first ten minutes, I want to go home and screw. After the first 20 minutes, I never want to screw again as long as I live.
Erica Jong, American writer, in *Playboy* **magazine**

I don't think pornography is very harmful, but it is terribly, terribly boring.
Noël Coward (1899–1973), British playwright

Porn fascinates us – media and public alike.
Jacqui Smith, British Labour Party politician, investigating pornography following the public discovery that her husband had charged porn videos to her expenses

Pornography is presumably intended to arouse sexual desire and procure solitary orgasm, against which, so far as I know, there has never been any law except that of a Scout master.
Anthony Burgess (1917–1993), British writer

POWER

The ultimate aphrodisiac.
Henry Kissinger, German-born political scientist and winner of the Nobel Peace Prize

What the proprietorship of these papers is aiming at is power, and power without responsibility – the prerogative of the harlot through the ages.
Stanley Baldwin (1867–1947), British Conservative politician and Prime Minister, attacking the press barons at a by-election meeting in 1931. Harold Macmillan, who was present, recalls his father-in-law, the Duke of Devonshire, commenting: 'Good God, that's done it. He's lost us the tarts' vote.'

A man in love is like a sparrow caught with birdlime; the more he struggles, the more he is entangled.
Madame de Staël (1766–1817), French writer

The men who really wield, retain, and covet power are the kind who answer bedside phones while making love.
Nicholas Pileggi, American screenwriter

If you live with a man you must conquer him every day. Otherwise he will go to another.
Brigitte Bardot, French actress turned animal-rights campaigner

My three husbands were afraid of me. I am a very powerful woman. They needed a woman, not a writer.
Nawal El Saadawi, Egyptian feminist writer, in the *Financial Times*, **2012**

There are no rules when it comes to love.
Taylor Swift, American singer

PREGNANCY AND PROCREATION

If I had a cock for a day I would get myself pregnant.
Germaine Greer, **Australian feminist writer**

If pregnancy were a book they would cut the last two chapters.
Nora Ephron (1941–2012), American screenwriter and director

A hen is only an egg's way of making another egg.
Samuel Butler (1835–1902), British author

The act of procreation and the members employed therein are so repulsive, that if it were not for the beauty of the faces and the adornments of the actors and the pent-up impulse, nature would lose the human species.
Leonardo da Vinci (1452–1519), leading figure of the Italian Renaissance

PROMISCUITY

Lady Capricorn, he understood, was still keeping open bed.
Aldous Huxley (1894–1963), British writer, in *Antic Hay*, **1923**

Eliot: It doesn't suit women to be promiscuous.
Amanda: It doesn't suit men for women to be promiscuous.
From *Private Lives*, **by Noël Coward (1899–1973), British playwright**

It is as absurd to say that a man can't love one woman all the time as it is to say that a violinist needs several violins to play the same piece of music.
Honoré de Balzac (1799–1850), French writer

The sexual freedom of today for most people is really only a convention, an obligation, a social duty, a social anxiety, a necessary feature of the consumer's way of life.
Pier Paolo Pasolini (1922–1975), Italian film director

You were born with your legs apart. They'll send you to your grave in a Y-shaped coffin.
Joe Orton (1933–1967), British playwright

No wearer of a lib' bodice has ever been famed for her promiscuity, and a rarity nowadays of both liberty bodices and virgins is undeniable.
Charlotte Bingham, British novelist

She is like measles. Everybody should go through the experience. Once you've had it, you never want to have it again.
A victim of the Grand Duchess Anastasia, who was notorious during the 1930s for entertaining young men

Latins are tenderly enthusiastic. In Brazil they throw flowers at you. In Argentina they throw themselves.
Marlene Dietrich (1901–1992), German-American actress and singer

I am always looking for meaningful one-night stands.
Dudley Moore (1935–2002), British actor and comedian

Conservatives say teaching sex education in the public schools will promote promiscuity. With our education system? If we promote promiscuity the same way we promote math or science, they've got nothing to worry about.
Beverly Mickins, American performance artist

PROSTITUTION

Prostitution gives her an opportunity to meet people. It provides

fresh air and wholesome exercise, and keeps her out of trouble.
Joseph Heller (1923–1999), American novelist, in *Catch 22*, **1961**

My method is basically the same as Masters and Johnson, only they charge thousands of dollars and it's called therapy. I charge fifty dollars and it's called prostitution.
Xaviera Hollander, Dutch writer and former prostitute

Romance without finance is a nuisance. Few men value free merchandise. Let the chippies fall where they may.
Sally Stanford (1903–1982), American madam and writer, in *The Lady of the House*, **1966**

Fines'd and curl'd hair in the amorous parts, a moist open clint, absence of the membrane hymen, shaggy and discoloured nymphae, the interior orifice of the womb widened, and the voice chang'd is no sufficient evidence of a woman's being a prostitute.
Nicolas Venette (1622–1698), French physician, giving advice to worried husbands in *The Mysteries of Conjugal Love Revealed*

There is something utterly nauseating about a system of society which pays a harlot 25 times as much as it pays its Prime Minister, 250 times as much as it pays its Members of Parliament, and 500 times as much as it pays some of its ministers of religion.
Harold Wilson (1916–1995), British former Prime Minister, referring to Christine Keeler and the Profumo Affair in 1963

Prostitutes believe in marriage. It provides them with most of their trade.
'Suzie', quoted in *Knave* **magazine, 1975**

It is a silly question to ask a prostitute, why she does it . . . these are the highest paid of professional women in America.
Gail Sheehy, American writer and social critic, in *Hustling*

This is virgin territory for whorehouses.
Al Capone (1899–1947), Italian-American gangster, on suburban Chicago

We're all hookers. What matters is dignity.
Mike Farren (1943–2013), British writer and musician associated with UK Underground

Punishing the prostitute promotes the rape of all women. When prostitution is a crime, the message conveyed is that women who are sexual are 'bad' and therefore legitimate victims of sexual assault. Sex becomes a weapon to be used by men.

Margot St James, American campaigner for the decriminalisation of prostitution, quoted in the San Francisco Examiner, **1979**

They're whores, and that's not a term of abuse. It's a good, honest, biblical word for an honourable profession of ancient lineage. They make love with men for a living and don't you ever think badly of them for that. Any woman worthy of the name would do the same if her children were hungry. Remember, never judge someone until you've walked a mile in their moccasins.

Allegra Taylor, Australian-born writer, in Prostitution: What's Love Got To Do With It?, **1991**

They sit down and drink tea, and the procuress leads in a Shouma saying, 'pay your respects to the guests' and the girl does so. Then she commands 'walk forward', 'turn around' – so the girl turns around to face the light, and thus to show her face. Then the woman asks, 'let us see your hands' so the girl pushes up her sleeves to reveal her hands, arms and her skin. At the command 'look at the guest' she glances sidelong at him, thus showing her eyes. Then she is asked 'how old are you' and she gives her reply, so the customer can hear her voice. The procuress says, 'walk around again', and pulls back the girl's skirt to reveal her feet.

Chen Dong-Yuan, Chinese writer, describing the ritual of selecting a young girl for concubinage, in A History of the Lives of Chinese Women, **1937**

I have often noticed that a bribe . . . has that effect – it changes a relation. The man who offers a bribe gives away a little of his own importance; the bribe once accepted, he becomes inferior, like a man who has paid for a woman.

Graham Greene (1904–1991), British novelist, in The Comedians, **1966**

If any of your women be guilty of whoredom, then bring your witnesses against them from among themselves, and if they bear witness to the fact, shut them up within their houses till death release them, or God make some way for them.

Qu'ran, central religious text of Islam, c.632 CE

I was mistaken for a prostitute once in the last war. When a GI asked me what I charged I said 'Well, dear, what do your mother and sisters normally ask for?'
Thora Hird (1911–2003), British actress, in *The Independent*, **1999**

When a guy goes to a hooker, he's not paying her for sex, he's paying her to leave.
Anon

I would like to be a beautiful male prostitute.
Lord Byron (1788–1824), British Romantic poet

I remember the first time I had sex – I kept the receipt.
Groucho Marx (1880–1977), American comedian

PUBERTY

All healthy persons, at the time of puberty, must certainly feel the passion of physical love. It is part of their health, and as a natural consequence as hunger or thirst, it is the most delightful of all the passions, and makes the greater part of human happiness.
Dr Michael Ryan (1800–1841), British physician, in *A Manual of Midwifery*, **1831**

PUNISHMENT

And if it's true, he should be parted from his bollocks.
Coal miner Kenny Mullins, on NUM President Arthur Scargill, after hearing reports of possible misuse of funds donated during the 1984–1985 miners' strike

Two mothers-in-law.
Lord John Russell (1792–1878), British Liberal politician and Prime Minister, on being asked what he would consider a proper punishment for bigamy

I think men should get penalty points on their licence for leaving towels on the bed and the loo seat up. They'll have to make up for it . . . in other ways.
Andrea McLean, British television presenter, on *Loose Women*

RAPE

I strongly feel that a rapist is a rapist, whether he is married to his victim or not.
John Patten, British Conservative politician, commenting on the law ruling that a husband can be guilty of raping his wife

RELATIONSHIPS

The easiest kind of relationship for me is with ten thousand people. The hardest is with one.
Joan Baez, American folk singer

No, I don't even use the word relationship. Unless you're screwin' your cousin; that's a 'relationship'.
Anon

Why marry again? He's got the T-shirt. I won't go to the wedding. There'll only ever be one Mrs Ecclestone.
Tamara Ecclestone, daughter of Bernie Ecclestone, President of Formula One, on the announcement of his engagement, 2012

I mean, if the relationship can't survive the long term, why on earth would it be worth my time and energy for the short term?
Nicholas Sparks, American writer and producer, in *The Last Song,* **2009**

I suffer from girlnextdooritis where the guy is friends with you and that's it.
Taylor Swift, American singer

I like my relationships like I like my eggs. Over easy.
Jarod Kintz, American writer, in *It Occurred to Me*

If I'm not interested in a woman I'm straightforward. Right after sex, usually say, 'I can't do this any more. Thanks for coming over.'
Vince Vaughn, American actor

A relationship isn't going to make me survive. It's the cherry on the top.
Jennifer Aniston, American actress

RELIGION

I went to a convent in New York and was fired finally for my insistence that the Immaculate Conception was a spontaneous combustion.
Dorothy Parker (1893–1967), American wit

If I had been the Virgin Mary I would have said no.
Stevie Smith (1902–1971), British poet

Personally, I can't see the appeal. Who would put their faith in a garment whose owner managed to get pregnant before she even reached for the top button?
Jaci Stephen, British journalist, commenting on a piece of cloth allegedly belonging to the Virgin Mary's nightdress, for sale in Britain

God is a gentleman. He prefers blondes.
Hal, in *Loot* **(1965) by Joe Orton (1933–1967), British playwright, 1965**

Adam and Eve had many advantages but the principal one was that they escaped teething.
Mark Twain (1835–1910), American writer

Whenever Christ was confronted by people in sexual disarray, he took good care to safeguard sexuality by reminding them that they had to avoid sin; that is to say, to use their sexuality in a fully human way.
Dr Jack Dominian, British relationship psychiatrist

If President Nixon's secretary, Rosemary Woods, had been Moses's secretary, there would only be eight commandments.
Art Buchwald (1925–2007), American humorist and *Washington Post* **columnist**

God, why didn't you make women first – when you were fresh?
Marc Chabot, played by Yves Montand (1921–1991), Italian-French actor and singer, in *On a Clear Day You Can See Forever*, **1970**

The good news is that Jesus is coming back. The bad news is that he's really pissed off.
Bob Hope (1903–2003), American comedian

To hear many religious people talk, one would think God created the torso, head, legs and arms, but the devil slapped on the genitals.
Don Schrader, American former pastor and gay activist

Life in Lubbock, Texas, taught me two things: One is that god loves you and you're going to burn in hell. The other is that sex is the most awful, filthy thing on earth and you should save it for someone you love.
Butch Hancock, American country music singer

I thank God I was raised Catholic, so sex will always be dirty.
John Waters, American film-maker and writer

I have a great respect for someone from a strict Catholic upbringing who can climax without reservation.
Robert Downey Jnr, American actor

I think the essence of Judeo-Christian teachings is very similar to *Playboy*.
Hugh Hefner, American founder of *Playboy* magazine

Sex is one of the nine reasons for reincarnation . . . the other eight are unimportant.
Henry Miller (1891–1980), American writer

REPUTATION

There are no good girls gone wrong, just bad girls found out.
Mae West (1893–1980), American actress

She: I've heard plenty about your love-making.
He: Oh, it's nothing
She: That's what I heard.
From *Laugh-In*, NBC TV, 1969

It's the good girls who keep the diaries; the bad girls never have the time.
Tallulah Bankhead (1902–1968), American actress

Funny, really. When you look at the things that go on these days my story reads like *Noddy*.
Diana Dors (1931–1984), British actress

I am as pure as the driven slush.
Tallulah Bankhead

A bad woman always has something she regards as a curse – a real bit of goodness hidden away somewhere.
Lady Trowbridge, British writer, in *The Millionaire*, **1907**

My literary reputation – or rather the lack of it – is the work of male reviewers who fear female sexuality and don't like successful women.
Erica Jong, American writer, quoted in *The Observer*, **1980**

Reluctant though one may be to admit it, the entire British aristocracy is seamed and honeycombed with immorality. If you took a pin and jabbed it down anywhere in the pages of Debrett's Peerage you would find it piercing the name of someone with a conscience as tender as a sunburned neck.
P.G. Wodehouse (1881–1975), British writer, in *Mulliner Nights*, **1933**

When the Himalayan peasant meets the he-bear in his pride, he shouts to scare the monster, who will often turn aside. But the she-bear thus accosted rends the peasant tooth and nail. For the female of the species is more deadly than the male.
Rudyard Kipling, (1865–1936), British writer, in *The Female of the Species*, **1911**

Sade brushes the lust off the labia of women asphyxiated in the smoky cell of sex.
Som Deva, Indian sexologist, describing the activities of the Marquis de Sade, in *The Marching Eros*, **1983**

The worst lay in the world. She was always drunk and she was always eating.
Peter Lawford (1923–1984), Anglo-American actor, on Rita Hayworth

I used to be snow white but I drifted.
Mae West (1893–1980), American actress

I hope there's a tinge of disgrace about me. Hopefully, there's one good scandal left in me yet.
Diana Rigg, British actress, in *The Times*, **1999**

Once they call you a Latin lover, you're in real trouble. Women expect an Oscar performance in bed.
Marcello Mastroianni (1924–1996), Italian actor

When a man is seen with a lot of women, it's 'Oh, which one did he grace?' But if a woman is seen with lots of men, she's just a slut.
Debra Winger, American actress

Nope, no sex scandals yet. But I'm open to offers!
John Cusack, American actor

ROMANCE

Give me my golf clubs, fresh air and a beautiful partner, and you can keep my golf clubs and the fresh air.
Jack Benny (1894–1974), American comedian

There is never any real sex in romance; what is more, there is very little, and that of a very crude kind, in ninety-nine hundredths of our married life.
George Bernard Shaw (1856–1950), Irish playwright

Oh, what a dear, ravishing thing is the beginning of an amour!
Aphra Behn (1640–1689), British writer, and one of the first professional female writers in English literature

I know a lot of people didn't expect our relationship to last – but we've just celebrated our two-month anniversary.
Britt Ekland, Swedish actress, speaking of her latest partner

To love oneself is the beginning of a life-long romance.
Lord Goring, in *An Ideal Husband* **by Oscar Wilde (1854–1900), Irish playwright**

She was a lovely girl. Our courtship was fast and furious – I was fast and she was furious.
Max Kauffman, American writer and wit

A silvery June afternoon. A June afternoon in Paris 23 years ago. And I am standing in the courtyard of the Palais Royal scanning its tall windows and wondering which of them belong to the apartment of Colette, the Grande Mademoiselle of French letters.
Truman Capote (1924–1984), American writer, quoted in the Daily Telegraph **magazine**

How can I be a maid and sleep every night with the King? When he comes to bed he kisses me, takes me by the hand and bids me 'Goodnight, Sweetheart,' and in the morning, he kisses me and bids me 'Farewell darling!' Is not this enough?
Anne of Cleves (1515–1557), fourth wife of Henry VIII, on being asked by her lady-in-waiting if she was still a maid

I don't know what the word means. It sounds as if it's something to do with knights in shining armour.
Daphne du Maurier (1907–1989), British writer and playwright, on romance

If there is to be any romance in marriage women must be given every chance to earn a decent living at other occupations. Otherwise no man can be sure that he is loved for himself alone, and that his wife did not come to the registry office because she had no luck at the labour exchange.
Rebecca West (1892–1983), British writer

The word 'romantic' doesn't exist in the male vocabulary in Leeds. A date means a walk round the pub and a packet of crisps if he's in a generous mood. If you're really lucky, he'll buy you a take-away.
A secretary from Leeds quoted in the Daily Mirror

As romantic as the sound of hogs being butchered.
Truman Capote (1924–1984), American writer, describing James Thurber and girlfriend making love

I am a romantic. Love affairs are the only real education in life.
Marlene Dietrich (1901–1992), German-American actress and singer

The human heart likes a little disorder in its geometry.
Louis de Bernières, British novelist, in Captain Corelli's Mandolin, **1993**

SEDUCTION

The resistance of a woman is not always proof of her virtue, but more often of her experience.
Ninon de Lenclos (1620–1705), French author and courtesan

A woman will sometimes forgive the man who tries to seduce her, but never the man who misses an opportunity when offered.
Charles Maurice de Talleyrand (1754–1838), former Prime Minister of the French Republic

The trouble with Ian is that he gets off with more women because he can't get on with them.
Rosamond Lehmann (1901–1990), British novelist, on Ian Fleming

Men who do not make advances to women are apt to become victims of women who make advances to them.
Walter Bagehot (1826–1877), British journalist and businessman

To succeed with the opposite sex, tell her you're impotent. She can't wait to disprove it.
Cary Grant (1904–1986), British actor

He in a few minutes ravished this fair creature, or at least would have ravished her, if she had not, by a timely compliance, prevented him.
Henry Fielding (1707–1754), British novelist

When Venus said, 'Spell no for me',
'N-O' Dan Cupid wrote with glee,
And smiled at his success:
'Ah, child,' said Venus, laughing low,
'We women do not spell it so,
We spell it Y-E-S.'
Carolyn Wells (1869–1942), American writer, in *The Spelling Lesson*, 1920

What [girls] love to yield they would often rather have stolen. Rough seduction delights them, the boldness of near rape is a compliment.
Ovid (43 BC–AD 17), Roman poet, in *The Art of Love*

I tried to charm the pants off Bob Dylan but everyone will be disappointed to learn that I was unsuccessful. I got close . . . a couple of fast feels in the front seat of his Cadillac.
Bette Midler, American actress, in *Rolling Stone* **magazine, 1982**

Shopping can be fun. It can be an emotional outlet. Women go shopping to buy friendship and flattery from the assistant. For some women, shopping is a sex compensation, so the shop must seduce the customer.
Raine Spencer, Lady Dartmouth, British politician and socialite

I distinguish between terror and fear. From terror one escapes screaming, but fear has an odd seduction. Fear and the sense of sex are linked in secret conspiracy, but terror is a sickness like hate.
Graham Greene (1904–1991), British novelist, in *Ways of Escape,* **1980**

Be it money or women. Dad loved the chase.
Tracey Emin, British artist, talking of her father in interview, 2012

Seduction is often difficult to distinguish from rape. In seduction, the rapist bothers to buy a bottle of wine.
Andrea Dworkin (1946–2005), American feminist writer

For women the best aphrodisiacs are words. The G-spot is in the ears. He who looks for it below there is wasting his time.
Isabel Allende, Chilean writer

Vampires are immortal, you can do whatever you want, and get away with it. And there's the seduction part, of course; sex is a big part of the vampire thing.
Jonny Lee Miller, British actor

SELF-CONTROL

My own reaction to these men with this powerful sex appeal is secretly and passionately responsive – but shamefully, and secretly. So, I long to acquiesce, to fling my flesh at their feet. To have them hurt and humiliate me, however they may wish. My instinctive urge is to accept the role of victim to their villainy

– I would do anything to engage their attention . . . but instead, alas, I practise control.
Molly Parkin, British writer and artist, in *Good Golly Miss Molly*

Fifty men outside? I'm tired. Send ten of them home.
Mae West (1893–1980), American actress

Just because a man has something that sticks out, doesn't mean he's got to put it anywhere and everywhere.
Goldie Hawn, American actress

SELF-KNOWLEDGE

Ah! Madam . . . you know everything in the world but your perfections, and you only know not those, because 'tis the top of perfection not to know them.
William Congreve (1670–1729), British playwright

Shame is the feeling you have when you agree with the woman who loves you that you are the man she thinks you are.
Carl Sandburg (1878–1967), American poet

I found that I became more sexually confident, that I could even have entertained the likes of empty-headed beach boys in my bed, if I'd found their bodies desirable enough.
Molly Parkin, British writer and artist, on her new-found confidence after divorce

Sexual freedom has become more important than identity. Indeed, it has superseded it. The modern philosophy states – I ejaculate, therefore I am.
Quentin Crisp (1908–1999), British writer, in *How to Become a Virgin*, **1981**

I am not the type who wants to go back to the land; I am the type who wants to go back to the hotel.
Fran Lebowitz, American writer, in *Social Studies*

My mother wanted me to understand that as a woman I could do pretty much whatever I wanted to, that I didn't have to use sex or sexuality to define me.
Suzanne Vega, American singer

A rampant cock. That's what I am to the world today, goddammit, a phallic symbol.
Errol Flynn (1909–1959), American actor

I believe when it comes to love, there's something intangible about who we are attracted to and I don't think I have a pattern.
Taylor Swift, American singer

SENSES

The intoxication of rouge is an insidious vintage known to more girls than mere man can ever believe.
Dorothy Speare (1898–1951), American screenwriter, in *Dancers in the Dark*, **1922**

Blake said that the body was the soul's prison unless the five senses are fully developed and open. He considered the senses the 'windows of the soul'. When sex involves all the senses intensely, it can be like a mystical experience.
Jim Morrison (1943–1971), American lead singer of The Doors

SEX

I'm having problems with boyfriend withdrawal.
Ulrika Johnsson, British television personality

Older women are best because they always think they may be doing it for the last time.
Ian Fleming (1908–1964), British writer of the James Bond novels

Whoever named it necking was a poor judge of anatomy.
Groucho Marx (1880–1977), American comedian

The only reason I would take up jogging is so I could hear heavy breathing again.
Erma Bombeck (1927–1996), American writer

Sex is not only a divine and beautiful activity: it's a murderous activity. People kill each other in bed. Some of the greatest crimes

ever committed were committed in bed. And no weapons were used.
Norman Mailer (1923–2007), American writer and political activist

I know nothing about sex, because I was always married.
Zsa Zsa Gabor, Hungarian-American socialite

When I'm good I'm very good, but when I'm bad I'm better.
Mae West (1893–1980), American actress

My own belief is that there is hardly anyone whose sexual life, if it were broadcast, would not fill the world at large with surprise and horror.
W. Somerset Maugham (1874–1965), British novelist

Maybe I'm not talented. Maybe I'm just the Dinah Shore of the '60s. The square people think I'm too hip and the hip people think I'm too square. And nobody likes my choice of men – everybody thinks I'm fucking the Mormon Tabernacle Choir.
Cher, American singer

It's like sex. You can't describe it until you've experienced it.
Stanley Kalms, founder and chairman of the Dixons Retail plc, talking about HD television

I don't see much of Alfred any more since he got so interested in sex.
Clara McMillen (1898–1982), wife of Alfred Kinsey, American sexologist and author of The Kinsey Report on sexual behaviour

The tragedy is when you've got sex in the head instead of down where it belongs.
D.H. Lawrence (1885–1930), British writer

Love is the answer, but while you're waiting for the answer, sex raises some pretty good questions.
Woody Allen, American actor and film-maker

You remember your first mountain in much the same way you remember having your first sexual experience, except that climbing doesn't make as much mess and you don't cry for a

week if Ben Nevis forgets to phone next morning.
Muriel Gray, TV presenter and writer, in *The First Fifty*, **1991**

I think I made his back feel better.
Marilyn Monroe (1926–1962), American actress, after a private meeting with John F. Kennedy

I get very sexually excited on stage. It's like making love to 9,000 people at once.
Prince, American singer

I'd rather have a nice cup of tea.
Boy George, British singer

Is sex dirty? Only if it's done right.
Woody Allen

There are a lot more interesting things in life than sex – like reading.
Jean Alexander, British actress who played Hilda Ogden in ITV's *Coronation Street*

Boats, cars, sex . . . you have to touch all of them lightly or they lose their glamour.
Mel Gibson, Australian actor

It's the most fun I ever had without laughing.
Woody Allen, American actor and film-maker, in *Annie Hall*, **1977**

Most of the time, women want it more than men. I do.
Donna Ewin, Page 3 girl

Sex is good for you. I'd rather die making love than in any other way.
Edward Woodward (1930–2009), British actor

People have always found my sex life of interest, but I can do without sex.
Pamella Bordes, photographer and former Miss India

They say sex is as good as a five-mile run. I don't think I move five miles making love, but we've got three bedrooms. Make of that what you will.
Michael Palin, British actor and writer

Good sex is absolutely wonderful for you – much better than jogging.
Jilly Cooper, British novelist

When two people make love, there are at least four people present – the two who are actually there and the two they are thinking about.
Sigmund Freud (1856–1939), Austrian psychoanalyst

Sex in a love relationship is always better. I know a lot more about sex now – there's no more of that frantic fumbling and groping that went on when you were young.
Paul Daniels, British magician

Lady Rumpers: And then you took me.
Sir Percy: I took you? You took me. Your land army breeches came down with a fluency born of long practice.
From *Habeus Corpus* by Alan Bennett, British playwright

I wish I had as much in bed as I get in the newspapers.
Linda Ronstadt, American singer

I'd like to do a love scene with him just to see what all the yelling is about.
Shirley MacLaine, American actress, on her brother Warren Beatty

There will be sex after death – we just won't be able to feel it.
Lily Tomlin, American actress and comedienne

I believe in sex and death – two experiences that come once in a lifetime.
Woody Allen, American actor and film-maker, in *The Sleeper*, 1973

I know it does make people happy but to me it is just like having a cup of tea.
Cynthia Payne, retired British party hostess, after her acquittal over the famous sex-for-luncheon-vouchers case, 1987

It was just one of those things which, if you had been to bed before marriage, you would presumably have known.
Barbara Cartland (1901–2000), British novelist

Watch sex. It is the key to success and the trap-door to failure.
Michael Shea (1938–2009), former press secretary to the Queen, and director of public affairs at Hanson plc

Last time I tried to make love to my wife nothing was happening, so I said to her, what's the matter, you can't think of anybody either?
Rodney Dangerfield (1921–2004), American comedian

I would rather go to bed with Lillian Russell stark naked than Ulysses Grant in full military regalia.
Mark Twain (1835–1910), American writer

If it weren't for pickpockets I'd have no sex life at all.
Rodney Dangerfield

Sex is nobody's business except for the three people involved.
Woody Allen

Sex is the biggest nothing of all time.
Andy Warhol (1928–1987), American artist

All this fuss about sleeping together. For physical pleasure I'd sooner go to my dentist any day.
Evelyn Waugh (1903–1966), British novelist

Nothing is so much to be shunned as sex relations.
Saint Augustine (AD 354–430), early Christian theologian

Are you going to come quietly or do I have to use earplugs?
Spike Milligan (1918–2002), British comedian, in *The Goon Show*

The physical union of the sexes . . . only intensifies man's sense of solitude.
Nikolai Berdyaev (1874–1948), Russian philosopher

They made love as though they were an endangered species.
Peter de Vries (1910–1993), American editor and writer

In sexual intercourse it's quality not quantity that counts.
Dr David Reuben, American psychiatrist and writer

Make love to every woman you meet. If you get five per cent on your outlays, it's a good investment.
Arnold Bennett (1867–1931), British novelist

Of the delights of this world man cares most for sexual intercourse, yet he has left it out of his heaven.
Mark Twain (1835–1910), American writer

Whatever else can be said about sex, it cannot be called a dignified performance.
Helen Lawrenson (1907–1982), American writer and magazine editor

Women complain about sex more than men. Their gripes fall into two major categories:
(1) Not enough
(2) Too much
Ann Landers (1918–2002), American writer

In fact, it's quite ridiculous, the shapes people throw when they get down to it. There are few positions more ridiculous to look at than the positions people adopt when they are together. Limbs everywhere. Orifices gaping. Mucus pouring out and in. Sweat flying. Sheets wrecked. Animals and insects fleeing the scene when the going gets rough. Noise? My dear, the evacuation of Dunkirk in World War Two was an intellectual discussion compared to it. Once in a while, of course, there's silence. Usually afterwards. It's called exhaustion.
Nell McCafferty, Irish playwright and feminist campaigner

I like a man what takes his time.
Mae West (1893–1980), American actress

It is depressing to have to insist that sex is not an unnecessary, morally dubious self-indulgence but a basic human need, no less for women than for men.
Ellen Willis (1941–2006), American left-wing writer and activist

Basically, heterosexuality means men first. That's what it's all about.
Charlotte Bunch, American feminist author and activist

Ducking for apples – change one letter and it's the story of my life.
Dorothy Parker (1893–1967), American wit

Some men are all right in their place – if they only knew the right places.
Mae West

In real life women are always trying to mix something up with sex – religion, or babies, or hard cash; it is only men who long for sex separated out, without rings or strings.
Katharine Whitehorn, British journalist

I'd rather have a good bowl of soup.
Margaret Houston, Edinburgh teacher, explaining her view on sex

All too many men still seem to believe, in a rather naive and egocentric way, that what feels good to them is automatically what feels good to women.
Shere Hite, German-American sex educator

I've tried several varieties of sex. The conventional position makes me claustrophobic. And the others either give me a stiff neck or lockjaw.
Tallulah Bankhead (1902–1968), American actress

The truth is that sex doesn't mean that much to me now.
Lana Turner (1921–1995), American actress

I am happy now that Charles calls on my bed chamber less frequently than of old. As it is, I now endure but two calls a week and when I hear his steps outside my door I lie down on my bed, close my eyes, open my legs and think of England.
Lady Alice Hillingdon (1857–1940), wife of George, second Baron Hillingdon

Oh, not at all – just a straight-away pounder.
Lillie Langtry (1852–1929), British music-hall performer, on being asked if the Prince of Wales was a romantic lover

My husband is German; every night I get dressed up like Poland and he invades me.
Bette Midler, American actress

As for the topsy-turvy tangle known as soixante-neuf, personally I have always felt it to be madly confusing, like trying to pat your

head and rub your stomach at the same time.
Helen Lawrenson (1907–1982), American writer and magazine editor

Conventional sexual intercourse is like squirting jam into a doughnut.
Germaine Greer, Australian feminist writer

When grown-ups do it it's kind of dirty – that's because there's no one to punish them.
Tuesday Weld, American child actress of the 1950s

The important thing in acting is to be able to laugh and cry. If I have to cry, I think of my sex life. If I have to laugh, I think of my sex life.
Glenda Jackson, British Labour Party politician and former actress

I didn't know how babies were made until I was pregnant with my fourth child five years later.
Loretta Lynn, American country music singer

I didn't get ahead by sleeping with people. Girls take heart.
Barbara Walters, American television personality

I have never been able to sleep with anyone. I require a full-size bed so that I can lie in the middle of it and extend my arms spreadeagle on both sides without being obstructed.
Mae West (1893–1980), American actress

I've only slept with the men I've been married to. How many women can make that claim?
Elizabeth Taylor (1932–2011), British actress

Personally, I like sex and I don't care what a man thinks of me as long as I get what I want from him – which is usually sex.
Valerie Perrine, American actress and model

I've never taken up with a congressman in my life . . . I've never gone below the Senate.
Barbara Howar, American writer

Ignorance of the necessity for sexual intercourse to the health and virtue of both man and woman, is the most fundamental error in medical and moral philosophy.
George Drysdale (1825–1904), American physician, in *The Elements of Social Science,* **1854**

So many Englishwomen look upon sexual intercourse as abhorrent and not as a natural fulfilment of true love. My wife considered all bodily desire to be nothing less than animal passion, and that true love between husband and wife should be purely mental and not physical . . . like so many Englishwomen she considered that any show of affection was not in keeping with her dignity as a woman and that all lovemaking and caresses should come entirely from the man and that the woman should be the passive receiver of affection.
Anonymous letter to Marie Stopes (1880–1958), British birth-control campaigner

I have long lost any capacity for surprise where sex is concerned.
Geoffrey Howard (Marmaduke Dixey, 1889–1973), British judge and writer

But did thee feel the earth move?
Ernest Hemingway (1899–1961), American writer, in *For Whom the Bell Tolls,* **1940**

No sex without responsibility.
Frank Pakenham, 7th Earl of Longford (1905–2001), Labour peer

'Sex,' she says, 'is a subject like any other subject. Every bit as interesting as agriculture.'
Muriel Spark (1918–2006), British novelist, in *The Hothouse by the East River,* **1973**

The reproduction of mankind is a great marvel and mystery. Had God consulted me in the matter, I should have advised him to continue the generation of the species by fashioning them of clay.
Martin Luther (1483–1546), German Catholic priest and seminal figure in the Reformation

This sex attraction, though it is useful for keeping the world peopled,

has nothing to do with beauty: it blinds us to ugliness instead of opening our eyes to beauty.
George Bernard Shaw (1856–1950), Irish playwright

It has to be admitted that we English have sex on the brain, which is a very unsatisfactory place to have it.
Malcolm Muggeridge (1903–1990), British writer and satirist

Sex is. There is nothing more to be done about it. Sex builds no roads, writes no novels and sex certainly gives no meaning to anything in life but itself.
Gore Vidal (1925–2012), American writer and wit

Sex is a pleasurable exercise in plumbing, but be careful or you'll get yeast in your drainpipe.
Rita Mae Brown, American feminist writer

Two young lovers left rescuers all at sea when they were caught making love in a rubber dinghy. People on shore at Saltdean, near Brighton, saw the little craft moving violently and thought two children were stranded. But rescuers were sent packing after the lovers told them they could cope on their own. A spokesman said, 'They saved some energy for the row home.'
Newspaper report, 1992

And remember, there's nothing these women won't do to satisfy their ever-moist groins; they've just one obsession – sex.
Juvenal (AD 60–130), Roman poet, in *Satires X*

I enjoy fucking my wife. She lets me do it any way I want. No women's liberation for her. Lots of male chauvinist pig.
Joseph Heller (1923–1999), American novelist, in *Something Happened*, **1974**

No one, thank goodness, advocates that people should go about with long green strands of snot dangling from their noses in the name of nasal freedom, yet quite a few people have been converted in recent years to a belief that it is permissible for them to inflict the sights, sounds and smells of their bodies on any innocent bystander in the name of 'sexual freedom'.
Quentin Crisp (1908–1999), British writer

The man and woman make love, attain climax, fall separate. Then she whispers, 'I'll tell you who I was thinking of if you tell me who you were thinking of.' Like most sex jokes the origins of the pleasant exchange are obscure. But whatever the source, it seldom fails to evoke a certain awful recognition.
Gore Vidal (1925–2012), American writer and wit

The zipless fuck is absolutely pure . . . and is rarer than the unicorn.
Erica Jong, American writer

Sex is one of the nine reasons for reincarnation. The other eight are unimportant.
Henry Miller (1891–1980), American writer, in *Big Sur and the Oranges of Hieronymus Bosch*, **1957**

Sex – the poor man's polo.
Clifford Odets (1906–1963), American playwright and director

In the case of very fascinating women, sex is a challenge, not a defence.
Lord Goring, in *An Ideal Husband* **by Oscar Wilde (1854–1900), Irish playwright**

Sex is like having dinner – sometimes you joke about the dishes, sometimes you take the meal seriously.
Woody Allen, American actor and film-maker

Sex ought to be a wholly satisfying link between two affectionate people from which they emerge unanxious, rewarded and ready for more.
Dr Alex Comfort (1920–2000), British sexologist and author of *The Joy of Sex*, **1972**

Have you not as yet observed that pleasure, which is undeniably the sole motive force behind the union of the sexes, is nevertheless not enough to form a bond between them? And that, if it is preceded by desire which impels, it is succeeded by disgust which repels. That is a law of nature which love alone can alter.
Pierre Choderlos de Laclos (1741–1803), French novelist, in *Les Liaisons Dangereuses*, **1782**

The total deprivation of sex produces irritability.
Elizabeth Blackwell (1821–1910), American physician and the first

woman to receive a medical degree in the US, in *The Human Element in Sex*

It's all this cold-hearted fucking that is death and idiocy.
D.H. Lawrence (1885–1930), British writer, in *Lady Chatterley's Lover*, **1928**

A well-bred woman does not seek carnal gratification, and she is usually apathetic to sexual pleasures. Her love is physical or spiritual rather than carnal, and passiveness in regard to coition often amounts to disgust for it. Lust is seldom an element in a woman's character, and she is the preserver of chastity and morality.
From *Sex and Sex Worship* **by Dr Otto A. Wall, c.1919**

To know women as well as I do: they are only unwilling when you compel them, but after they're as enthusiastic as you are.
Jean Giraudoux (1882–1944), French playwright, in *Tiger at the Gates*, **1935**

Sex is exciting only when it is a subtle and pervasive part of the relationship between men and women, varying in its form from adolescence to old age, and dies only with death if is properly nourished in life.
Pearl Buck (1892–1973), American novelist

The Kama Sutra is the Mrs Beeton of sex.
Aldous Huxley (1894–1963), British writer, quoted in the *Sunday Times*, **1973**

Sex is interesting, but it's not totally important. I mean it's not even as important (physically) as excretion. A man can go seventy years without a piece of ass, but he can die in a week without a bowel movement.
Charles Bukowski (1920–1994), American writer, in *Notes on a Dirty Old Man*

Sexual intercourse is kicking death in the ass while singing.
Charles Bukowski

When a man and a woman of unorthodox tastes make love the man could be said to be introducing his foible into her quirk.
Kenneth Tynan (1927–1980), British theatre critic, *The Guardian*, **1975**

It is better to be first with an ugly woman than the hundredth with a beauty.
Pearl Buck, in *The Good Earth*

Sex is very, very important. It's part of daily life like breathing, communicating, touching.
Felicity Kendal, British actress

Sex was best in the afternoon, after a shower.
Ronald Reagan (1911–2004), American actor and 40th President of the United States

Sex has never been an obsession with me. It's just like eating a bag of crisps. Quite nice, but nothing marvellous. Sex is not simply black and white.
Boy George, British singer

Sex is a bad thing because it rumples the clothes.
Jacqueline Kennedy Onassis (1929–1994), wife of President John F. Kennedy

Good sex is like good bridge. If you don't have a good partner, you'd better have a good hand.
Mae West (1893–1980), American actress

Slept with everybody to get to the top.
LaToya Jackson, American singer and sister of Michael Jackson, of Madonna

Software is like sex: it's better when it's free.
Linus Torvalds, Finnish software engineer and founder of Linux

The fact is I am not having sex. But I feel absolutely ripe for the, what would you say? Plucking?
Angelina Jolie, American actress

There's no sex in Middle Earth.
Ian McKellen, British actor

SEX APPEAL

If a man doesn't look at me when I walk into a room, he's gay.
Kathleen Turner, American actress

Nothing risqué, nothing gained.
Alexander Woollcott (1887–1943), American columnist with *The New Yorker*

We need heroes. Whether or not it pleases you, Mr Connery, we have decided that you will be our hero.
Anne, Princess Royal, at a film première

I thought I couldn't afford to take her out and smoke as well. So I gave up cigarettes. Then I took her out and one day I looked at her and thought: 'Oh well', and I went back to smoking again, and that was better.
Benny Hill (1924–1992), British comedian, on a girlfriend he had when earning 27 shillings 6 pence a week

These are very confusing times. For the first time in history a woman is expected to combine intelligence with a sharp hairdo, a raised consciousness with high heels, and an open, non-sexist relationship with a tan guy who has a great bod.
Lynda Barry, American cartoonist and writer, in 'Why are Women Crazy?' **cartoon in** *Esquire* **magazine, 1984**

Good rock stars take drugs, put their penises in plaster of Paris, collectivise their sex, molest policemen, promote self-curiosity, unlock myriad spirits, epitomise fun, freedom and bullshit. Can the business anarchist on your block match that?
Richard Neville, Australian journalist, in *Playpower*, **1970**

I can't speak for women, but I find Mikhail Gorbachev attractive as a man's man. It's an extraordinary combination of intelligence, baldness and serenity.
Sean Connery, British actor

I'm more the thinking woman's crumbling ruin. I always wear the same suit on the programme so people don't notice me.
Melvyn Bragg, British broadcaster and writer, on the suggestion that he was 'the thinking woman's crumpet'

I have had propositions, but I don't take them up. The family can't understand how anyone can fancy me. But then, neither can I.
Barry Norman, British broadcaster and film critic

Many a man in love with a dimple makes the mistake of marrying the wrong girl.
Stephen Leacock (1869–1944), Canadian political scientist and writer, in *Literary Lapses*, **1910**

I'm in my 70s. What could she possibly see in me – is she into necrophilia or something?
Dirk Bogarde (1921–1999), British actor, on a request by Madonna to include him in her book *Sex*

Glenda Jackson, when she stepped up to accept her Oscar wrapped in an old horse-blanket and with her curlers almost hidden under a used tea towel, she yet generated more real sexuality than any of the so-called 'glamour' stars in the Hollywood Bowl. A corrosively intelligent actress. The thinking man's Hilda Ogden.
Henry Root (aka Charles Donaldon, 1935–2005), in *The World of Knowledge*, **1982**

Scotsmen are metaphysical and emotional, they are sceptical and mystical, they are romantic and ironic, they are cruel and tender, and full of mirth and despair.
Rachel Annand Taylor (1876–1960), British writer, in *William Dunbar*, **1931**

Plunging necklines attract more attention and cost less money.
Shelley Winters (1920–2006), American actress, quoted in the *Sunday Times*, **1971**

She sounded like the Book of Revelations read out over a railway station public-address system by a headmistress of a certain age, wearing calico knickers.
Clive James, Australian broadcaster, describing Margaret Thatcher on television

All a writer has to do to get a woman is to say he's a writer. It's an aphrodisiac.
Saul Bellow (1915–2005), American writer

If Canada is underdeveloped, so is Brigitte Bardot.
H.R. MacMillan (1885–1976), Canadian forestry industrialist

Brigitte Bardot on the screen is not simply a selfish delinquent. She has freshness, charm and a touch of mischievousness. She is irresponsible and immoral, but not deliberately cruel.
Reported in *The Observer*, **1959**

He who hath a long and great nose is an admirer of the fair sex, and well accomplished for the war of Venus.
Aristotle (384–322 BC), Greek philosopher

It's a rare man who can be that tough on the field and also have his own line in underwear.
Barack Obama, 44th President of the United States, meeting David Beckham at the White House, 2012

I fancied David long before I met him. I had no idea who he was, but I remember thinking he was gorgeous.
Victoria Beckham, British fashion designer and former Spice Girl, on husband David, in *The Beckhams* **by Andrew Morton**

What's so fucking wrong with being a sex symbol?
Kris Kristofferson, American actor and country music singer

I've always wanted to be a sex symbol, but I don't think I am . . . I can't imagine anyone thinking that I was sexually attractive. And if they do, where the fuck are they?
Sinéad O'Connor, Irish singer

If I've still got my pants on in the second scene . . . I think they've sent me the wrong script.
Mel Gibson, Australian actor

I think of myself as a sex symbol for men who don't give a damn
Phyllis Diller (1917–2012), American actress

Sexiness is all in the eye of the beholder. I think it should be Absolutely. My sex appeal, whatever it might be, isn't obvious . . at least to me.
Sharon Tate (1943–1969), American actress and model

Sex appeal is not on purpose.
Heather Locklear, American actress

Sex appeal is in the workplace every day of the week. I'm not saying that's the only calling card, but it's a whole crayon box.
Barbara Corcoran, American entrepreneur

SEX EDUCATION

Edinburgh's Director of Education, referring to sex education, is reported to have said: 'Teachers noticed a new look in children's eyes after an experimental course.'
Reported in the *Sunday Express*

Few of them wished to proceed to further education. The girls were dreaming of boys and babies, and the boys of sheep and whisky.
Reported in the *Glasgow Evening Times*

All teaching in all subjects aims to stimulate interest. It would be odd if this were not true of sex lessons.
Roger Probert, Birmingham headmaster, 1973

The only unnatural act is that which you cannot perform.
Alfred Kinsey (1894–1956), American sex psychologist and author of The Kinsey Report

Sex is like math. Add the bed, subtract the clothes, divide the legs and hope you don't multiply.
Anon

don't just go birdwatching during mating season because I'm some kind of deviant voyeur. No, pornithology makes real contributions to science too.
Benson Bruno

f you want to get laid go to college. If you want an education go to the library.
Frank Zappa (1940–1993), American musician

An intellectual is a person who's found one thing that's more interesting than sex.
Aldous Huxley (1894–1963), British writer

Sex education may be a good idea in the schools, but I don't believe the kids should be given homework.
Bill Cosby, American actor and comedian

In my day we didn't have sex education, we just picked up what we could off the television.
Victoria Wood, British comedienne

SEXIST

If I really felt I was being sexist in my shows, I'd stop. As it is, my fan mail from women carries every kind of postmark from around the world – and every kind of suggestion.
Benny Hill (1924–1992), British comedian

Ted needs someone to be there 100 per cent of the time. He thinks that's love. It's not, it's babysitting.
Jane Fonda, American actress, on the break-up of her marriage to Ted Turner

SEX ON THE AIR

Millions buy certain newspapers so they can read about sex and boobs. I give it to them over the air.
Tony Blackburn, British radio presenter, claiming that the secret of his success on Radio London was the free and frank way sex was discussed on his programme; a few months after his claim, Radio London was disbanded

Only yesterday a cab driver told me he had driven into the back of a car when I asked a woman to twang her suspenders. I love stockings and suspenders. I even wear them myself to prove I'm not sexist. It's a turn-on.
Tony Blackburn

Sex is like air, it's not important unless you aren't getting any.
John Callahan (1951–2010), American cartoonist

Only failing to possess a current TV licence or having sex during transmission of an Act of Worship would see you fed to the lions and dismissed.
Kate Adie, British foreign correspondent, of her time at the BBC, in *The Kindness of Strangers*

Love doesn't drop on you unexpectedly, you have to give off signals, sort of like an amateur radio operator.
Helen Gurley Brown (1922–2012), American author and editor

SEX AND FILMS

There are a lot of chicks who get laid by the director and still don't get the part.
Claudia Linnear, American soul singer

A movie without sex would be like a candy bar without nuts.
Earl Wilson (1907–1987), American columnist

Do not think that the solution to man's solitude is a line of men masturbating and a line of women masturbating.
Lina Wertmüller, Italian film director

Sex is emotion in motion.
Mae West (1893–1980), American actress

Even if the whole thing, including what she did on the screen, has evolved from the sort of girl she was, her life and career still seem to have been dreamed up by one of her scriptwriters.
David Shipman (1932–1996), British film critic and writer, on the actress Clara Bow

I love you.
Harry Belafonte, American singer, when asked which phrase he overused

Being a sex symbol is rather like being a convict.
Raquel Welch, American actress

The bikini made me a success.
Ursula Andress, Swiss actress, recalling the bikini she wore in the film *Dr No*

Don't play no faggots.
Sylvester Stallone, American actor, advising fellow actors

My dad told me: 'Anything worth having is worth waiting for.' I waited until I was 15.
Zsa Zsa Gabor, Hungarian-American socialite

This film business, perhaps more so in America than in Europe, has always been about young sexuality. It's not true of theatres, but in America, film audiences are young. It's not an intellectual cinema in America.
Jaqueline Bisset, British actress

Usually when you see females in movies, they feel like they have these metallic structures around them, they are caged by male energy.
Björk, Icelandic singer

Sex was never as neat as the movies made it. Real sex was messy. Good sex was messier.
Laurell K. Hamilton, American novelist, in *Blue Moon*

Sweating is sexy.
Farrah Fawcett (1947–2009), American actress

Young actors often don't think of the consequences of doing nudity or sex scenes. They want the role so badly that they agree to be exploited, and then end up embarrassing family, friends, and even strangers.
Natalie Portman, American actress

I remember doing the sex scene in *Red Rock West*. I had to kiss Nic Cage and then look like I was going down on him. And he couldn't do anything – he just had to lie there.
Lara Flynn Boyle, American actress

SEX AND ROCK 'N' ROLL

A game is a closed field, a ring of death with, oh, sex as the centre. Performing is the only game I've got.

Jim Morrison (1943–1971), American lead singer of The Doors

Pop music is sex and you have to hit them in the face with it.
Andrew Loog Oldham, British band manager

The wriggling ponces of the spoken word.
D.G. Bridson, British radio producer, on disc jockeys

Purgative of all frustrations. It's like going to Confession when I was ten years old. The weight of wanking would lift from my brain as I told the priest I'd masturbated X times. At gigs it's the same thing.
Bob Geldof, Irish singer and political activist

Rock and roll is about cocks and jiving and the odd bloody nose . . . and about people like us talking seriously about the social order.
Jean-Jacques 'JJ' Burnel, French-born guitarist with The Stranglers, in the New Musical Express, **1979**

You're all a bunch of fucking idiots. Your faces are being pressed into the shit of the world. Take your fucking friend and love him. Do you want to see my cock?
Jim Morrison taking a direct approach with female fans

The hippies wanted peace and love. We wanted Ferraris, blondes and switchblades.
Alice Cooper, American singer

Sex was a competitive event in those days and the only thing you could take as a certainty was that everyone else was lying, just as you were.
Bob Geldof, in his autobiography Is That It?

It's hard to maintain a one-to-one relationship if the other person is not going to allow me to be with other people.
Axl Rose, American musician and lead singer with Guns 'n' Roses

People are like, 'Well, she doesn't know the Sex Pistols.' Why would I know that stuff? Look how young I am. That stuff's old, right?
Avril Lavigne, Canadian singer

We're great, Jo and me. We're pals and I guess sex has a lot to do with it. She's also brilliant at clearing a room. So protective, so devoted. I can't believe how much she loves me.
Ronnie Wood, British musician with the Rolling Stones, on his ex-wife

SEX SYMBOL

A sex symbol becomes a thing. I hate being a thing.
Marilyn Monroe (1926–1962), American actress

Can't act . . . voice like a tight squeak . . . utterly unsure of herself . . . unable even to take refuge in her own insignificance.
From a Columbia Pictures report on a young Marilyn Monroe

A vacuum with nipples.
Otto Preminger (1905–1986), Austro-Hungarian film director, on Marilyn Monroe

She was good at playing abstract confusion in the same way that a midget is good at being short.
Clive James, Australian broadcaster, on Marilyn Monroe

Marilyn was mean. Terribly mean. The meanest woman I ever met around this town. I have never met anybody as mean as Marilyn Monroe or as utterly fabulous on the screen, and that includes Garbo.
Billy Wilder (1906–2002), Austrian-born American film director

To put it bluntly, I seem to be a whole superstructure with no foundation. But I'm working on the foundation.
Marilyn Monroe

What's so fucking wrong with being a sex symbol?
Kris Kristofferson, American actor and country-music singer

Being a sex symbol is a heavy load to carry, especially when one is tired, hurt and bewildered.
Clara Bow (1905–1965), American silent-film actress

I am not a sex symbol.
Jason Isaacs, British actor

I don't know what it means to be a sex symbol. When I look at myself on a magazine cover I don't see it as me, but as someone painted, fluffed, puffed and done up.
Jennifer Aniston, American actress

He wishes. No, I had the Levi's guy on my wall, not a picture of William, sorry.
Kate Middleton, Duchess of Cambridge, in interview, 2011

SEX TOYS

There are a number of mechanical devices which increase sexual arousal, particularly in women. Chief among these is the Mercedes-Benz 380SL convertible.
P.J. O'Rourke, American writer and political satirist

Sometimes a cigar is just a cigar.
Sigmund Freud (1856–1939), Austrian psychoanalyst, on being asked by a student whether his cigar smoking was a symbolic activity

Maybe I'll make a 'Mary Poppins' movie and shove the umbrella up my ass.
Marilyn Chambers (1952–2009), American pornographic actress and vice-presidential candidate

Det-Inspector Roy Penrose said in a statement read to the court that a booklet advertising artificial male organs was found by police at Miss Jones's home in May. They also found a vibrating device hidden inside a pouffe. The hearing continues today.
Report in the *Birmingham Post*, quoted in *Private Eye* magazine

Our first declared confrontation was over sex. As part of my new-broom policy at Mount Street, I systematically invaded cupboards and drawers throwing out old make-up bottles, other women's clothes, and objects that could only have been there for sexual use: a cork on a long string attached to a hotwater bottle, a pair of Victorian knickers, and a single black stocking.
Kathleen Tynan (1937–1995), Canadian journalist, on married life with Kenneth Tynan

Caller: I was really disgusted when I opened the parcel and all these dangly bits fell out, I was so embarrassed.
Radio presenter: Did you not realise you had sent off for a sex aid?
Caller: No, I bought it to surprise my daughter. A few years ago I bought her an inflatable deer to sit in her garden. It looked good, very realistic – until the kids punctured it. So, I thought I'd buy her the sheep to replace it!
Conversation on LBC Radio talk show, March 1992, regarding a product marketed as the 'Love Ewe'

Kinky is using a feather. Perverted is using the whole chicken.
Anon

I'm all for bringing back the birch, but only between consenting adults.
Gore Vidal (1925–2012), American writer and wit

A woman with a well-stocked toy drawer isn't dependent on anyone and is unlikely to hurl herself at a lowlife just for nooky.
Arianne Cohen, American writer, in *Marie Claire* magazine, 2008

My boyfriend has a sex manual but he was dyslexic. I was lying there and he was looking for my vinegar.
Victoria Wood, British comedienne

The best sex I have ever had was with my vibrator.
Eva Longoria, American actress

SEXUAL FANTASY

Deaf and dumb (except when I ask her to talk dirty); her fathe owns a wine store; gives me no crap about anything on earth; give

me all over body massages, and doesn't say things like, 'Have you come, can I get dressed now?'
Anon

Dear Sir,
I hope I am not a prude, but I feel compelled to lodge a protest concerning the ever-increasing flood of obscenity in dreams. Many of my friends have been shocked and sickened as myself by the filth that is poured out nightly as soon as our eyes are closed. It is certainly not my idea of home entertainment. Night after night, the most disgraceful scenes of perversion and bestiality are perpetuated behind my eyelids . . . it is imperative that official action should be taken.
Kenneth Tynan (1927–1980), British theatre critic, in *The Sound of Two Hands Clapping,* **1978**

Of course, as a teenager my sexual fantasies were full of Anita Ekberg and the usual giant Nordic goddesses. That is until Brigitte Bardot became the 'love of my life' in the late '50s. All my girlfriends who were dark-haired suffered under my constant pressure to become Brigitte. By the time I married my first wife (who was, I think, a natural auburn), she too had become a long-haired blonde with the obligatory bangs.
I met the real Brigitte a few years later. I was on acid and she was on the way out.
John Lennon (1940–1980), British singer with The Beatles

I consider myself the zenith of sexual perversion.
Woody Allen, American actor and film-maker

SEXUALITY

Sexuality is something like nuclear energy, which may prove amenable to domestication, through scruple, but then again may not.
Susan Sontag (1933–2004), American writer and political activist, in *Styles of Radical Will,* **1969**

No man can be held throughout the day by what happens throughout the night.
Sally Stanford (1903–1982), American madam and writer, in *The Lady of the House,* **1966**

Her body is arranged the way it is to display it to the man looking at the picture. The picture is made to appeal to his sexuality. It has nothing to do with her sexuality . . . women are there to feed an appetite, not to have any of their own.
John Berger, British writer, on the construction of advertising images, in *Ways of Seeing*, **1972**

To ask women to become unnaturally thin is to ask them to relinquish their sexuality.
Naomi Wolf, American feminist writer, in *The Beauty Myth*, **1991**

Sins become more subtle as you grow older. You commit sins of despair rather than lust.
Piers Paul Read, British writer

I just came into my own sexuality at 30. I don't think it's something you can deeply experience at 18 or any time before that.
Eva Longoria, American actress

I'm proud of my sexuality. I embrace it. It's just another part of me.
Adam Lambert, American singer

I just want to be known for things other than my sexuality.
Eva Mendes, American actress

Sexuality is such a part of life, but sexuality in the movies – I have a hard time finding it.
Catherine Deneuve, French actress, in *Premier*, **1993**

You walk off the plane in Rio, and your blood temperature goes up. The feel of the wind on your face, the water on your skin, the taste of the food, the music, the sexuality; Brazilians are very comfortable in their sexuality.
Amy Irving, American actress

We shouldn't feel restricted by our sexuality, and our sexualit doesn't have to be a cultural choice.
Neil Tennant, British lead singer of the Pet Shop Boys

I admit I have a tremendous sex drive. My boyfriend lives 40 mile: away.
Phyllis Diller (1917–2012), American actress

SEXY

. . . as a vandalised laundromat.
Victoria Wood, British comedienne

. . . as a side of bacon in the deep freeze.
Les Dawson (1934–1993), British comedian

. . . as a man making love with his socks on.
Anon

Madame Bovary is the sexiest book imaginable. The woman's virtually a nymphomaniac but you won't find a vulgar word in the entire thing.
Noël Coward (1899–1973), British playwright

Being bald is an unfailing sex magnet.
Telly Savalas (1922–1994), American actor

It's a flesh market, you won't find finer flesh anywhere.
Julia Morley, British chairwoman of the Miss World contests

Shakespeare is the sexiest great writer in the language.
A.L. Rowse (1903–1997), British historian

Well built without being the slightest bit sexy, like a junior minister's wife.
Denis Norden, British comedy writer

Perhaps it was time to stretch a bit. The truth is, I didn't want to do those glamorous leading-men roles for ever. I'm much better at playing villains, or slightly villainous guys. It's more fun and it's definitely more sexy.
Michael Douglas, American actor

I've spent time with her and she's everything a man could want. She's a very warm, beautiful, intelligent and sexy lady.
Sylvester Stallone, American actor, on Sarah Ferguson, the Duchess of York

George Moore unexpectedly pinched my behind. I felt rather honoured that my behind should have drawn the attention of the great master of English prose.
Ilka Chase (1900–1978), American actress and novelist

You don't have to hit anybody on the head with four-letter words to be sexy.
Eartha Kitt (1927–2008), American singer and actress

I am the world's sexiest man.
Noël Coward (1899–1973), British playwright

My ass is way too big.
Marilyn Monroe (1926–1962), American actress, asked about her body

I'm not a sexy person in real life.
Tina Turner, American singer

The sexiest thing in the world is to be totally naked with your wedding band on.
Debra Winger, American actress

What I do is so extreme. It's meant to make guys think: I don't know if this is sexy or just weird.
Lady Gaga, American singer

The hottest bitch in heels right here.
Rihanna, Barbadian singer

I like to feel sexy. I know my husband thinks I'm sexy. I think he is too. But I don't go out half-naked with 'sex' written across my back.
Catherine Zeta-Jones, British actress

SINS

Nothing makes one so vain as being told that one is a sinner.
Lord Henry, in *The Picture of Dorian Gray* **by Oscar Wilde (1854–1900), Irish playwright**

Few love to hear the sins they love to act.
Pericles, in *Pericles* **by William Shakespeare (1564–1616), British playwright**

SUCCESS

A lot of executives keep up the pretence of being solid community members when they are sleeping with their secretaries. Hef's honest. He isn't burdened by success.
Christie Hefner, American former CEO of Playboy Enterprises, on her father

Anyone can have a key to the executive washroom, but once a woman gets inside, what is there? A lavatory.
Germaine Greer, Australian feminist writer

The secret is to marry an older woman.
Peter Tickner, about to celebrate 74 years of marriage – both he and his wife Rose are 100 years old

For a penniless, pregnant, Brazilian girl, Ron's a prime catch.
Charmain Brent, on hearing that her train-robber husband, Ronnie Biggs, had found another woman

Beardsley is now on top and working hard to get it.
Jim Rosenthal, British television sports commentator, on Peter Beardsley's soccer technique

My biggest problem all my life was men. I never met one yet who could compete with the image the public made out of Bette Davis.
Bette Davis (1908–1989), American actress, quoted in *Conversations in the Raw*

If I wrote a play about my own life people would be far more shocked. I feel sex is a good thing. It makes people better people, and I think that desiring and loving, and even having people, is the best thing life has to offer.
Nell Dunn, British playwright, commenting on her play *Up The Junction*

You have to admit that most women who have done something with their lives have been disliked by almost everyone.
Françoise Gilot, painter and mistress of Picasso, 1987

Winning a Grammy sure helped me get laid.
Bonnie Raitt, American blues singer

For marriage to be a success, every woman and every man should have her and his own bathroom. The End.
Catherine Zeta-Jones, British actress

TALL STORIES

Girl: I saw you the other day at the corner of Hollywood and Vine winking at the girls.
Rudy Vallee: I wasn't winking, that's a windy corner. Something got in my eye.
Girl: She got in your car too.
From *The Rudy Vallee Show*, c.1929

We were rehearsing a love scene and Whitney needed help.
Kevin Costner, American actor, when caught kissing Whitney Houston behind a trailer on film set

It was so romantic. He just took it out and put it on the table in Soho.
Kathryn Holloway, British presenter of *TVAM*, showing off her engagement ring to viewers

The more undeveloped the country, the more overdeveloped the women.
John Kenneth Galbraith (1908–2006), Canadian economist, in *Time*, 1969

No woman came amiss to him if they were very willing and very fat. The standard of His Majesty's taste made all those ladies who aspired to his favour and who were near the statutable size strain and swell themselves like frogs in the fable to rival the bulk and dignity of the ox. Some succeeded and others burst.
Philip Stanhope, 4th Earl of Chesterfield (1694–1773), writing about King George I

Girls are always presuming I've kept my heterosexual virginity.
David Bowie, British singer

Hell, if I'd jumped all the dames I'm supposed to have jumped, I'd never had time to go fishing.
Clark Gable (1901–1960), American actor

TEMPTATION

The only way to get rid of temptation is to yield to it . . . I can resist everything but temptation.
Lord Darlington, in Lady Windermere's Fan **by Oscar Wilde (1854–1900), Irish playwright**

What makes resisting temptation difficult for many people is they don't want to discourage it completely.
Franklin P. Jones (1908–1980), American journalist

I am not over-fond of resisting temptation.
William Beckford (1760–1844), British novelist

Do you really think it is weakness that yields to temptation? I tell you that there are terrible temptations which it requires strength, strength and courage to yield to.
Sir Robert Chiltern, in An Ideal Husband **by Oscar Wilde (1854–1900), Irish playwright**

Why resist temptation – there will always be more.
Don Herold (1889–1966), American cartoonist

A little of what you fancy does you good.
Marie Lloyd (1870–1922), British music-hall entertainer

Ah, why did God,
Creator wise that peopled highest heaven
With spirits masculine, create at last
This novelty on earth, this fair defect
Of nature, woman?
John Milton (1608–1674), British poet, in Paradise Lost, **1667**

The right education of the female sex, as it is in a manner everywher neglected, so it ought to be generally lamented. Most in th depraved later age think a woman learned and wise enough if sh can distinguish her husband's bed from another's.
Mrs Hannah Woolley (1623–1675), British governess, *Th Gentlewoman's Companion,* **1675**

When once the woman has tempted us, and we have tasted th forbidden fruit, there is no such thing as checking our appetite whatever the consequences may be.
George Washington (1732–1799), first President of the United State

THERAPY

They all sit around feeling very spiritual, with their mental hand on each other's knees, discussing sex as if it were the art of Fugu
Jimmy Porter, in *Look Back in Anger* **by John Osborne (1929–1994 British playwright**

Writing songs has a therapeutic effect, and it either kills off lov or wins the heart of the lover.
Shakira, Colombian singer

With me, nothing goes right. My psychiatrist said my wife and should have sex every night. Now, we'll never see each other!
Rodney Dangerfield (1921–2004), American comedian

TIME

Is there a cure for a broken heart? Only time can heal your broke heart, just as time can heal his broken arms and legs.
Miss Piggy, in *Miss Piggy's Guide to Life,* **1981**

Sex and drugs were simply not discussed in our culture at th time.
Gloria Estefan, Cuban-born American singer

TRADITION

I was raised in the Jewish tradition, taught never to marry a gentile woman, shave on a Saturday and, more especially, never to shave a gentile woman on Saturday.
Woody Allen, American actor and film-maker

In the old days you went from ingénue to old bag with a stretch of unemployment in between.
Julie Walters, British actress

I've never felt the constraints of social acceptability.
Joanna Lumley, British actress

I am not wanting to make too long a speech tonight, as I am knowing your old English saying: 'Early to bed and up with the cock.'
Anonymous Hungarian diplomat

Your traditional well-built woman, meaning large breasts, small waist, good butt, good legs. That's my sexual ideal.
John Travolta, American actor

TRUE CONFESSIONS

When I have one foot in the grave I will tell the truth about women. I shall tell it, jump into my coffin, pull the lid over me and say, Do what you like now.'
Leo Tolstoy (1828–1910), Russian novelist

I don't care what is written about me so long as it isn't true.
Dorothy Parker (1893–1967), American wit

A good source of humour is the relationship between the sexes. And it is always the man who comes off worst in what I do – never the woman. Terrible things happen to me and the other men in my shows. Teeth come out; we get knocked on the head hard. But the girls retain their dignity: it is the men who are the idiots. And that is true in real life as well.
Benny Hill (1924–1992), British comedian

A woman reading *Playboy* feels a little like a Jew reading a Nazi manual.
Gloria Steinem, American feminist writer

I never know how much of what I say is true.
Bette Midler, American actress

At certain times I like sex – like after a cigarette.
Rodney Dangerfield (1921–2004), American comedian

Look, Mr President, I might sleep with them, but I'm damned if I'll eat lunch with them.
William H. Lawrence (1916–1972), American politician, to President John F. Kennedy, on the subject of admitting women to the all-male Gridiron Club

It's all right letting yourself go, as long as you can get yourself back.
Mick Jagger, lead singer of the Rolling Stones

I like making love myself and I can make love for about three minutes. Three minutes of serious fucking and I need eight hours' sleep and a bowl of Wheaties.
Richard Pryor (1940–2005), American comedian, from *Richard Pryor in Concert,* **1980**

Take up car maintenance and find the class is full of other thirty something women like me, looking for a fella.
Marian Keyes, Irish novelist, in *Last Chance Saloon,* **1999**

I like children, I have my wonderful niece, but I knew early on that my energies were meant to go somewhere else.
Nancy Dell'Olio, Italian lawyer and media personality

I left High School a virgin.
Tom Selleck, American actor

I understand women perhaps because I have a very effeminate streak.
Rod Stewart, British singer

I've got lots of good friends. I could have affairs. I can read a book at night, put the cat on the end of the bed. I can pick up my passport and go to France. I don't have to ask anybody.
Joanna Lumley, British actress

I've had my cock sucked by five of the big names in Hollywood. I wanted more than anything to get some little part.
James Dean (1931–1955), American actor

I love women . . . If I could get into it, it would be great. But you know, it don't mean a thing if it ain't got that schwing.
Sharon Stone, American actress, asked if she had ever had sex with a woman

Everybody makes me out to be some kind of a macho pig, humping women in the gutter. I do, but I put a pillow under them first.
James Caan, American actor

I approach love differently now that I know it's hard for it to work out.
Taylor Swift, American singer

I always wear a matching set, a nice thong and a bra.
Cheryl Cole, British singer

VAGINA

The vagina walls are quite insensitive in the great majority of females . . . there is no evidence that the vagina is ever the sole source of arousal, or even the primary source of erotic arousal in any female.
Alfred Kinsey (1894–1956), American sex psychologist and author of The Kinsey Report, in *Sexual Behaviour in the Human Female*, **1953**

In the third stage they get their pleasure chiefly from the little penis that they have on the outside of their bodies, called the clitoris, and are mostly interested in having that organ stimulated. In the adult stage they get their greatest pleasure from the vagina, which can be used much more effectively to give pleasure to a male partner.
Eric Berne (1910–1970), British psychiatrist, in *A Layman's Guide to Psychiatry and Psychoanalysis*, **1969**

A lovely ring that I wear in a very special place. One of my (vaginal) lips . . . it's pierced, and he thought that this part of my body had made a lot of money and fame, and it deserved a present.
Marilyn Chambers (1952–2009), American pornographic actress and vice-presidential candidate, on a gift bought for her by Sammy Davis Jr

I'm open to love. But guys should have to earn it. Because the minute they get it, they want something else.
Rihanna, Barbadian singer

Amazing! Astonishing! Still can't get over the fantastic idea that when you're looking at a girl, you are looking at somebody who is guaranteed to have on her – a cunt! They all have cunts! Right under their dresses! Cunts for fucking!
Philip Roth, American novelist, in *Portnoy's Complaint*, **1969**

VERBOSITY

For three days they went at it without repose, showing the way the millrace flows, and how the industrious spindle goes. They gave the lamb suck, they startled the buck, they tried on the finger ring for luck. They cradled the child, they kissed the twins, they polished the sword till it had not a speck, they taught the sparrow how to peck, they made the camel show his neck, and fed the bird at the barley bins. They gave the little pigeon seed, and put the rabbit out to feed, with many another pretty deed, till they blew a hole in the shepherd's reed.
From *The Arabian Nights*, **a collection of Arabic folk tales**

VICES

One reason I don't drink is that I want to know when I'm having a good time.
Lady Nancy Astor (1879–1964), first woman to sit as an MP in the House of Commons

Cocaine isn't habit-forming. I should know – I've been using it for years.
Tallulah Bankhead (1902–1968), American actress

It seems impossible to root out of an Englishman's mind the notion that vice is delightful, and that abstention from it is privation.
George Bernard Shaw (1856–1950), Irish playwright, in *Mrs Warren's Profession: The Author's Apology,* **1893**

Vice is a creature of such hideous mind that the more you see it the better you like it.
Finley Peter Dunne (1867–1936), American writer

Fat people are brilliant in bed. If I'm sitting on top of you, who's going to argue?
Jo Brand, British comedienne

How like herrings and onions our vices are in the morning after we have committed them.
Samuel Taylor Coleridge (1772–1834), British poet

What maintains one vice would bring up two children.
Benjamin Franklin (1706–1790), one of the Founding Fathers of the United States

Society punishes not the vices of its members, but their detection.
Marguerite, Countess of Blessington (1789–1849), Irish writer

The closer you get to vice, the less gilt and glamour you find there is to it.
Sophie Tucker (1887–1966), Russian-American singer and actress

Permissiveness is simply removing the dustsheets from our follies.
Edna O'Brien, Irish novelist, in *Goodbye Baby and Amen*

It depends on what the meaning of 'is' is.
Bill Clinton, 42nd President of the United States, giving evidence to the Grand Jury, contending that his statement 'There's nothing going on between us' had been truthful

The focus on my appearance has really surprised me. I've always been a size 14 to 16. I don't care about clothes. I'd rather spend my money on cigarettes and booze.
Adele, British singer

Publishing a sophisticated men's magazine seemed to me the best possible way of fulfilling a dream I'd been nurturing ever since I was a teenager. TO GET LAID A LOT.
Hugh Hefner, American founder of *Playboy* **magazine**

Just because society, and government, and whatever was different 100 years ago, doesn't mean that people didn't have sex, pick their nose or swear.
Kate Winslet, British actress

But you know there's still an argument, there's still ten states that outlaw premarital sex, and many more states where adultery is still outlawed and a crime.
Liam Neeson, British actor

VIRGINITY

I thought of losing my virginity as a career move.
Madonna, American singer

All the evidence I've seen says that sex before marriage isn't a good idea. Women are born virgins and sex is something that is added to them. They are not incomplete without it.
Victoria Gillick, who campaigned, unsuccessfully, to prevent girls under 16 being prescribed the pill without their parents' consent

I said it ten years ago that in ten years' time it would be smart to be a virgin. Now everyone is back to virgins again.
Barbara Cartland (1901–2000), British novelist

What men desire is a virgin who is a whore.
Edward Dahlberg (1900–1977), American writer

Nature abhors a virgin – a frozen asset.
Clare Boothe Luce (1903–1987), American writer and politician

A simple maiden in her flower is worth a hundred coats-of-arms.
Alfred, Lord Tennyson (1809–1892), British poet laureate, in *Lady Clara Vere de Vere*, **1833**

Although it is true that the hymen is often relaxed in virgins, or broken and diminished by accidents independent of all coition, such accidents are very rare, and the absence of the hymen is assuredly a good ground for strong suspicion.
T. Bell, in *Kalogynomia, Or The Law of Female Beauty, Being The Elementary Principle of that Science*, **1821**

Nothing is more horrible than the terror, the sufferings, and the revulsion of a poor girl, ignorant of the facts of life, who finds herself raped by a brute. As far as possible we bring them up as saints, and then we hand them over as if they were fillies.
George Sand (Amantine Lucile Dupin, 1804–1876), French writer, in a letter, 1843

The men you meet aren't naive enough to expect virgins but they certainly don't want to hear about the 'ghosts' of your past life. Yet I can't imagine a man sticking around much after two or three months if you hadn't slept together.
From *Out of the Doll's House* (1988) by Angela Holdsworth, TV producer and writer

Sire, four virgins wait without.
Without what?
Without food and clothing.
Give them food and bring them in.
From *Only on Sundays* (1967) by Katharine Whitehorn, British journalist

I hate a woman who seems to be hermetically sealed in the lower regions.
Sydney Smith (1771–1845), British writer and Anglican cleric

It is one of the superstitions of the human mind to have imagined that virginity could be a virtue.
Voltaire (François-Marie Arouet, 1694–1778), French writer and philosopher, in *Notebooks*, 1778

With regards to sexual relations, we should note that in giving herself to sexual intercourse, the girl renounces her honour. This is not, however, the case with men, for they have yet another sphere for their ethical activity beyond that of the family.
Georg Hegel (1770–1831), German philosopher, referring to unmarried girls, in *The Philosophy of Right*, 1821

It will be quite sufficient for the memorial of my name and for my glory if, when I die, an inscription be engraved on a marble tomb, saying, 'Here lieth Elizabeth, which reigned a virgin and died a virgin.'
Queen Elizabeth I (1533–1603), in answer to a request by the Speaker in the Lower House that she should marry

Michael is not interested in girls and sex. He is definitely still a virgin and doesn't believe he has missed anything.
Chris Tervit, tour manager for Michael Jackson

VIRILITY

There is no known way of increasing male sperm production.
Dr Virginia E. Johnson (1925–2013), American sexologist

Virility is an illness which is best avoided.
Sir Nicholas Goodison, British Chairman of the Stock Exchange

Sex at age 90 is like trying to shoot pool with a rope.
George Burns (1896–1996), American actor and comedian

I'm never through with a girl until I've had her three ways.
John F. Kennedy (1917–1963), 35th President of the United States

VIRTUE

Pleasure is something that you feel that you should really enjoy which is really virtuous, but you don't, and sin is something that you're quite sure you shouldn't enjoy but you do.
Ralph Wightman, British BBC broadcaster, speaking on *Any Questions*, **1961**

Virtue is its own revenge.
E.Y. Harburn (1898–1950)

Be virtuous and you will be eccentric.
Mark Twain (1835–1910), American writer

Most plain girls are virtuous because of the scarcity of opportunity to be otherwise.
Maya Angelou, American poet

What is virtue but the trade unionism of the married?
Don Juan, in Man and Superman **by George Bernard Shaw (1856–1950), Irish playwright**

There are few good women who do not tire of their role.
François, Duc de La Rochefoucauld (1613–1680), French writer

I cannot love anyone if I hate myself. That is the reason why we feel so extremely uncomfortable in the presence of people who are noted for their special virtuousness, for they radiate an atmosphere of the torture they inflict on themselves. That is not a virtue but a vice.
Carl Jung (1875–1961), Swiss psychiatrist and writer

Assume a virtue, if you have it not.
Hamlet, in Hamlet **by William Shakespeare (1564–1616), British playwright**

Dost thou think, because thou art virtuous, there shall be no more cake and ale?
Sir Toby Belch, in Twelfth Night **by William Shakespeare (1564–1616), British playwright**

Who can find a virtuous woman? For her price is far above rubies. The heart of her husband doth safely trust in her, so that he shall have no need of spoil. She will do him good and not evil all the days of her life.
From the Bible, Proverbs 31: 10–12

Most good women are hidden treasures who are only safe because nobody looks for them.
Dorothy Parker (1893–1967), American wit

Woman's virtue is a man's greatest invention.
Cornelia Otis Skinner (1899–1979), American actress

Virtue, like a dowerless beauty, has more admirers than followers.
Marguerite, Countess of Blessington (1789–1849), Irish writer

Virtue is not photogenic.
Kirk Douglas, American actor

Girls are sacrificed to family convenience, or else marry to settle themselves in a superior rank . . . If some widow did not now and then fall in love, love and hymen would seldom meet, unless at a village church.
Mary Wollstonecraft (1759–1797), British feminist writer, in *A Vindication of the Rights of Women*, **1792**

WEALTH

I think people still want to marry rich. Girls especially . . . It's simple. Don't date poor boys. Go where the rich are . . . You don't have to be rich to go where they go.
Sheilah Graham Westbrook (1904–1988), British-born American writer, in the *Los Angeles Times*, **1974**

A gold rush is what happens when a line of chorus girls spot a man with a bankroll.
Mae West (1893–1980), American actress, in *Klondike Annie*, **1936**

WEATHER

I had a good eight inches last night.
Ulrika Johnsson, British television personality, talking about overnight snowfalls

Well, what happened last night, was it a storm?
Lisa Maxwell, British television presenter, to weathergirl Trish Williamson, the day after the hurricane of 1987

Some people might wake up tomorrow and find they've had an inch or two.
Michael Fish, British BBC weatherman

The strongest winds will be around the backside.
Bill Giles, British weatherman, discussing expected stormy weather in the east of Britain

Personally, I've got a very fine five-inch.
Patrick Moore (1923–2012), British television astronomer, on *The Sky at Night*

Sex in the open air? No. I can't be bothered. If he can't afford a room, I'm not going.
Jane McDonald, British singer and television presenter

The storm caused by our god, sex, sends us all to our ruin by the shortest route.
Elfriede Jelinek, Austrian writer, in *Lust,* **1989**

WEDDINGS

Of all actions of a man's life his marriage does least concern other people; yet of all actions of our life it is more muddled with by other people.
John Sleden (1584–1654), British scholar specialising in Jewish law

If it were not for the presents, an elopement would be preferable.
George Ade (1866–1944), American playwright and newspaper columnist

That is ever the way. 'Tis all jealousy to the bride and good wishes to the corpse.
J.M. Barrie (1860–1937), British writer

The 'Wedding March' always reminds me of the music played when soldiers go into battle.
Heinrich Heine (1797–1856), German poet

It has been said that a bride's attitude towards her betrothed can be summed up in three words: aisle, altar, hymn.
Frank Muir (1920–1998) and Denis Norden, British comedy writers, in *Oh, My Word!*

WIVES

You cannot pluck roses without fear of thorns, nor enjoy a fair wife without danger of horns.
Benjamin Franklin (1706–1790), one of the Founding Fathers of the United States

I think of my wife and I think of Lot
And I think of the lucky break he got.
William Cole's 'Marriage Couplet', from *The Oxford Book of American Light Verse*

The wife who submits to sexual intercourse against her wishes or desires, virtually commits suicide, while the husband who compels it, commits murder.
Victoria Claffin Woodhull (1838–1927), American leader of the woman's suffrage movement

She okays all my scripts. In my marital contract it's written that I can't do any sex scenes.
Dustin Hoffman, American actor, on his wife

He who can't do any better goes to bed with his own wife.
Spanish proverb

Of course, I do have a slight advantage over the rest of you. It helps in a pinch to be able to remind your bride that you gave up a throne for her.
Edward VIII, Duke of Windsor (1894–1972)

Take my wife . . . please.
Henny Youngman (1906–1998), British-American violinist and comedian

Many a man owes his success to his first wife and his second wife to his success.
Jim Backus (1913–1989), American actor

Translations (like wives) are seldom faithful if they are in the least attractive.
Roy Campbell (1901–1957), South African poet, in *Poetry Review,* **1949**

The trouble with my wife is that she is a whore in the kitchen and a cook in bed.
Geoffrey Gorer (1905–1985), British writer and anthropologist, in *Exploring the English Character*, **1955**

If a man stays away from his wife for seven years, the law presumes the separation to have killed him; yet according to our daily experience, it might well prolong his life.
Lord Darling (1849–1936), former Lord Chief Justice of England

The husband was a teetotaller, there was no other woman, and the conduct complained of was that he had drifted into the habit of winding up every meal by taking out his false teeth and hurling them at his wife.
Arthur Conan Doyle (1859–1930), British author of the Sherlock Holmes mysteries, in *A Case of Identity*, **1891**

Wives are young men's mistresses, companions for middle age, and old men's nurses.
Francis Bacon (1561–1626), British philosopher

I chose my wife, as she did her wedding-gown, not for a fine glossy surface, but such qualities as would wear well.
Oliver Goldsmith (1730–1774), Anglo-Irish writer

He will hold thee, when his passion shall have spent its novel force,
Something better than his dog, a little dearer than his horse.
Alfred, Lord Tennyson (1809–1892), British poet laureate, in *Locksley Hall,* **1835**

London is full of women who trust their husbands. One can always recognise them, they always look so thoroughly unhappy.
Oscar Wilde (1854–1900), Irish playwright

The woman who cannot evolve a good lie in defence of the man she loves is unworthy the name of wife.
Elbert Hubbard (1856–1915), American writer and philosopher

Good wives and private soldiers should be ignorant.
Pinchwife in *The Country Wife* **by William Wycherley (1640–1716), British playwright**

If a woman has her PhD in physics, has mastered in Quantum theory, plays flawless Chopin, was once a cheerleader, and is now married to a man who plays baseball, she will forever be 'Former Cheerleader Married to Star Athlete'.

Maryanne Ellson Simmons, American writer and artist, and wife of Milwaukee Brewers catcher Ted Simmons

Many men owe their success to their wives. I owe my wife to my success.

Anon

Reading someone else's newspaper is like sleeping with someone else's wife. Nothing seems to be precisely in the right place, and when you find what you are looking for, it is not clear then how to respond to one.

Malcolm Bradbury (1932–2000), British academic, in *Stepping Westward*, **1965**

Never feel remorse for what you have thought about your wife; she has thought much worse things about you.

Jean Rostand (1894–1977), French biologist and writer, in *Le Marriage*, **1927**

When a man opens a car door for his wife, it's either a new car or a new wife.

Prince Philip, Duke of Edinburgh

If the husband is the criminal, he escapes with little or no injury to either fame or fortune. If the wife be the criminal, the perceptions of the world and her incapacity to make honourable provision for herself, compel her to join the ranks of prostitutes.

T. Bell, in *Kalogynomia, Or The Law of Female Beauty, Being The Elementary Principle of that Science*, **1821**

Your wives are your fields, so go into your fields whichever way you like.

Qu'ran, central religious text of Islam, c.632 CE

My wife doesn't care what I do when I'm away as long as I don't have a good time.

Lee Trevino, American pro golfer

When a man steals your wife, there is no better revenge than to let him keep her.
Sacha Guitry (1885–1957), French writer and director

WOMANHOOD

You sometimes have to answer a woman according to her womanishness, just as you have to answer a fool according to his folly.
Trefusis, in *An Unsocial Socialist* **by George Bernard Shaw (1856–1950), Irish playwright**

Women in drudgery knew they must be one of four: whores, artists, saints and wives.
Muriel Rukeyser (1913–1980), American poet and feminist, in 'Beast in View', *Wreath of Women,* **1944**

I get the impression that she loves life, and people too . . . she doesn't write like a man but like a 100 per cent woman, a female, sometimes, a 'bitch'. In many ways she is more forthright, more honest, more daring than most male authors.
Henry Miller (1891–1980), American writer, on *Fear of Flying* **by Erica Jong, in the** *New York Times*

Probably the most successful mode of rearing girls, so as to bring them to the full perfection of womanhood, is to retard the period of puberty as much as possible . . . It is the duty therefore, of the mother to enjoin on her daughter the frequent use of cold baths, free exercise in the open air, or in cool, well-ventilated rooms, to provide plain and digestible diet for her, and to insist on abstinence from hot tea and coffee.
E.H. Ruddock (1882–1875), British physician, *The Common Diseases of Women*

You may marry or you may not. In today's world that is no longer the big question for women. Those who grab onto men so that they can collapse with relief, spend the rest of their days shining up their status symbol and figure they never have to reach, stretch, earn, grow, face dragons or make a living again, are the ones to be pitied. They, in my opinion, are the unfulfilled ones.
Helen Gurley Brown (1922–2012), American author and editor, in *Sex and the Single Girl,* **1963**

The nicest women in our 'society' are raving sex maniacs. But being just awfully nice they don't, of course, descend to fucking – that's uncouth – rather they make love, commune by means of their bodies and establish sensual rapport.
Valerie Solanas (1936–1988), American radical feminist writer, in *Born Female*, **1968**

To be a liberated woman is to renounce the desire of being a sex object or a baby girl. It is to acknowledge that the Cinderella–Prince Charming story is a child's fairy tale.
Clare Boothe Luce (1903–1987), American writer and politician, 1974

If you're vivacious and a bit wild, they call you mad. That's the thing about being a woman and successful. If you were a bloke, you would just be eccentric.
Tracey Emin, British artist

Man may have discovered fire, but women discovered how to play with it.
Candace Bushnell, American writer and creator of *Sex and the City*

All women do have a different sense of sexuality, or sense of fun, or sense of like what's sexy or cool or tough.
Angelina Jolie, American actress

Every woman needs a man to discover her.
Charlie Chaplin (1889–1977), American film-maker

Men may have wars, but women have their periods.
Robin Williams, American actor

WOMEN

Women are like banks, boy. Breaking and entering is a seriou business.
Joe Orton (1933–1967), British playwright, in *Entertaining M Sloane*, **1964**

Aren't women prudes if they don't and prostitutes if they do?
Kate Millett, American feminist writer

With women, I've got a long bamboo pole with a leather loop on the end of it. I slip the loop around their necks so they can't get away or come too close. Like catching snakes.
Marlon Brando (1924–2004), American actor

What do you think: women – a mistake? Or did He do it to us on purpose?
Daryl Van Horne, played by Jack Nicholson, American actor, in *The Witches of Eastwick*, **1987**

A beautiful woman who gives pleasure to men serves only to frighten the fish when she jumps in the water.
Kwang Tse, Taoist philosopher, fourth century

God did it on purpose so that we may love you men instead of laughing at you.
Mrs Patrick Campbell (1865–1940), British actress, in reply to a male acquaintance who asked why women seem to have no sense of humour

You don't know a woman until you have had a letter from her.
Ada Beddington Leverson (1862–1933), British writer

Women are like dogs really. They love like dogs, a little insistently. And they like to fetch and carry and come back wistfully after hard words, and learn rather easily to carry a basket.
Mary Roberts Rinehart (1876–1958), American crime writer

Being a woman is of special interest only to aspiring male transsexuals. To actual women, it is simply a good excuse not to play football.
Fran Lebowitz, American writer

I should like to know what is the proper function of women, if it is not to make reasons for husbands to stay at home, and still stronger reasons for bachelors to go out.
George Eliot (Mary Ann Evans, 1819–1880), British novelist

There are two kinds of women: those who want power in the world, and those who want power in bed.
Jacqueline Kennedy Onassis (1929–1994), wife of President John Kennedy

Behind almost every woman you have ever heard of stands a man who has let her down.
Naomi Bliven, American writer

A woman can look both moral and exciting . . . if she also looks as if it was quite a struggle.
Edna Ferber (1885–1968), American Pulitzer Prize-winning writer

A liberated woman is one who has sex before marriage and a job after.
Gloria Steinem, American feminist writer

Nine times out of ten a woman had better show more affection than she feels.
Jane Austen (1775–1817), British novelist

We have drugs to make women speak, but none to keep them silent.
Anatole France (1844–1924), French writer

There are three intolerable things in life – cold coffee, lukewarm champagne, and overexcited women.
Orson Welles (1915–1985), American film-maker

Both women and melons are best when fairly ripe.
Spanish proverb

All women are trollops.
French proverb

Watch out for women's tricks!
From the libretto of The Magic Flute**, opera by W.A. Mozart (1756–1791), Austrian composer**

Woman is the wrath of Zeus.
Greek proverb

The costliest women are the ones who cost nothing.
Alfred de Musset (1810–1857), French poet and playwright

A woman uses her intelligence to find reasons to support her intuition
G.K. Chesterton (1874–1936), British writer

Women are one of the Almighty's enigmas to prove to men that He knows more than they do.
Ellen Glasgow (1873–1945), American novelist

Women are most fascinating between the ages of 35 and 40 after they have won a few races and know how to pace themselves. Since few ever pass 40, maximum fascination can continue indefinitely.
Christian Dior (1905–1957), French fashion designer

There's nothing so similar to one poodle dog as another poodle dog, and that goes for women too.
Pablo Picasso (1881–1973), Spanish artist

A lady is known by the product she endorses.
Ogden Nash (1902–1971), American poet

Women should be obscene and not heard.
John Lennon (1940–1980), British singer with The Beatles

Women never know when the curtain has fallen. They always want a sixth act, and as soon as the interest of the play is entirely over, they propose to continue it.
Lord Henry, in *The Picture of Dorian Gray* **by Oscar Wilde (1854–1900), Irish playwright**

It was a woman who drove me to drink, and I never had the courtesy to thank her for it.
W.C. Fields (1880–1946), American actor and comedian

A woman is but an animal, and an animal not of the highest order.
Edmund Burke (1729–1797), Irish writer and politician

A pessimist is a man who thinks all women are bad. An optimist is one who hopes they are.
Chauncey Depew (1834–1928), US Senator and attorney

There are lots of good women who, when they get to heaven, will watch to see if the Lord goes out nights.
E.W. Howe (1853–1937), American writer and editor

I'm just a person trapped inside a woman's body.
Elayne Boosler, American comedienne

A woman, especially if she has the misfortune of knowing anything, should conceal it as well as she can.
Jane Austen (1775–1817), British novelist, in *Northanger Abbey,* **1817**

You know women as well as I do. They are only willing when you compel them, but after that they're as enthusiastic as you are.
Jean Giraudoux (1882–1944), French playwright, in *Tiger at the Gates,* **1935**

Girls are taught from childhood that any exhibition of sexual feeling is unwomanly and intolerable; they also learn from an early age that if a woman makes a mistake it is upon her and upon her alone that social punishment will descend.
Mary Scharlieb (1845–1930), British gynaecological surgeon and writer, in *The Seven Ages of Woman,* **1915**

Solitary women exhibit pseudo-masculine efficiency, a determined practical competence which they might expect or demand from a husband if only they had one.
Anthony Storr (1920–2001), British psychiatrist, in *Human Aggression,* **1968**

She is Venus when she smiles; but she's Juno when she walks, and Minerva when she talks.
Ben Jonson (1572–1637), British playwright

I am a source of satisfaction to him, a nurse, a piece of furniture, a woman – nothing more.
Sophia Tolstoy (1844–1919), Russian writer and wife of Leo, in *A Diary of Tolstoy's Wife*

And a woman is only a woman, but a good cigar is a smoke.
Rudyard Kipling (1865–1936), British writer, in *The Betrothed*

The ten properties of a woman:
YE. I. Is to be a merry chere
YE. II. To be well placed
YE. III. To have a broad forhead
YE. IIII. To have broad buttocks
YE. V. To be hard of ward
YE. VI. To be easy to leap upon
YE. VII. To be good at long journey

YE. VIII. To be well sturring under a man
YE. VIIII. To be always busy wt ye mouth
YE. X. Ever to be chewing on ye bridle
From Sir Anthony Fitzherbert's *Boke of Husbandry*, **1568**

Nature placed the female testicles internally . . . woman is a most arrogant and extremely intractable animal; and she would be worse if she came to realise that she is no less perfect and no less fit to wear breeches than man . . . I believe that is why nature, while endowing her with what is necessary for procreation, did so in such a way as to keep her from perceiving and ascertaining her sufficient perfection.
P. Borgarucci, sixteenth-century Italian anatomist

God created woman. And boredom did indeed cease from that moment – but many other things ceased as well! Woman was God's second mistake.
Friedrich Nietzsche (1844–1900), German philosopher

The judgment of God upon your sex endures even today; and with it inevitably endures your position of criminal at the bar of justice. You are the gateway to the devil.
Tertullian (AD 160–220), Roman theologian

A woman's place is in the wrong.
James Thurber (1894–1961), American writer and cartoonist

Woman are not much but they are the best other sex we have. When children cease to be altogether desirable women cease to be altogether necessary.
John Langdon-Davies (1897–1971), British writer and war correspondent

There is only one real tragedy in a woman's life: the fact that her past is always her lover, and her future invariably her husband.
Mrs Chevely, in *An Ideal Husband* **by Oscar Wilde (1854–1900), Irish playwright**

A woman's whole life is a history of the affections.
Washington Irving (1783–1859), American writer

It is assumed that a woman must wait motionless, until she is wooed. That is how the spider waits for the fly.
George Bernard Shaw (1856–1950), Irish playwright, in *Man and Superman: Epistle and Dedicatory*

Woman reduces us all to a common denominator.
Patiomkin, in *Great Catherine* **by George Bernard Shaw**

The fickleness of the women whom I love is only equalled by the infernal constancy of the women who love me.
Charteris, in *The Philanderer* **by George Bernard Shaw**

Many women still feel it's not their right to look at erotic photos of men. They also have trouble finding the words to express their sexuality. We're going to have to create a new language.
Pauline Brown, editor of *For Women* **magazine**

[For] once a woman has given her heart you can never get rid of the rest of her body.
Lord Foppington, in *The Relapse* **by Sir John Vanbrugh (1664–1726), British playwright**

If you really worship women they'll forgive you everything, even if your balls are dropping off.
Lawrence Durrell (1912–1990), British writer

Anyone who says he can see through women is missing a lot.
Groucho Marx (1880–1977), American comedian

A womane is a worthy wyght
She serveth a man both daye and nyght,
Therto she puttyth alle her myght,
And yet she hathe but care and woo.
Anon, from *Medieval English Lyrics: A Critical Anthology*, **by R.T. Davies, 1991**

There are two kinds of women – goddesses and doormats.
Pablo Picasso (1881–1973), Spanish artist

I never realised until lately that women were supposed to be the inferior sex.
Katharine Hepburn (1907–2003), American actress

I'm not denyin' the women are foolish: God Almighty made 'em to match the men.
George Eliot (Mary Ann Evans, 1819–80), British novelist

WHAT WOMEN WANT

Despite my 30 years of research into the feminine soul, I have not yet been able to answer . . . the great question that has never been answered: what does a woman want?
Sigmund Freud (1856–1939), Austrian psychoanalyst

Any idiot would know women's needs are simple. All we want is your basic millionaire/brain surgeon/criminal lawyer/great dancer who pilots his own Lear jet and owns oceanfront property. On the other hand, things being what they are today, most of us will settle for a guy who holds down a steady job and isn't carrying an infectious disease.
Linda Sunshine, American author

Women want men, careers, money, children, friends, luxury, comfort, independence, freedom, respect, love and a three-dollar pantyhose that won't run.
Phyllis Diller (1917–2012), American actress

What this woman wants, with all due respect to Sigmund Freud, is for men to stop asking that question and to realise that women are human beings, not some alien species. They want the same things men want.
Diane White

'd like to own Texas and lease Colorado.
Rita Mae Brown, American feminist writer

Freedom from pain, security, creature comforts, and an end to loneliness. When you get down to the basics, it's still the same old story, a fight for love and glory.
Alice Kahn, professor in speech-language pathology at Miami University, Ohio

Vain man is apt to think we were merely intended for the world's propagation and to keep its human inhabitants sweet and clean;

but, by their leaves, had we the same literature he would find our brains as fruitful as our bodies.
Mrs Hannah Woolley (1623–1675), British governess, in *The Gentlewoman's Companion*, **1675**

That's a dumb question: only a fraud like Freud could make a problem out of an opportunity.
Edward Abbey (1927–1989), American writer, on being asked what women want

Implicit obedience.
Horace Rumpole, from *Rumpole of the Bailey* **by John Mortimer (1923–2009), British barrister turned writer**

Men.
Malcolm Forbes (1919–1990), American publisher of *Forbes* **magazine**

Money, power, love, sex (until they get married), adulation, children and control. Of these, children cause the most trouble. Women also want equal rights and equal pay for equal work, and I agree with them 100 per cent, though on some days it is hard to figure out how a species that controls 97 per cent of the money and all the pussy can be downtrodden.
Larry L. King (1929–2012), American playwright

Do you know what the women in this town are really after? They want jewels in their bank vaults, Chanel clothes in their wardrobe, a Porsche in their garage, a tiger in their bed – and an ass of a husband who pays for it all.
Shobhaa De, Indian writer

Oh Charles – a woman needs certain things. She needs to be loved, wanted, cherished, sought after, wooed, flattered, cossetted, pampered. She needs sympathy, affection, devotion, understanding, tenderness, infatuation, adulation, idolatry – that isn't much to ask, Charles.
From *Round the Horne*, **BBC Radio comedy series, created by Barry Took (1928–2002) and Marty Feldman (1934–1982)**

What else do they want in life but to be as attractive as possible to men? Do not all their trimmings and cosmetics have this end in view, and all their baths, fittings, creams, scents as well – and a

those arts of making up, painting, and fashioning the face, eyes and skin? Just so. And by what other sponsor are they better recommended to men than by folly?
Erasmus (1466–1536), Dutch Catholic priest, humanist and writer, in *The Praise of Folly*, **1509**

I like them on their knees, in the kitchen, doing the dusting. In return, I feed them, wine them, make them laugh, occasionally – and give them a punch on the nose and a good kicking when they need it. They're happier that way. They feel secure.
Oliver Reed (1938–1999), **British actor**

When it comes to being a good lover, a guy has to ask a girl what she wants and be willing to give it to her.
Jenna Jameson, American former pornographic actress

WOMAN'S ROLE

It is a man's place to rule, and a woman's to yield. He must be held up as the head of the house, and it is her duty to bend so unmurmuringly to his wishes, that the rest of the household will follow her example, and treat him with the due respect his sex demands.
From *Woman and the Times We Live In*, **by Sarah Ann Sewell, 1869**

As a general rule, a modest woman seldom desires any sexual gratification for herself. She submits to her husband, but only to please him; and, but for the desire of maternity, would rather be relieved from his attentions.
William Acton (1813–1875), British physician, in *The Functions and Disorders of the Reproductive Organs*, **1865**

Maids must be wives and mothers, to fulfil the entire and holiest end of woman's being.
Fanny Kemble (1809–1893), British actress and writer, in *Woman's Heart*

You've done all the hard work, you've brought up the children, you've run the home and then suddenly you're completely invisible.
Lynda Bellingham, British actress, speaking of women over 50

X-RATED

All women think they're ugly, even pretty women. A man who understood this could fuck more women than Don Giovanni. They all think their cunts are ugly . . . they all find fault with their figures . . . even models and actresses, even the women you think are so beautiful that they have nothing to worry about, do worry all the time.
Erica Jong, American writer

Nobody, including the Supreme Court, knows what obscenity is.
Norman Dorsen, American professor at the New York University School of Law

I never trust a man unless I've got his pecker in my pocket.
Lyndon B. Johnson (1908–1973), 36th President of the United States

Yes, I went to see one the other night called *Jilly* [about a girl who] goes to the dentist for a fillin' and a drillin', and frankly I enjoyed it a lot more than I did *Heartburn* with Jack Nicholson and Meryl Streep, for a couple of reasons. One, Meryl Streep is a dog. She's a good actress, but the girl is a dog. She reminds me a lot of Cordie Mae Poovey, a girl I went to high school with. She played a great trumpet, but goddamn she was ugly.
Lewis Grizzard (1946–1994), American writer, on being asked if he watched X-rated movies

I always wanted to be an animated character. And basically that's what I do now. I'm kind of an X-rated Cinderella.
Cher, American singer

A question asked in a Surrey school exam went: 'Why do cocks crow early every morning?' A twelve-year-old replied: 'My dad says they have to make the most of it while the hens are asleep.'
Reported in the *Peterborough Daily Telegraph*, 1983

After four martinis, my husband turns into a disgusting beast. And after the fifth, I pass out altogether.
Anon

An adult western is where the hero still kisses his horse at the end, only now he worries about it.
Milton Berle (1908–2002), American comedian and actor, in *Variety*

The word 'fuck' appears thirty times, the word 'cunt' fourteen times, the word 'balls' thirteen times, 'shit' six times, 'arse' and 'piss' three times apiece.
Mervyn Griffiths-Jones (1909–1979), British prosecuting counsel at the trial for obscenity of D.H. Lawrence's novel *Lady Chatterley's Lover*, **1960**

I doubt if there are any rational people to whom the word 'fuck' would be particularly diabolical, or totally forbidden.
Kenneth Tynan (1927–1980), British theatre critic, speaking on BBC TV, 1965

To be human is to be fucked. To know that you're fucked right off the bat.
Murray Schisgal, American writer, in *Playboy* **magazine, 1975**

There are times when I like sex and times when I don't. When I'm in the mood for it, I like nothing better. But I don't enjoy cruelty. I hate it when somebody I don't know comes out wearing a rubber diving suit with a battleship in one hand and a jar of Vaseline in the other.
Barbara Hutton (1912–1979), American actress and socialite

Wouldn't it be wicked to be a grandma one day and have that cover hanging on the wall in your grandson's garage.
Lily Cole, British supermodel, commenting on her racy cover shoot for French *Playboy*, **2012**

After loss of identity, the most potent modern terror is loss of sexuality, or, as Descartes didn't say, 'I fuck therefore I am.'
Jeanette Winterson, British writer, in *Art and Lies*, **1994**

He wanted to fuck her loudly on a hard bed with rain beating on the windows
Don DeLillo, American writer, in *Mao II*, **1991**

YOUTH

They think youth has got him where he is, beside me. This isn't so. I think it was his fart that fascinated me first, and the way he commented on it. No one that I was involved with at the time ever acknowledged their farts. 'Smell this,' he said, and gave me a bisto

sniff. 'I always think the best have something of mushroom on toast about them – don't you?' And we hadn't even been to bed – it was while we were both undressing.
Molly Parkin, British writer and artist, on her younger husband

How absurd and delicious it is to be in love with someone younger than yourself. Everyone should try it.
Barbara Pym (1913–1980), British novelist

My girlfriend has married an old man;
I have married a younger.
Her old man is witty, sexy and strong;
Mine's the same. But mine will last longer.
Molly Parkin

Perhaps at fourteen every boy should be in love with some ideal woman to put on a pedestal and worship. As he grows up, of course, he will put her on a pedestal the better to view her legs.
Barry Norman, British broadcaster and film critic, in *The Listener* **magazine, 1978**

I love the Guides (I'm still a supporter), and rose to the heady heights of patrol leader. Camping was the bit I enjoyed most, especially if it involved getting together with the Scouts.
Lesley Garrett, British soprano

I would go to seedy places in the New York area and dance on tables, with drunken men whipping out their hoo-has.
Goldie Hawn, American actress

Believe me, you can get into a lot of trouble being sixteen years old in a foreign country with no adult telling you when to come home.
Cameron Diaz, American actress

I wish all teenagers can filter through songs instead of turning to drugs and alcohol.
Taylor Swift, American singer

Actually I get asked for my ID card because I look too young.
Nancy Dell'Olio, Italian lawyer and media personality, describing what happens when she rarely goes out without make-up

Sex is great until you die, but it's never as great as when you were a kid, when it was a mystery.
David Duchovny, American actor

The fact is that young people are going to have sex whether you like it or not.
Emma Thompson, British actress

INDEX